"I have been waiting for this book! [...] many Christians like myself have [...] recruited into the church solely so [...] miss the primary calling on my life; I [...] my purpose! He tells stories about people of faith who are doing precisely that in very different ways. 'They are all about bringing people into a place of welcome and hospitality and, more, to believing, in faith, that the welcome of God will also be tasted'. I am inspired to do the same."

Debra Green OBE, Founder and Director, Redeeming Our Communities (ROC)

"At last a book that gives us the full sweep of God's missional heart and our part in his grand plan of renewal. This book is accessible, inspiring and biblically rooted in the key texts that make up the seven facets of missional theology. Kelly draws on his own adventurous missional journey, blending into the book his love of art, poetry and storytelling, alongside some serious missional theology. This is not, however, simply a creative academic book: I found it personally challenging, spiritually deepening and missionally motivating."

Rev Roger Sutton, Director of GATHER and co-chair of the Trafford Borough Partnership, Greater Manchester

"Gerard is such a unique writer – with the soul of a poet, the mind of an academic and the style of a novelist, he makes reading both pleasant and purposeful. You will love this book. Wisdom and insight leak brilliantly from every page."

Cathy Madavan, Speaker, writer, member of Spring Harvest planning group and author of *Digging for Diamonds*

"Is Gerard Kelly telling stories, or is he teaching theology? His genius is that he wouldn't answer a question like that. Just like Jesus. In these stories you will find yourself and your purpose, because you will find the beautiful, brazen mission of God artistically illuminated."

Andy Flanagan, Singer-Songwriter and Director of Christians on the Left

"Gerard Kelly is a master storyteller and this book tells the Master's story but it also tells your story and mine. The Seven Stories that Shape Your Life is a missional curriculum – a tool to help followers of Jesus to see how their lives are connected to the story and mission of God. Yet this is no dry text book. It's more like the menu for a great banquet. Kelly invites us to sit at his table so we can hear from theologians, contemporary commentators, poets and musicians, Biblical heroes and ordinary Christians, and then turns to us so we can tell our story too. For the 'greatest story ever told' must be told afresh in each generation through the storied lives of all who believe it."

Jim Memory, European Christian Mission (ECM) and Redcliffe College (UK)

"What always appeals to me about Gerard's writing and speaking is that his word pictures and perspectives help me to see familiar things in new light, to make fresh application of age-old truths in our contemporary settings, and to take a fresh, candid look at myself. This book is no exception. This book is the author's invitation to us 'to imagine an engagement with the mission of our maker that more fully embraces his story.' So what are we waiting for?"

Jeff Fountain, Director, Schuman Centre for European Studies

"I always felt that my personal mission was doing God's will in the places I was called – in my case into frontline politics as an MP. This is why the book resonated and made sense of a life I thought I had tried to lead – our mission is Gods will. To know your life is significant in the eyes of God and to use your calling to achieve this is a powerful message for all of us who feel we may have failed if we are not called to traditional mission. If you want to understand your role in God's mission to create heaven on earth there is no better place to start than this book by Gerard Kelly."

Andy Reed, OBE, Director, SageImpact Ltd, MP for Loughborough 1997 to 2010

THE SEVEN STORIES THAT SHAPE YOUR LIFE

Discover your God given purpose

Gerard Kelly

MONARCH
BOOKS

Oxford, UK, and Grand Rapids, USA

Text copyright © 2016 Gerard Kelly
This edition copyright © 2016 Lion Hudson

The right of Gerard Kelly to be identified as the author of this work has been asserted by him in accordance with the Copyright, Designs and Patents Act 1988.

All rights reserved. No part of this publication may be reproduced or transmitted in any form or by any means, electronic or mechanical, including photocopy, recording, or any information storage and retrieval system, without permission in writing from the publisher.

Published by Monarch Books
an imprint of
Lion Hudson plc
Wilkinson House, Jordan Hill Road,
Oxford OX2 8DR, England
Email: monarch@lionhudson.com
www.lionhudson.com/monarch

ISBN 978 0 85721 634 2
e-ISBN 978 0 85721 635 9

First edition 2016

Acknowledgments

Scripture quotations marked "NLT" are taken from the Holy Bible, New Living Translation, copyright © 1996, 2004. Used by permission of Tyndale House Publishers, Inc., Carol Stream, Illinois 60188. All rights reserved.

Scripture quotations marked "NIV" are taken from the Holy Bible, New International Version Anglicised. Copyright © 1979, 1984, 2011 Biblica, formerly International Bible Society. Used by permission of Hodder & Stoughton Ltd, an Hachette UK company. All rights reserved. "NIV" is a registered trademark of Biblica. UK trademark number 1448790

Scripture quotations marked "KJV" are taken from the Authorized (King James) Version: rights in the Authorized Version in the United Kingdom are vested in the Crown. Reproduced by permission of the Crown's patentee, Cambridge University Press.

Scripture quotations marked "The Street Bible" are taken from "The Word on the Street". Copyright © 2003, 2004 by Rob Lacey, formerly titled "The Street Bible". This title is also available as a Zondervan ebook product. Visit www.zondervan.com/ebooks for more information.

Scripture quotations marked "NKJV" are taken from the New King James Version®. Copyright © 1982 by Thomas Nelson. Used by permission. All rights reserved.

Excerpts pp. 83 and 269–70 taken from *The Ragamuffin Gospel: Good News for the Bedraggled, Beat-up, and Burnt Out* by Brennan Manning, copyright © 1990 by Brennan Manning. Used by permission of WaterBrook Multnomah, an imprint of the Crown Publishing Group, a division of Penguin Random House LLC. All rights reserved.

A catalogue record for this book is available from the British Library

Printed and bound in the UK, August 2016, LH26

Contents

Foreword — 7
Introduction — 10

Chapter:

1 **Creation**: Walk with the Worldmaker — 40
2 **Vocation**: Depend on the Dreamgiver — 84
3 **Liberation**: Be Changed by the Chainbreaker — 121
4 **Formation**: Hold on to the Heartseeker — 162
5 **Limitation**: Find Strength in the Faithbuilder — 205
6 **Incarnation**: Follow the Footwasher — 240
7 **Restoration**: Be Filled by the Firestarter — 277

Endword — 318
Endnotes — 320

Foreword

It is a great gift, sometimes, for the familiar to be made strange.

Good art does this: an arresting line in a poem makes us think again about the familiar, realize it is different from what we had always assumed. A well-taken photo can make us see something, even in our own children, that we had never consciously noticed before. A great painting invites us to see reality differently, often precisely by exaggerating and distorting what was seen.

The art of public speaking is all in making the familiar strange. To re-awaken hope in those who have dismissed all politics as corrupt and irrelevant. To convince jaded consumers that this product is different. To challenge a church congregation to actually live truths they have always believed.

In my own world of the university, most good teaching starts the same way. What if something we've always thought was obvious isn't? What if the evidence in that area is flawed? Students arrive at university confident in what they think; we try hard to confuse them, to make the familiar strange, before encouraging them to reconstruct a set of convictions more carefully.

It is a great gift, sometimes, for the familiar to be made strange.

In this book, Gerard Kelly makes the familiar strange. He takes the Christian story we all know so well, and looks at it from an oblique angle, showing us sides of the story we had never seen before. Many of us have heard the gospel told in four stories: creation, fall, redemption, and final consummation. Gerard does not say that this is wrong, but he does say that there are other ways of looking, ways that will help us to see more of the glory of God's story.

There is a story that he does say is wrong: the gospel as a pyramid selling scheme, people being converted in order to convert others. The problem here is not, as he makes clear, with a missional account of God's purpose. Rather, this is an unbearably thin account of what Christian mission is all about. Right at the beginning of the life of the church, Irenaeus, saint, pastor and, probably, martyr, wrote that "the glory of God is a human being fully alive". We are called not just to decision, but to life in all its fulness. This is the gift of God in Christ, made real by the Spirit.

Gerard offers us seven stories to understand our missional calling. Created and called by God, we are set free and remade, but also circumscribed, because God has come in Jesus to save us, and to send us to be a part of his purposes in restoring all things. The mission is God's; it is our purpose and our privilege to be called to be a part of it. The goal is the renewal of creation, not an escape from a failing world.

The vision of this book is delightfully—and rightly—positive. God is at work, and God's purposes will not be frustrated. The vision of this book is also profoundly realistic. We bring with us the baggage of wounds and failures which distort us, and God renews our lives so that we may be a part of the renewal of the life of the world. So stated, this sounds like a story we are all familiar with, but Gerard's genius is to retell it in ways that are profoundly new.

It is a great gift, sometimes, for the familiar to be made strange.

I want, finally, to say a word about the author. As I journey on in life, I count it one of the greatest privileges God has given me that I get to meet and learn from some wonderful, godly, and wise people who are doing more for God's Kingdom than I could ever imagine. Gerard and Chrissie Kelly are up at the top of that list. Through the churches they have planted, and the leaders they have encouraged, they have done more for the progress of the gospel in continental Europe than anyone else I have met or heard of. Gerard writes with a reality, a vulnerability, an honesty, that is instantly powerful; he combines this with deep practical wisdom and an evident love for God's people.

This book is full of stories of real people who so often (although the theme is hidden in the telling) have benefitted enormously from Gerard's work. God has used his ministry to bring healing, truth, salvation, to so many. And that "so many" includes me. When (it happens too rarely) I know I will be with Gerard because we are both speaking at the same conference or whatever, I look forward to the occasion, knowing that I will meet Jesus in meeting him, knowing that I will learn to be a better minister of the gospel through observing his example. I have never yet been disappointed.

I can narrate Christian theology in all the standard ways—it is my job. But every time I have been with Gerard, he has challenged me to understand differently, to look from a new angle, to hear a different voice. And every time, that challenge has made me a better follower of Jesus.

It is a gift, sometimes, for the familiar to be made strange.

Dr Stephen Holmes
Senior Lecturer in Theology, Head of School of Divinity, University of St Andrews

Introduction

> No one knew what they were joining. Or who they were joining. Or, really, why they were joining. But join they did! Problem was, I didn't know what they were joining either. And soon, as the numbers rose into the hundreds, and as the word spread around the world, I really had to come up with something...
>
> Danny Wallace[1]

Comedian Danny Wallace is now widely known as the man who started a cult by accident.[2] Two years into the twenty-first century, he left a job at the BBC and found himself with time on his hands. He was bored. Attending the funeral in Switzerland of his great-uncle Gallus Breitenmoser, he discovered that the old man, back in the 1940s, had started his own commune to escape the monotony of village life. Intrigued and inspired, Wallace decided to pay homage to this eccentric heritage. He put an announcement in *Loot*, the London small-ads paper, with the two words "Join Me" and his mailing address. The only requirement of those responding was that they send a passport photograph. Within weeks the responses began and Wallace was soon looking at the small, smiling faces of schoolteachers, mechanics, salespeople, clergy, children, and pensioners: all willing to pledge allegiance to his cause without actually knowing what it was. Before long the new "joinees" began to ask their nonplussed leader what exactly their shared task was to be. What had he invited them to join him *for*? Recruitment, as Danny Wallace discovered, is just the first step, and the easiest. Once you have your army, you have to *do* something with them.

Danny Wallace's experience produced a very funny book, *Join Me*, and led on to other eccentric projects but it also – and this too was by accident – laid bare a deep fault line in all religious experience. Joining a faith movement is one thing. Finding out what it's for is a deeper process altogether.

Over three decades my wife, Chrissie, and I have worked with individuals, families, and churches to stimulate a deeper connection with God's purposes in the world. For the past fifteen years this work has been carried out through the Bless Network, whose training base in France is shaping the lives of people of faith from many nations. Through hundreds of conversations we have come to see two glaring truths that all too often are ignored by the teaching programmes of local churches.

The first is that too many of those who have accepted the Christian faith are not entirely sure what to do with it. They have joined but are still waiting to be told what for. Worse still, the language in which the faith has been explained to them has revolved almost exclusively around receiving. This is what faith can do for you. The question of what you can do with your faith is left unanswered for a significant number of believers.

The second is that this lack really matters. There is a point of personal growth in the faith journey at which it becomes imperative to make a serious and sustainable connection to God's mission in the world. Finding faith is an important step. Finding purpose is what makes it a lifetime's journey. Human beings are designed for creative engagement with their environment: in one area or another and at some level we are all wired to *achieve*. It is achieving, not receiving, that gives meaning to our lives.

For too long our churches have advertised personal salvation as if it were, in and of itself, our goal. It is not only the Evangelicals on TV who fall into this trap. Sacramental and liturgical expressions of faith are just as readily misapplied. If receiving the Eucharist is only about my personal standing with God, what good does the enterprise of church achieve? We are like doorkeepers at a five-star hotel, holding wide the door to usher our guests inside, but caring little about what happens once they're through. Fine for the doormen – they can count scalps, register guests, and pat themselves on the back for having found so many – but, for the guests themselves, this is not remotely enough. Decision-based mission doesn't begin to answer the most important question of all: the question *why*. Why am I here? Why am I even alive? If my maker has now revealed himself as my redeemer, why has he done it? What is the purpose of this whole faith enterprise?

The evangelical tribe I've been part of for more than four decades has tended to fall back on a simplistic answer to this key question. Why have I been recruited? Simple: so that I can recruit others. My introduction to the Jesus Movement of the 1970s was very much on this basis. We were saved in order to lead others to salvation. I was enlisted as an enlister, and since the goal was always to enlist as many as possible, that should have been enough. We thought we would spend the rest of our lives evangelizing, and die happy, having told the world about Jesus. As I grew in faith I discovered that my questions were not all about "how to win others". I found myself asking, rather, how this faith was supposed to shape my life. What did my beliefs have to say about art, business, the media, and all the thousand and one other aspects of culture that people care about? In parallel with a generation raised on Jesus, I began to wonder what a whole-life discipleship might look like. What if the mission of God was more than personal salvation? What if I had been recruited not just to recruit others, but for some larger, more complex task? I discovered in myself gifts that didn't seem to have a place in personal "witness". What were they for? Did God want me to use them, or ignore them? I found myself hungering for a definition of mission that took in a wider view of the world without losing the passion and energy the Jesus Movement had given me.

For many of us in the twenty-first-century Western church, the "recruited to recruit" paradigm has now completely run out of steam. It is being artificially kept alive in sections of the church with a particular passion for doing so, but, for thousands – perhaps millions – of believers, it no longer motivates. This is hardly surprising, since it doesn't really make sense. Joining just so that you can invite others to join simply pushes back the *why* question until it gets heavier and heavier, and eventually falls on you. Like every pyramid and Ponzi scheme, a church fuelled by its search for recruits will ultimately collapse on itself. There has to be a deeper "why". The Danny Wallace option makes for good comedy. It doesn't make for a sustainable faith.

A Missionary Curriculum?

What does make faith meaningful is finding purpose. The deepest satisfaction, it seems, comes from finding our place of service and usefulness, knowing that our lives have meaning in the purposes of God. The word we use to describe this "why" of faith is mission, but all too often this is the very word around which our misunderstandings most accrue, like old hair congealing in a drainpipe. Defining exactly what Christian mission is has never been an easy task. David Bosch touches on no fewer than twelve accepted meanings of the word,[3] and makes the plea that mission should remain, to some extent, undefined.[4]

At its most basic, mission is another way of saying *purpose*, but in the church it has taken on less helpful meanings. Some of the most widespread and problematic assumptions are:

1. **That mission always means travel**. Missionaries are those who go overseas while most of us stay put, so most of us, by definition, are not missionaries. The contrast used in our language between "home" and "the mission field" captures this dilemma perfectly. How can our home context be an arena of God's mission if it isn't overseas? The problem arises because at the heart of mission there is a "from–to" dynamic – a breaking out of comfort and conformity to "go" where life is less straightforward. It is entirely wrong, though, as many of us are now discovering, to equate this "from–to" movement exclusively with geography and travel. The arc of the mission of God is a movement from the self to the other – not from Abingdon to Addis Ababa.

2. That mission is for missionaries. This is a related problem, where only those who carry the title "missionary" are assumed to have a mission. In the Catholic Church, for example, the phrase "pray for more vocations" is taken to mean that we need more priests and nuns. The idea that we all have a vocation has been lost. Whatever happened to God's army of ordinary people?

3. That the only mission of faith is to spread the faith. This is a version of the "recruited to recruit" problem, in which it is assumed that the only purpose of the church is to increase the size of the church. The problem here is not that mission never involves sharing faith: it is that sharing faith is not a big-enough definition of God's purposes in the world. When a believer says, "I can't be part of God's mission because I'm not good at sharing my faith", then you know that God's mission has been narrowly defined and poorly understood.

4. That whatever else mission is, it is not part of my ordinary life. This is perhaps a summary of the other three problems. Over here is my life: my concerns; my ambitions; my dreams; my activities; my routine – in effect, everything that makes me human – and over here is God's mission. Whatever the latter turns out to contain, I can be sure it won't have a lot to do with the former.

Your response may be to see these as old-fashioned ideas, in which case be thankful. Our understanding of mission is changing. We are shaking off old habits. The fact remains, though, that in the mainstream of our churches too many people labour under the oppressive shadows of such misunderstandings. Not all of us believe all these things to be true, by any means, but for most of us some version of each of these will be hiding somewhere in the cupboards of our faith. I know this is true because I see the look on people's faces when I tell them that my job is about helping them engage in "mission". I've never been a proctologist, but I suspect the reaction may be similar. Worse still, we are slow to replace these outdated ideas with more wholesome concepts. It's all very well clearing out the closets and ditching old ideas, but if we don't replace them with more useful pictures we risk losing mission altogether.

Sadly, the missions community, of which I am a long-term member, must bear a share of the blame for this situation. All too often, individuals who do overcome their ill-founded fears of mission and present themselves for service are offered training that confirms precisely the misunderstandings we've just listed. They are congratulated for *not* being ordinary; for being willing to travel; for having a vocation; for being willing to share their faith; for accepting the hard road of sacrifice and dissatisfaction. It is precisely at the moment that they depart from their everyday lives that we welcome them as "missionaries". We have developed sophisticated mechanisms for selecting and training the chosen few who are willing to serve. We have no message, it seems, for the many. Church leaders, for their part, have too often accepted the status quo, offering an approach to discipleship that for ordinary people hardly touches on the realities of God's mission in the world. If we are to see a wholesale realignment of our churches with the priority of connecting God's people with God's purposes, we have a lot of changing to do.

What is the answer to this stalemate in missional thinking? It is twofold: to come to an understanding of God's mission that includes and empowers *all* God's people, and to develop discipleship resources to help each believer find their place. Writing to the church in Ephesus, Paul describes a process of discipleship that will continue "until we all come to such unity in our faith and knowledge of God's Son that we will be mature in the Lord, measuring up to the full and complete standard of Christ."[5] *All* is one of Paul's favourite words in this letter, and the maturity he's talking about is the maturity of purpose and service. The process he is describing, which will go on until all of us are implicated, is the process of equipping God's people for their purpose.[6] It is the discovery, development, and deployment of the gifts God has given to each of us and to all of us. Nothing short of this vaulting ambition is worthy of being called mission.

If we are to recover the missionary energy that created the church in the first place, and has kept it alive to this day, we are going to need:

- To appreciate anew the sheer breadth of God's mission in the world. The full scope of mission is perhaps best summarized as "*what God wants*": any definition more narrow will not do justice to the biblical record. Jesus urged us to pray, after all, "May your Kingdom come soon. May your will be done on earth, as it is in heaven."[7] I don't often hear the Lord's Prayer cited as a guide to mission, but surely that's what it is. If it is always the will of God for the will of God to be done, we know at least where mission begins. Samuel Escobar writes, "It is necessary to correct the tendency to base mission on a few selected texts from the New Testament. What has to be grasped is God's purpose for humankind as revealed in Scripture, and the missionary thrust of the whole history of salvation. This will throw new light on the nature of mission."[8]

- To grasp the role of God's people in the delivery of his mission. Paul's formula in Ephesians 3:10 can be stated as "all the colours of God's wisdom, through all the calling of God's people, to every corner of the world."[9] Can we begin to see that mission is the sum total of the gifts God has given all of us, fully discovered, developed, and deployed? This includes sharing faith, because sharing faith is what some of us are called to and gifted for, but there is so much more. God's mission is as wide and as varied as the gifts he has given to his people.

- To see discipleship as essentially this process of *connecting God's people with God's purposes*. If we are all to come to maturity, we are going to need tools and teaching that aid this process, and a view of Christian growth that prioritizes the embracing of purpose for all believers. Being equipped for God's purposes means finding out what God is doing in the world, discerning what your part in it is, and speaking life to the gifts you have been given for fulfilling it.

These three tasks add up to the embracing of a missional curriculum – an approach to teaching and equipping in our churches that sets for itself the lofty goal of seeing all Christ's followers connected to his purpose in the world. If people are the centre of God's plan, as the Bible clearly suggests, then connecting people to purpose will be the core business of the church.

Connecting Your Call

Over many years of working with believers from all points on the Christian compass, we have encountered many who have a faith, and are glad of it, but who don't have a clear purpose for living. Those who do have a strong sense of purpose all too often struggle to connect it in any meaningful way with their faith. The few who are able, by contrast, to connect the purpose of their lives with God's intentions for our world discover that they are in turn enabled:

- To know that their lives are significant in the purposes of their maker. They find out what they were born for. Connection with God's mission triggers in them a deep response. The more fully we know *why* we are alive, the more truly alive we are.

- To live well in the balanced place of loving and being loved. What could be more satisfying than a life in which you both receive blessing and see blessing released to others? Witness the number of business people who dedicate the first half of their lives to gaining wealth and the second to giving it away. The joy of *giving* turns out to be a higher goal than that of *gaining*.

- To live their faith sustainably, not burning out with the short-term fire of a rocket on Bonfire Night, but living and serving for the long game. Connection with God's mission should never be mistaken for mere *activism*. It is something more complex; a fuller expression of who we are, poured into a purpose we know to be much greater than ourselves.

This approach to mission does not exclude the narrow range of activities we have traditionally associated with the term, but it completes them. It sets them like jewels alongside the other thrilling, life-wide tasks God is calling us to. It invites all of us to surrender to God's purposes, and to support one another in the diversity of the adventures God has for us. Let me offer three examples from our own small church community in France.

Mylene and Thierry are from New Zealand and France respectively, and live in the city of Caen in Normandy. Mylene had always dreamed of owning her own business, and she realized several years ago that what she really longed to do was to open a coffee house. She didn't have the backing she needed, or the training, but she did have a vision. Two years ago she left her job to concentrate on gaining the skills she needed to open Caen's first new-generation coffee shop. In those two years great miracles have happened, and Keys & co, at the time of writing, has come through its first very successful month of trading, with Mylene, Thierry, and their daughter Stéphanie joyfully serving the people of Caen. Throughout this family's journey we have prayed for them as a church, speaking life and blessing into their dream. Why? Because they have committed Keys & co to being a kingdom space; a place where God is pleased to dwell; a "Bethel", where heaven touches earth. Mylene, Thierry, and Stéphanie are praying daily that Keys & co will serve the purposes of God in Caen. They want their café to be successful, because their mission needs to be sustainable, but the goal is the kingdom: life brought to the city; the wisdom of God made known to the rulers and authorities in the heavenly realms. Keys & co is as vital a part of God's strategy for the city of Caen as is the church we are working to plant there, and we have prayed for it in that light.

Fiona is English, and recently heard the call of God to love and serve the refugees living in "The Jungle", the ramshackle camp on the edge of Calais. For three months Fiona has led a team serving chai tea and lunch to hundreds of people each day. With the demolition of the camp she is moving from a "Chai Hut" to a "Chai Van" as we equip a former ambulance to deliver the same service to a more dispersed migrant population. Fiona's journey to Calais is an illustration of how the call of God works. A graduate of the London School of Theology, she is passionate about worship and mission, and has sensed over many years a twofold purpose: to love and serve Muslims, and to pray for the world's most dangerous places, a number of which she has visited. As she saw all that was unfolding in Calais, she came alive to a new sense of God's call. She saw that God was bringing Muslim people to Europe, desperately in need of being loved and served. More than this, she discovered that of the nine most dangerous places on earth to be or to become a Christian, seven were represented in the population of the Jungle. What is Fiona longing for as she serves chai tea to desperate people? That even the Jungle, surely one of the most desolate corners of France, will become a kingdom space; a place where God is pleased to dwell. The goal, once again, is kingdom: the purposes of God inching forward on planet earth through the willing surrender of human energies and capacities.

Tim and Jane are an English couple who have lived in France for ten years. They run a bed and breakfast but are also language teachers, offering instruction by immersion to both children and adults, who are welcomed into their home. Through a series of recent miracles, they have the capacity to expand their business and are developing a hundred-acre site near Tours as a combined campsite, guest house, and language school. The project will be two years in the making, and one of the earliest decisions was to designate a permanent prayer room at the very centre of the site. The property is along one of the pilgrim routes leading ultimately to Santiago de Compostela, and the new venture will revive a lost local tradition of welcoming pilgrims. As Tim and Jane walk the site, discussing their project with architects and contractors, they have one key goal in mind: that this, too, will be a kingdom space. They want holidaymakers, language students, pilgrims, and visitors to find themselves in a place where it is easy to know God; where heaven touches earth; where prayer is as accessible an activity as play.

The diversity of these three projects is self-evident: a city café; an "SOS Chai" truck in a refugee slum village; a campsite and language school. There are common threads, though, that link them. They are all entrepreneurial, reflecting the passion and giftedness of their creators. They each represent an effort to see that passion overlapping somehow with the purposes of God. They are all about bringing people into a place of welcome and hospitality and, more, to believing, in faith, that the welcome of God will also be tasted. They are about loving people; taking them seriously; letting them know that they matter. They are *missional* in the deepest sense of the word. We *know* that many people will be blessed through these projects – more than would be reached by persuading Mylene, Thierry, Stéphanie, Fiona, Tim, and Jane to focus all their efforts on "evangelism" and church activities. People will meet God; they will find faith; they will be helped in their need – it just won't be in the same way that we might expect if all these individuals were "missionaries". The projects will thrive, and will last, because they are moving in the direction of the gifts God has given to these people, rather than against the tide of their lives and dreams.

If you talked to any one of these missional leaders you would be left in no doubt as to their passion. They are creative, committed go-getters. Each of them, in order to come to this place, has needed to show courage. Courage, sometimes, to resist the pressure to conform to a more mainstream understanding of mission. Courage to pursue a sense of God's call that they felt strongly but which others had to be persuaded of. Courage to see their "secular" activities as significant in the purposes of God. Courage to know that tea and coffee, and the smile they are served with, can be agents of the kingdom of God.

These brief pictures of what happens when individuals find their place in the purposes of God are small illustrations of a much larger process, a much wider movement. It is a movement in which ordinary believers are discovering the immense joy of connecting with the mission of God in the world. It is a movement, I believe, that offers great hope to the tired churches of the West, struggling as they are in the ruins of Christendom.

This movement rests on the recognition of the intrinsic value and giftedness of every human being. The mission of God is a human potential movement because:

- The gifts that fuel it are present already in God's army of ordinary people. Mission is about releasing what God has invested in us all.

- The breadth of its footprint is matched by the diversity of the gifts God has given. It needs all of us to engage because God's gifts have been so widely and variously dispersed.

- The process of mission is a reflection of these same convictions – it is when we see, celebrate, and communicate the immense value of every human being that we begin to see something of the plan of God for them.
- Ultimately, the call of God on every life is to a purpose. Those who don't yet know that they belong to Christ are also called – not only to receive salvation, but to become active themselves as agents of the kingdom.

Mission is sparked when I realize that I matter to God – I have a part to play in his plans. It is sustained when I realize that this is also true of others. Mission says "You matter". It says it to me and it asks me to say it to others.

Surprised by Joy?

At the heart of this broader understanding of mission is an invitation to joy. Finding out why I am alive; exploring and expressing the gifts God has given me; tasting a life of purpose and meaning; inviting others to do the same – these are joyful, celebratory activities. Our problem is that we have come to see God's mission as essentially *miserable*. It seems harsh to put this in such brutal words, but the reality is that many believers think of mission in terms of duty and drudgery, and not of joy. Mission is what we really should do but don't really want to. If there's something we do want to do there's a good chance it won't qualify as mission. If there's something we've never wanted to do, or somewhere we've never wanted to go, guess what? Yep, mission! Contrast this with the magnificent words of pioneer missiologist Lesslie Newbigin:

> There has been a long tradition which sees the mission of the Church primarily as obedience to a command. It has been customary to speak of "the missionary mandate." … If one looks at the New Testament evidence one gets another impression. Mission begins with a kind of explosion of joy… The mission of the Church in the pages of the New Testament is more like the fallout from a vast explosion, a radioactive fallout which is not lethal but life-giving.[10]

Can we begin to dream of such an understanding taking hold of our churches? Can mission again become "an explosion of joy" for all God's people?

A House of Seven Stories

> Honest stories respect our freedom; they don't manipulate us, don't force us, don't distract us from life. They bring us into the spacious world in which God creates and saves and blesses.
>
> EUGENE PETERSON[11]

In this exciting movement of connecting God's people to God's purposes, our particular area of concern has been to explore in some depth the pathways by which ordinary believers can move towards a deeper alignment with God's plan for their lives. There are other areas that need attention – the training of our leaders and the teaching programmes of our churches to name but two – but the calling we have sensed has been to work at the grass roots, helping individual followers of Jesus to find their place in his purposes. Our explorations in this area have taken on a dual emphasis, of *understanding* and *activation*, leading us to identify two specific needs that human beings have in their struggle to connect with their maker's intentions:

First, we need a coherent understanding of who God is and what he wants. We need an overarching narrative that we can embrace and believe in: a story that makes sense not only of the world in which we live, but of our own place in it. This is a fundamental human need. Stories are the maps in which we read and therefore navigate our landscape, and it is primarily by stories that the Bible speaks to us. The people of God are a storied people. One of the great tragedies of the contemporary church is that we can use all the right words but still end up telling the wrong story. Of course we'll get lost, if the maps we are using have misread our terrain.

Second, as we embrace this deeper story, we need tools and entry points that enable us to connect with it. Becoming missional – connecting at the deepest level with the mission of God in our world and activating our own part in it – is a process. It cannot be the work of a moment or the fruit of one decision. It unfolds, in our experience, in a number of stages, each one of which is vital to the overall goal of connection, always with the ultimate aim of more fully integrating the story into our lives and our lives into the story.

A missionary curriculum will address these twin goals: articulating the breadth of the story of God and highlighting the key steps by which the individual believer can connect with it. In the course of the many conversations we have had with those looking for such a connection, we have found ourselves coming back time and time again to the same key concepts. These are steps or stages in the faith journey that many of us seem to struggle with and which, properly understood and acted on, open up to each of us the possibility of finding our place in God's plans for our world. Too many Christians are frustrated, guilt-ridden, and exhausted from trying to find their place in a story that doesn't make sense in the first place, and when it does has no place for them. The result is a colossal switch-off from the whole concept of mission. The energy they might have used in loving God and serving their neighbours gets channelled elsewhere, not because they don't care but because they don't see a clear way forward.

The stories God tells about us are not like this. They don't weigh us down with an unbearable burden of responsibility for an unattainable goal. They liberate us; they speak into the very marrow of our dry bones the command to get up and dance. God's stories are life-giving.

In a previous book, *The Prodigal Evangelical*,[12] I developed an overview of God's mission in the world built on four words: beautiful, broken, forgiven, and invited. This suggested that the overarching story of God, in its impact on humanity, is framed by four bold descriptors:

- We are *beautiful* because we owe our existence to a careful, creative, loving maker, whose image persists in us no matter how hard we try to obliterate it.

- We are *broken* because the story of God takes seriously the unavoidable fact that there is something in us that is not as it should be – the crack that runs through everything runs through my heart.

- We are *forgiven* because, in Christ, our maker has come to us and has accomplished, in and of himself, all that is necessary for our full and final reconciliation: the prodigal father waits only to embrace us.

- We are *invited* because every human being has a place at the table of God; every name is on the guest list; your attendance is anticipated – you have only to respond.

This is the trajectory of the story of God, as it arcs from the splendour of our origins, through our lostness and the foundness he responds with, to our invitation to the banquet at the end of the universe. As we have explored the application of these four words to our life and mission we have found them resonating in many unexpected corners, from the creation of art to the consolation of refugees. We have also, however, sensed a need to go further in our exploration of God's mission. Specifically, we have been challenged to respond to an urgent question: how do I *connect* with this great story? How can I, beautiful, broken, forgiven, and invited as I am, find my place in the story God is telling in my world? This, surely, must be the very heart of my participation in God's mission, that I should find my place in his story?

In seeking to respond to this question, we have identified seven stories that have their proper place in the overarching narrative of God's intentions for our world and that each speak to a different aspect of our place in his plans. Like tributaries joining one great river, these seven threads flow into the wider picture of God's mission: they are the stories our maker is using in each of our lives to bring us into line with his purposes.

Why seven *stories*? Why not seven steps, or seven principles, or seven habits? Because *story* is the basic category by which we understand God's purposes and find our place in his plans. The Bible, our primary source in this process, is a repository of stories, but so is the world we live in. Brands, products, friendships, careers, rivalries, films, books – non-fiction as much as fiction – faith systems, philosophies, scientific theories – these are all stories. They are the narratives we use to make sense of our world and find our place in it. They are the drawings on the walls of the caves we live in. They codify and journal the world we know and speculate about the world beyond our knowledge. We are storied creatures. This has been an implicit truth of the Christian faith from its very beginnings. We know that we live by stories and for the most part we know where to find them.

"The best stories", Michael Novelli writes, "give us a glimpse of ourselves – they show us who we are and who we could be. God's story is like this. It stretches from the beginning of time, across our lives, and into the future. It tells of a great and faithful Creator who reveals the most beautiful way to live in rhythms of love, peace, and sacrifice."[13]

The seven stories we have identified as points of connection to the wider story of God are:

Creation – The story of who you are, of where you are, and of how you came to be here. Your participation in God's mission starts right here, with his original intention.

Vocation – The story of your calling and purpose and of a path uniquely fitted to you. God's mission is a partnership: your dreams for your life woven into God's dream for his world.

Liberation – The story of the prison cell God brings you out from and the promise he is leading you into. God's mission is a journey from slavery to freedom.

Formation – The story of your affections, the things that matter most to you, and God's desire to win your heart through worship. God's mission comes to birth in a life abandoned to his love and mercy.

Limitation – The story of God's presence in the places in your life, and the places your life takes you, that are hard for you. The mission of God is an adventure of discovering his purposes even in the pain of exile.

Incarnation – The story of the journey God himself has taken to come to you and end your alienation. Mission is not what you can do for God. It is everything that God has done for you.

Restoration – The story of the gifts God has given you, the greater gifts he has for you, and his plan that you should share them with your neighbour. Mission is joining God in the making of a whole new world.

Each of these seven is:

- **Rooted in Scripture.** Not only do they arise from specific incidents recorded in the Old and New Testaments, they are also threads that run through the biblical narrative from beginning to end. The Exodus, for example, is a specific event in Israel's history. It can be pinned down to key passages in the book of the same name. Freedom, on the other hand, and God's desire to liberate his people from every form of slavery, resound on the Bible's every page, from the Genesis announcement "You are free"[14] to the final shout of tears dried and sufferings brought to an end.[15] In the Exodus event God's liberating intentions break the surface, as visible as a lake in the sunlight; but they are fed by an underground stream that flows from our deepest past towards God's promised future. These seven stories, likewise, are among those that can be discerned as threads woven into the whole tapestry of God's story.

- **Active in our lives.** These are stories we have found over thirty years of ministry to be "active" in the lives of individuals. They are familiar landmarks, sites we have come back to time and again as we have worked to help God's people connect with God's purposes. For each of the seven there are men and women in Scripture who help us to see God's workings, but for each there are also examples all around us. Since these seven stories represent, in our view, the intentions of our maker, they are arguably present in the life of every human being. These are the questions we are all trying to answer, even when we don't know we're doing it. Like a set of pistons designed to take their proper place in an engine assembly, we were *made* for connection with our maker. To live in disconnection from the creator is to live at less than our full potential. In all of our lives these stories are doing their work, calling us to live in that vital place of connection where we know and are known.

- **Complementary.** These are the seven threads, we believe, that when woven together enable individuals to live passionately, sustainably, and fruitfully in connection to God's mission in the world. They are not chronological or systemized, to be followed sequentially in the sense of a Twelve Step programme. Rather, they are seven stories that are present in some form in the life of every human being and are each significant to us as a thread we need to give attention to at different times and in varying measure. Together they form a well-rounded picture of what it means to connect to God's mission in the world.

- **Lastly, each is in a very real sense *your* story.** Somewhere in your life, each of these stories is at work. They are rooted in stories the Bible tells, for sure, but they are also the stories we all live. They are not seasons, in the sense of something we pass through, though there may be times when we are more aware of one than another. The truth is that they are all at work in us all the time. Our creation story is being revealed to us each day; our freedom story is an ongoing journey; our limitation story is always there, even though we often pay it no heed. Listening to each of these stories, letting it shape you, acknowledging your place in it, and seeing the next steps – these are movements towards maturity. If you are prepared to look closely enough at your own life, you will find these stories present. Not only that, but your engagement with them will be the same as, but different from, that of everyone around you. We all have fingers but no two of us share the same prints.

We all live these stories; we are all the recipients of our maker's love and attention; we are all moving towards or away from his intentions for us: but no two of us have identical journeys. Our God is far too creative for such duplication.

"Throughout history", Michael Novelli tells us, "societies have passed on their values, beliefs and traditions through stories. Woven into the fabric of our cultures, families and communities, they're the strands that bind us together. Stories define who we are."[16]

Can we begin to imagine an engagement with the mission of our maker that more fully embraces his story? Are we ready to hear and respond to the stories God is telling about us?

The Crowd in the Cloud

> The unity of the Bible is discovered in the development of life with God as a reality on earth, centred in the person of Jesus. We might call this The Immanuel Principle of life. This dynamic, pulsating, with-God life is on nearly every page of the Bible. To the point of redundancy we hear that God is with people... These varied stories form a mosaic illustrating how the "with" life works in all circumstances of human existence, both in specific historical periods and through all times.
>
> RICHARD FOSTER AND KATHRYN A. HELMERS[17]

"Since we are surrounded by such a huge crowd of witnesses to the life of faith," the writer to the Hebrews says, "let us strip off every weight that slows us down, especially the sin that so easily trips us up. And let us run with endurance the race God has set before us."[18] Part of the Bible's role is to place before us the experiences of those who have gone before. Each of the seven stories we will explore together will touch on the lives of several biblical figures, from Adam and Eve, through Abraham to Jesus and beyond. They are your crowd in the cloud, cheering you on: the generations who have gone before you to field test the ways of God. God's mission, in this sense, is crowdsourced. You are not asked to work out, on your own, what faith should look like. You don't have to dredge up from within yourself the courage to move on. Your adventure with God is not a solo quest. Rather, you are free to draw on a library of lives, a colourful collection of stories describing life with God. Wikipedia defines crowdsourcing as "the practice of obtaining needed services, ideas, or content by soliciting contributions from a large group of people, and especially from an online community, rather than from traditional employees or suppliers".[19] From Abel to the Prophets, the names cited in Hebrews 11 bookend a hundred others – every life a treasure store of wisdom and encouragement. These are people who have pressed on, in the past, in the ways of faith; who have believed in things they didn't live to see. Hearing the stories God is telling about us is in part about engaging with this crowd in the cloud. They help us, in a number of ways, to see the human scale of God's mission. Specifically, they enable us to know:

- That it is faith, not fitness, that we celebrate. If you're looking for a list of Bible heroes who had it all together, if you want a study in success – look elsewhere. These are flawed heroes. They are included not because they found perfection but because they followed where God led them. They believed, and belief shaped their lives. The list of those who really made it, who never got it wrong, who serve infallibly as moral guides, would be much shorter. Scratch that: it would be empty but for one name. The faces in faith's gallery are there precisely for the errors they have made. Their stories matter because you can learn from their mistakes. The growth in our age of a prosperity gospel has led some to believe that faith is linked to winning. Winners have faith; losers don't. But faith, in the Hebrews 11 parade, is not about winning – it's about keeping going, even when you seem to be losing. Business leaders sell their self-serving books by offering the secret of success. Heroes of the faith don't. They share with us, rather, their vulnerability; their weakness; their inability to do what is asked of them: but they tell us, for all this, that they have persisted in trusting God. I'll take a loser with faith any day over a winner with nothing but a theory.

- Secondly, that different contexts require different actions. These are people who, in their context and with all their limitations, tried to work out what it was that God was asking them to do. They did their best to separate the signal from the noise; they forged a path through the fog. If we model our faith on theirs, we will do the same: listening hard in our own culture for the whisper our frantic lives so easily drown out. Faith is a pursuit of precision engineering. The station we are tuning to is a narrow band easily passed over by those in too much of a hurry. The writer to the Hebrews is not asking us to duplicate the lives of these people but to emulate their passion, to be as committed in our time and place as they were in theirs to discerning the ways of God. Follow their example; don't reproduce their actions. Be moved by the intense focus with which they pursued the promise of God. Learn from them this energy, this strength of purpose, this determination. How many of us miss out on the destination God has for us because the bus is too slow and we get off three stops early?

- Thirdly, that faith is about something we don't see. Not a never-never land hidden behind the sky, but a promise of what God wants to do that isn't done yet. Faith is the capacity that enables us to see beyond the evidence; to believe beyond the barriers of time and place. As Martin Luther King Jr said, "Faith is taking the first step even when you don't see the whole staircase." There is a thread running through the lives of every man and woman on the Hebrews 11 list: a cord drawing them outward from themselves towards God's future. It didn't feel the same to any two of them. For each of them the act of finding that thread was unique, fitted to their own particularities. But it was the same cord, knotted every century or so and stretching from the dawn of time towards the universe's final consummation. It's the same cord Jesus held; that Peter grabbed onto; that John and Phoebe and Mary had a hand on. It's the cord each one of us is invited, in our own world, to take hold of: the thread that points us beyond ourselves, that ultimately will draw us out of our blinkered limitations into light. The very notion that

Abel and Abraham are connected, that Rahab and the Prophets share a story, is evidence for the substance of this thread. They are all different, but they all grabbed the same cord. They prove in their diversity that we can too.

"This is what the past is for!" Corrie ten Boom writes in *The Hiding Place*. "Every experience God gives us, every person He puts in our lives is the perfect preparation for the future that only He can see."[20]

Don't project onto your Bible heroes the issues and assumptions of today. They are not you. They don't live in your world. But get to know them. Get to know their world, and learn from them what it took to cling to God. See them, in their trials and in their triumphs, reaching out beyond their limitations to take hold of God's promised future. They are your online community, your crowd in the cloud. Let them be for you a source of strength and courage.

Choosing to interact with the stories recorded for us by generations past is important, but equally important is choosing *how* to interact with them. Stories are not shopping lists, or rule books. They are not instruction manuals. They don't present information in ordered tables, or indicate a desired response with diagrams and arrows. There is only one way to encounter a story if you want to learn from it. You have to let it reach you from the inside. Eugene Peterson writes a moving account of a couple who became members of a congregation he led:

> Anthony Plakados was a thirty-five-year-old truck driver in my congregation. Anthony grew up in a Greek home, conventionally Catholic, but none of it rubbed off. He

left school after the eighth grade. He told me that he had never read a book. And then he became a Christian, got himself an old King James Bible with small print and read it three times in that first year of his conversion. Anthony was off and running, Mary, his wife was interested, but also a bit bewildered by all this and asked a lot of questions. Mary had grown up a proper Presbyterian, gone to Sunday School all her growing up years, and was used to a religion of definitions and explanations. When Mary's questions got too difficult for Anthony, he would invite me to their trailer-house home, papered with Elvis Presley posters, to help him out. One evening the subject was the parables – Mary wasn't getting it. I was trying to tell her how to read them, how to make sense of them, I wasn't getting on very well, and Anthony interrupted. "Mary, you got to live 'em, then you'll understand 'em; you can't figger 'em out from the outside, you got to git inside 'em – or let 'em git inside you." And Anthony hadn't read so much as a word of John Calvin.[21]

Imagine yourself following a trail through dense jungle alongside a wide, full river. You are conscious every step of the great, flowing body of water at your side, but you can't always get close to it. At times the banks are too steep; at other times the foliage too thick. You lose sight of the water for a while, knowing its presence only by sound. On occasions you follow by pure instinct. Intermittently along the trail, though, you stumble across magnificent access points. Here you find a small wharf for canoes to tie up to; here a wide, lazy beach; here a fishing spot; here a swimming hole created by a turn in the river's course. At each of these you stop for a while, marvelling at the closeness of the water and the joy of interacting with it. The river invites you in. The points of access make possible your response.

Join me, then, as we journey through the seven stories that make up the story of God in the world, and which invite you to find your own life in it. Each of the seven will offer you, I hope, opportunities to consider your connection with God's mission and to embrace it more fully. The end result, I pray, will be a map of the purposes of God for the world: a user's guide to a life of significance and meaning. You may notice as you explore these seven access-points to God's river that each is introduced through one of the Bible's great women. This is deliberate. From Eve onwards, women play a huge role in God's plan, and yet their stories are too often overlooked. Might we find new things in the story of God if we look for a moment through their eyes?

"If a story is not about the hearer he will not listen," John Steinbeck warned. "And here I make a rule – a great and interesting story is about everyone or it will not last."[22] I can only promise you that these seven stories, among the greatest ever told, *are* about everyone. They are about you.

CHAPTER 1

Creation:
Walk with the Worldmaker

> You have a **CREATION** story.
> It is the story of who you are,
> of where you are,
> and of how you came to be here.
> Your participation in God's mission starts right here,
> with his original intention.

A Game in Two Halves

> Bone of my Bone thou art, and from thy State
> Mine never shall be parted, bliss or woe.
>
> JOHN MILTON, *PARADISE LOST*[23]

Genesis 3:20 reads, "Then the man – Adam – named his wife Eve, because she would be the mother of all who live."[24] My Bible offers a footnote that tells me "*Eve* sounds like a Hebrew term that means 'to give life'". Helpful, but a footnote all the same, as if that's all that she herself was. The marginalization of Eve is one of the greatest sins and tragedies of the church. Untold damage has been done by the assumption that Adam is the protagonist of this drama. We'll nominate him for the Best Actor award. She can have Best Supporting Actress. The only time some people even mention Eve is when they point out that she was the first to take the fruit. They usually forget to ask where Adam was. *Beside her* is the answer[25] – mute, and complicit from his eyeballs to his toes.

Did the serpent speak to Eve because he thought she might be weaker than Adam, or because he saw that where she led, Adam would follow? It's interesting that Adam didn't join in the conversation, even though he was present for it. The text does, in this sense, contrast Adam with Eve: but this is not to credit him with obedience. At best it is to highlight his passivity. At least Eve showed some *interest* in what God had said.

I raise these questions not to read a twenty-first-century approach to gender back into an ancient text, but rather to discover what is there. It has always intrigued me that the one part of this narrative quoted by both Jesus and Paul is so ill-fitting to the cultures both were raised in.[26] Both affirm the Genesis prescription – that a man will leave his father's house and be joined to his wife – but neither lived in a culture with this practice. The reverse was normative throughout the ancient world. In many places it still is. When a man asks a girl to marry him, he takes her from her father's house and she is joined to him. We know this is true because it is the form that Jesus uses when he borrows from local marriage custom to explain his own intentions for his people.[27] Even in our culture, to this day, it is more common for a wife to take her husband's name than the reverse. And the priest or pastor frogmarched in to marry them will ask the congregation *"Who gives this woman to be married to this man?"* It is the girl who is "given away" by her father, not the groom – as you might expect if Genesis were taken seriously. How could we miss this, in so many cultures, through so many generations? Because the bias towards male supremacy, like that towards our own race, runs so deep in us.

What I read in this text is not hierarchy but partnership. There are moments when Adam clearly has the lead, but there are others when he follows. Eve is not a bit player in this drama, brought on to make her husband's sex life better. She is not the product of necessity. She is given to him – they are given to each other – as companion. Not only that: she is the perfect partner. God believes in partnership. He is trinity, three persons living in a circle of perpetual love. He knows what equality means, and respect, and he wants Adam to know it too. So much so that the task the man is given, with its emphasis on populating a planet, won't even get past the starting gate unless he and the woman learn to dance.

The Genesis presentation of Eve tells me:

- That before our cultures developed those awkward differences in status between genders, men and women were called to work in partnership together.

- That it is to them both that the task of ruling and subduing God's good earth is given, their job description set up in such a way that they have to co-operate to fulfil it.

- That this joint call is for a reason. Men and women are the two halves of humanity, and it is humanity that God invites into his partnership.

What I read in Adam's naming of his wife is *honour*. He is giving her a title of respect. And there's more. This naming takes place *after* the eating of the fruit. It is a response, in some way, to the whole discovery of nakedness and shame, to God's disappointment. It is after the ground has been cursed, and pain has been promised in childbirth. Is Eve afraid? Is Adam? How do they see the adventure that now lies before them? I wonder if Adam is trying somehow to comfort his wife: "Cheer up, love. You still get to be the mother of everyone who'll ever live!" Her role is future-focused. She is not mired in disappointment and regret. She has a job to do. The mother of all humanity. Now that *is* a place of honour.

Eve, for me, is the ultimate symbol, the reminder, that God's original intention was to partner with humanity, and for humanity to partner with one another. Human community and communion with God go hand in hand, and both are born in Eden. It is from this point – from God's original intention – that we must begin to trace the arc of the story of mission.

Creation: The Story So Far

> The reality with which we have to deal is the story – the story that begins before the creation of the world, ends beyond the end of the world, and leads through the narrow road that is marked by the names of Abraham, Isaac and Jacob, Moses, Amos, Paul and, name above every name, Jesus.
>
> LESSLIE NEWBIGIN[28]

Kate Adie's 2006 book Nobody's Child[29] explores the often-ignored subject of "foundlings": people who were abandoned at birth and have no knowledge, perhaps well into adulthood, of who their parents are or were. Adie herself was adopted, and she writes very movingly of the experience of having to make up answers to simple, everyday questions. "Do you have any brothers or sisters?" "Where were you born?" "When is your birthday?"

The earnestness and passion with which foundlings are driven to find out about their past signals a powerful truth: origins matter. Our history is a building block of our identity. If we want to know who we are, we need to know where we come from; and what is true for the individual is also true for humanity. If we are to know who we are – what it means to be human in this most human-shaped world – then we need to know where we come from. Origins matter: this is the crux of the "creation debate". "Creation" matters to me not so much as an argument with which to refute this or that theory of science, but as a fundamental statement of what *is*.

To be a "creationist" is to believe that the God we worship is the maker of heaven and earth. It is not to make any claim of understanding exactly how the world came into being, nor how long it took, nor what we might have reported had we been there to witness the process. To affirm the biblical account of creation is to assert that the universe is the work of a loving, personal being who has called into existence a multifaceted, achingly beautiful world and has placed human beings within it to manage, rule, and love it at his side.

To say that the One God we worship is the Creator of all things is to make a foundational philosophical statement. It is to say that all reality – all that we can see and know and experience and enjoy – has its origin in the love of God. It is to say that personality and purpose, mind and meaning, are at the heart of all things. Some believing scientists talk of *intelligent design* as a fundamental quality of the creation, but to be true to the Genesis account we should more accurately speak of *loving intention*. A universe conceived in the bosom of a loving, personal, purposeful God will be a different place from the aftermath of an accidental explosion. It matters that our planet is not a random collection of purposeless atoms, because if *it* is, then *we* are, and no meaning is possible for us. But if our world has meaning then so do we, and there is the possibility of a life of purpose.

This is, perhaps surprisingly, the starting point of all Christian mission. Christians too often begin their theological journey at Calvary, as if the story of salvation begins with the death of Jesus. But Calvary is not the beginning of our story; Eden is. God does not first enter the drama as our redeemer but as our creator. To put this into very blunt terms, the first statement of the Christian gospel is not "Jesus died for you". It is "God made you". The Genesis narrative gives us a picture of God's intentions for us that is still in place, and still speaking, even as the last words of the book of Revelation fade. God has never deviated from his original intentions for us, and the persistence of his plan – his sheer, dogged determination to see his dream fulfilled – is what fuels mission. *Original intention* is the underlying condition in which all mission takes place.

Three core truths, on which all we know about God's mission in the world is founded, emerge in the Bible's very first chapters. Your creation story is the starting point for understanding who God is, who you are, and how the two might be connected. The Genesis narrative tells me:

- Who God is. The Hebrew view of God, Tom Wright asserts, "can be summed up in a single phrase: creational and covenantal monotheism".[30] God is personal. He has made the world. He is intimately and lovingly involved with the world he has made. This God is faithful, committed, generous, artful. God is my "Father in heaven" – a loving parent who overwhelms me with his generosity and favour and yet whose every word to me is backed by the unfathomable depth of his power as the maker of all things. How can the utterly "other" – the all-powerful, the ultimate "beyond" – be intimate with me? Here is the mystery of our faith, and the mark and measure of God's generosity. All this, from the very beginning, is implicit in the story the book of Genesis tells. God's power is revealed in the very act of creation; his character in the loving care with which he makes each creature; his covenantal love in the gentle words he speaks to his first human friends.

- Who I am. Belief in creation also tells me something about myself. It tells me I am a creature. I have been called into being by this loving God. I live in response to his will and purpose. My identity, my nature, my functioning, my life in the world – none of these are random. They do not flow from chance events sparked by a cold universe, like lottery balls thrown from a machine. They flow, rather, from loving intention. Before all else, I am loved – if I would only know it. Not only am I a creature, loved and valued, I am more still: I am a creature made in the image of the maker. I am creative because he is creative; relational because he is relational; alive because he is alive. The life breath of the divine parent fills my very lungs; the pulse of my maker drives my heart. If I want to know what I am called to be, I need only to look to the source, whose reflection I am. God has not left me without clues to my identity.

He has left his fingerprints all over me. He has etched his image in my soul.

- Why I'm here. Because before all else I am loved, I can live purposefully. The search for purpose is the deepest need of the human soul. Here in the West we have proved, if it ever needed proving, that when all other needs are met, the need for purpose remains. To live well, I must live meaningfully – and if there is meaning I can endure all other forms of loss. To acknowledge God as creator is to assert that this meaning does not have to arise from within me. Rather, it is spoken over me. The God who hovered above a primal universe – formless and empty, wreathed in darkness – and spoke the words that called all meaning into being and all being into meaning, hovers, also, over my life. He calls me from nothingness to substance; from non-being to being; from aimlessness to life and fruitfulness. Over the addict, reduced to emptiness by chemical abuse, he hovers, calling forth life. Over the prostitute, wreathed in the darkness of the sins of others, he hovers, calling forth light. And over the consumer, sated with indulgence and abundance and yet empty of hope, he hovers, calling forth meaning and reality.

Without this sense of who God is, who I am, and how my life can have intrinsic meaning, there can be no understanding of mission at all. If "mission" is another way of saying "purpose", then only in a purposeful universe can it have meaning. The Genesis narrative drips with God's *intentionality*. It is he who speaks identity and meaning into every aspect of the world he makes, including, ultimately, me. I have a mission because my maker has intention. I don't know how it can be possible to live with purpose; to rest secure in the embrace of loving intention; to know who I am and where I come from, without kneeling before the God who has made me. I know there are many who claim freedom, and dignity, in the denial of God as their maker. But I cannot. I can't imagine meaning without creation. Creation, for me, is the cornerstone of all else. It is who God is. It is who I am. It is where I come from. It is all I ask for in the vast and boundless adventure that is the universe he has made. A missional theology starts with the primary and foundational distinction between Creator and Creation. God is my maker. I am made. All else flows from this assertion.

Freedom, Fear and Fruit

> The first prohibition ever issued by God to humanity, in Genesis 2:16, begins with the words "You are free…"
>
> ANON[31]

The Genesis account of the making of the world sets out the context of God's mission by telling me who God is, who I am, and how my life as his creature can have meaning, but it does even more in putting in place the foundations for mission. It describes the process by which the first human beings are invited into partnership with their creator, and the basis on which that partnership became flawed. In doing so it traces very clearly the contours of the central problem to which all mission is in some sense a response.

The framework of the story is simple. It is a drama in four acts.

In Act 1 the curtain rises on a world that God has made to be abundant in its goodness. Into this world he places a number of living creatures and from among them he chooses one species – the human race, represented by Adam and Eve – to be his co-regents. Their task will be to develop those parts of the world that are as yet untamed; to extend the boundaries of God's garden to the very edges of the planet, until the whole world is filled with a God-ordered, fruitful human society.

In Act 2 God's human partners are given the choice to continue in a relationship of trust and dependence or to strike out on their own, separate from the kindness of their maker. They choose independence over intimacy and claim for themselves the higher knowledge that previously only the creator has held. They seek, in simple terms, instead of serving God to become gods.

In Act 3 the maker discovers the choice his human partners have made and is forced, in response, to limit the scope of their power. The responsibility of taming the wilderness is still theirs, but the conditions in which they must do it have changed, robbed as they are of the core relationship with God that would have made their task much easier.

Act 4 of this drama, as we are told the story, is stretched over human history. The "what happens next?" of Genesis is the drama we spend each day confronting, the reality of a world that is beautiful but broken, of a humanity that still shows traces of the magnificence intended by the maker, and yet is capable of destruction and dysfunction beyond imagining. **Act 4** is the setting into which mission arrives; the dilemma our pursuit of God will or will not resolve. There is no mystery as to the outcomes of **Acts 1 to 3**. They are our story, written into our history, a past record coded into the very strands of our DNA. **Act 4**, though, has still to reach its end. This is where we come in. This is our challenge.

The importance of this story to the Bible's structure cannot be overstated. It is the backdrop of both Old and New Testaments. It is the setting that makes sense of Moses and the Law; of Israel and Jerusalem; of exile; of Jesus. It is the prologue that, even today, reads meaning into my life, into my struggle. Three words that sum up this drama help more than any others to set a context for the pursuit of Christian mission.

The first is **responsibility**. If Genesis tells us nothing else, it tells us that humanity has been given special responsibility. We are like all other creatures and yet unlike any. We are animal and yet so evidently more. We have reason; language; skills of creativity and dexterity no other creature shares. We have tools. We make fire. We write poetry. With these many gifts, the story tells us, comes a task commensurate with their breadth. We are so much more than the animals *because we are to care for them*. We are set apart from the natural world *because we are to cultivate it*. We have skills in language and toolmaking *because it is our job to civilize*. We are set in self-conscious, intentional relationships *because we are called to community*. All that we have been given, we have been given for a purpose, and that purpose is to work at God's right hand to fulfil all the potential of the world he has made. We are given it half-formed, half-finished. The world's completion is where we come in.

The second significant word is **freedom**. "You are free," God tells us in Genesis 2:16, before he tells us anything else. Free because our maker loves us, and freedom is the necessary condition by which love is actualized. Where there is no freedom – where I am given neither the capacity nor the right to reject the one who loves me – the condition I live in is not love. It is slavery. Love, in order to be love, requires freedom, and the freedom offered to God's first human partners tells us much about the nature of his love. His desire is that we should work with him by choice, not by coercion. We are to obey him – to do the right thing – because we choose to, not because by threat of violence we are forced to. The goal is obedience in freedom or no obedience at all. This is the golden standard, the rule God himself, all-powerful as he may be, has chosen to submit to. The call to freedom will be uttered again in Scripture. It will surface often as the mission of God in the world unfolds – and its place as a foundation stone in God's intention for his world will never be forgotten. The very future of creation depends on this: that human beings – the creatures God has chosen to so designate – will seek after righteousness and justice *because they want to.*

The third word that is central to this drama, that forms a bridge between responsibility and freedom, is **trust**. It is through trust that God intends his human friends to learn the meaning of responsibility and freedom. It will be because they trust him – because the relationship of intimacy he has offered them means more to them than the potential rewards of independent experiment – that they will stay close, and walk the path marked out for them. A crucial aspect of the world God sets in motion is *human participation in the life of God*. It is as human beings participate in the life of God that they are able to bear good fruit – but they have a choice about this. Obedience will not be the fruit of duty or of a desperate need to seek approval. It will be the fruit of trust. We know that trust is central, if unspoken, in the set-up of this story, because it is trust that is lost when the man and woman make their unwise choice. What is the first thing the maker does after his chosen creatures have betrayed him by seeking to usurp his role? He comes looking for them.[32] His plan is to walk with them in the garden just as he might do on any other evening. Despite their fall from grace, he seeks them still. He has not turned his back on them, nor is he angry. And yet a distance has grown up between them. Why? Because they fear him. Because, in place of trust, shame has taken hold of their hearts. God even asks them why they hide from him. It is Adam who responds, "I was afraid, because I was naked."[33] God's next question is remarkable: "Who told you that you were naked?"[34]

In other words, who told you to be afraid of me? Who gave you this shame? Who persuaded you that you could no longer trust me? It wasn't God who turned his back on humanity. It was humans, trading trust for fear and dependence for shame, who ran to hide.

Act 4, then, the segment of the drama we are part of, is shaped by these four conditions:

1. That the responsibility given to the human family remains. We still hold the task of bearing God's image; of reflecting his character; of ruling over our fellow creatures in his place. As regards the creation mandate, nothing has changed – except that it will be much harder now.

2. That the central dilemma of our brokenness is our loss of trust. Because we have lost our capacity to trust our maker, a rift has grown, and time has made it wider. We cannot rule as God would have us rule because trust is a condition of participation in God's life without which, on our own, we will rule falsely.

3. That nothing will be put right until trust is restored. Intimacy between creature and creator is essential to the right governance of planet earth, and until that key relationship is fixed, everything will be somewhat broken, somehow cracked, never quite what we might hope that it could be.

4. That we, too, will wallow in brokenness, turning in evertighter circles of despair, until our intimacy with God is made right. We will never be fully human, never live the life intended for us, never inherit all God has for us until the rift in our family is repaired. Participation in the life of God is the key to full humanity.

For the writers of Genesis, this **Act 4** world is the setting we are born into. It is the world as we find it; the challenge we are each presented with. As the mission of God unfolds and history carries us through Moses to David and Solomon; through the prophets and into exile; from exile to Jesus, to Paul and the apostles of the church, this will always be the background assumption. Made beautiful, we are born broken. The world as it should be will never be ours without repair – but with repair all things are possible. God has never given up on his dream.

Essential to this Genesis narrative is the assertion that human creatures were made not for independence but for dependence. The freedom that is our intended habitat is not the absence of all restraint, but the acceptance of the one restraint that matters: a relationship of trust. What is the mission of God, the goal for which the Holy Spirit is sent into the world? What is the plan our maker is working to? What is his end game? The restoration of trust. God is working towards trust restored, and from trust restored to the rebooting of our first creational command. No word of Scripture has ever cancelled or countermanded that first pronouncement of blessing and command over the human family. It was, is, and always will be God's will that we should "be fruitful and multiply. Fill the earth and govern it. Reign over the fish in the sea, the birds in the sky, and all the animals that scurry along the ground."[35]

The incredible assertion of the biblical narrative is that God remains committed, despite everything, to his human co-regents. He still wants us, and he still wants us to trust him. He will not re-establish control through violence or coercion. He will not impose martial law. He won't bully us and he won't beat us. He will wait for trust to be restored, and he will commit the whole future of creation to his strong belief that it can be. God has never changed his plan. He has never abandoned his intention to rule the world through human agency. Forming culture, caring for creation, cultivating the earth to bring out fruitfulness and fullness – these remain the desires of God for us. Mission is whatever needs to happen to make this possible again. Whenever and wherever the will of God moves from *not being done* to *being done*, the mission of God is fulfilled.

What is the mission of God *for*? For putting humans back where they belong. To expand this somewhat, we might say that the mission of God is:

- To see the human family restored to full participation in the life of God, so that

- Our "ruling and subduing" of the world reflects his wisdom, imaging his character, so that

- The earth itself is fruitful, fulfilling its potential and reflecting God's goodness and glory.

Once you see that this is what God wants, you realize that echoes of this mission surface through the many stories of the Bible. You hear it in the promise of the prophets that "[as] the waters fill the sea, the earth will be filled with an awareness of the glory of the Lord".[36] You find it in Jesus as he urges us to pray, "May your kingdom come soon. May your will be done on earth, as it is in heaven".[37] You see it in Paul as he writes that God's purpose is "to use the church to display his wisdom in its rich variety to all the unseen rulers and authorities in the heavenly places".[38] It resonates to the very final scenes of the Bible, where John sees "the holy city, the new Jerusalem, coming down from God out of heaven like a bride beautifully dressed for her husband". And hears "a loud shout from the throne, saying, 'Look, God's home is now among his people! He will live with them, and they will be his people. God himself will be with them. He will wipe every tear from their eyes, and there will be no more death or sorrow or crying or pain. All these things are gone forever'".[39]

The mission of God is grounded in original intention. What God wants is what God has always wanted: and you are part of it.

Beyond the Garden Wall

> The divine plan of extending salvation to the ends of the earth is the major thrust of the Scriptures from beginning to end... God's saving plan for the whole world forms a grand frame around the entire story of Scripture.
>
> KOSTENBERGER & O'BRIEN[40]

When Gilles, the friendly farmer who manages the land adjacent to ours, ripped out the hedge and fencing that runs the length of our approach, it was astounding how much difference it made. The whole vista as you approach our property was opened up – I even spotted houses that I didn't know were there. Fences are in many ways arbitrary, but we let them define our world. Walls, boundaries, borders – no matter how thin or ethereal they are, we treat them as solid lines. It's only when you take them away that you realize how much you've taken them for granted.

There is a positive side to this tendency. Several years ago psychologists observing children at play noticed a pattern they had not seen before. In a playground surrounded by a good strong fence, children will occupy all the space available to them. They will run and play right up to the fence, exploring its edges and claiming its corners. Where a playground is unfenced, by contrast, the same children will stay closer to its centre. They will tend to huddle, constantly assessing how far they are from the mid-point and leaving a wide border: a kind of no-go zone where the fence would otherwise be. They use distance to create the security a barrier would normally provide. Fences help us, then, to fully occupy and explore the ground given to us. I don't have to keep my furniture piled in the centre of the room under a tarpaulin – my strong walls allow me to arrange it, securely and safely, to the very edges of the room.

As with all such things, this positive coin of safety has a flip side. We are not meant to huddle like frightened children. The world beyond our fences calls to us.

There is an intriguing episode in the Genesis creation narratives that reflects on this reality. After the cataclysmic event we refer to as "the fall", when the relationship of trust between the creator and his favourite creatures is broken, Adam and Eve are evicted from the garden of Eden. God turfs them out, sending them into the implied wilderness beyond and even going as far as to place angels with flaming swords at the gate to stop them getting back in.[41] It's an aspect of the story not much talked about these days, but a century or two ago it featured strongly, highlighted particularly in Milton's *Paradise Lost*. Even now it is described in most translations as a "banishment". God can no longer rely on his friends to obey him so he must force them from the paradise he made for them.

But here's the odd thing about this understanding: according to Genesis 1:28–30, it was always God's plan for Adam and Eve to move beyond the garden. The whole earth was given to them to fill and cultivate; they were to move out and bring the touch of God to the wilderness, taming and managing the earth. This outward movement is reflected in the Bible's wider narrative, which moves from the garden to a city. The civilization of planet earth was Plan A, not Plan B. God had made a garden to set things in motion, but the task of moving further out, of bringing fruitfulness to the wilderness, was all ours.

So why the drama? Why the eviction notice reinforced by flaming swords? Even acknowledging that chapters 1 and 3 of Genesis draw on two distinct accounts of creation, the juxtaposition of these two ideas is intriguing. In the first instance God invites his human creatures to populate the whole earth; in the second he ejects them from the garden to make sure that they do.

There are a number of ways of reading the text, but what we do know is that the element that did not previously exist in Adam and Eve's relationship with God, but came in after their fall, was their fear. Before the cataclysm they relate to God with innocent trust. After it they are afraid of him. Might it be that he had to *evict* them rather than *invite* them to move beyond the garden as he had always intended, because in their fear they were determined to stay put? God has to kick them because otherwise they're going nowhere. Fear is what keeps us huddling behind our fences, instead of moving with God into the adventure of taming the wilderness.

Why does this matter to us today? Because for centuries we have been using the walls and fences of religion to hide behind instead of hearing God's call to engage with the world. Our religious practices all too often are about trying to recreate the garden, rather than pressing on to build the city. We take some small corner of God's world – my family; my church; my tribe; my nation – and we make *that* our paradise, ignoring God's desire for the whole earth to know his peace and presence.

There are echoes of this same dynamic in the New Testament. It has always intrigued me that the word the apostle Paul reached for to describe the gatherings of the new church movement was *ecclesia*. In the current usage of his day, this could be applied to "a gathering of citizens coming together to discuss their concern for their city". The word is used in this sense in Acts 19. What a stunning description of the church: a group of active, interested, creative human beings thinking about the future of their city / planet / world. Not a self-selecting cosy club hiding behind its own fences.

Boundaries matter. They help us to understand territory and make the best of what is given to us. But they are not definitive. Jesus didn't teach us to pray for God's will to be done in our little garden. He dared us to pray for an earth-wide kingdom. Mission comes alive when we reconnect with the sheer scope – the audacity – of God's ambitions.

The Message is the Medium

> Inscribed on the very heart of God's grace is the rule that we can be its recipients only if we do not resist being made into its agents; what happens to us must be done by us. Having been embraced by God, we must make space for others in ourselves and invite them in – even our enemies.
>
> MIROSLAV VOLF [42]

Once we acknowledge the model presented in Genesis, in which participation in the life of God leads to a life of wisdom and therefore of fruitfulness, extending to the very ends of the earth, we immediately see a further liberating truth. The goal of the mission of God and its central methodology are the same. The message is its own medium.

The vision God is moving towards and his chosen means of achieving it are of the same substance:

- The goal is people drawn into participation in the life of God. The means? God's people drawn more fully into participation in his life.

- The reason is that these people will then express their gifts according to God's wisdom, reflecting his character. How will this be achieved? Through God's people discovering, developing, and deploying their gifts in accordance with his wisdom.

- The ultimate result of this will be fruitfulness in the created world: a stewarded creation releasing its good fruits. How will this come about? Through the people of God bearing good fruit in the world.

The apostle Paul picks up this unexpected convergence of mission and method in his letter to the church in Colosse. In greeting his Christian friends in that city, Paul rejoices that the Good News that came to them "is going out all over the world. It is bearing fruit everywhere by changing lives, just as it changed your lives from the day you first heard and understood the truth about God's wonderful grace".[43]

A little later he confesses his ambitions for them, saying that "we have not stopped praying for you since we first heard about you. We ask God to give you complete knowledge of his will and to give you spiritual wisdom and understanding. Then the way you live will always honour and please the Lord, and your lives will produce every kind of good fruit. All the while, you will grow as you learn to know God better and better."[44]

In the first instance, the Colossian believers *are* the fruit of the Good News. In the second, they *bear* the fruit. God calls us to both realities: to be fruit and to bear fruit. That which God does for us he then asks to do through us: the recipients of his mission become its agents, and, since the end goal is fruitfulness, the pattern stays the same. Drawn into full participation in the life of God, we become fruitful, and God's mission is both fulfilled (we are its fruit) and extended (we are fruitful).

This pattern is essential to our understanding of God's mission. "What happens to us must be done by us." Our changed lives are the fruits of grace and we bear the fruits of grace in the world. As soon as we are recipients of God's mission we become its agents, and the goal of both is fruitfulness. In this sense the two questions "what is the end goal of God's mission?" and "what is the means by which God's mission is achieved?" receive exactly the same answer: "human beings bearing fruit".

I am drawn into engagement with God's mission in the world because he sees me as a diamond, not as coal. He sees value in me: gifts he has given; potential for fulfilment and fruitfulness. My engagement in his mission is my path to the fulfilment of that potential. God will see the good in me; will draw it out. Polished and perfected, I will bear fruit, shining in the gifts my maker sees in me. All the while, as this process goes on, I find a second change at work. Even as God reveals the jewel he sees in me, I begin to see the same in others. I long, as he longs, for other human beings to be seen as he sees them; for them to know their worth and status; for their gifts to be discovered and de-cobwebbed. I ache, as he aches, for the fruitfulness and freedom of humanity. The basis on which I am drawn into God's mission is also my motivation for engaging in it. He sees the good in me, and will not waste it. He asks me to see the good in others, and to fight for it.

Can I look into the eyes of another human being and see them as God sees them? I am beginning to embrace his mission. Is my heart broken, as his is, by the things that rob them of his goodness? I have moved a small step further. Can I *tell* them – that he loves them; that they matter; that the value they have in his eyes is beyond their wildest estimation? A bigger step. Can I *show* them, by my actions, standing with them to champion their cause? Better still.

Can I dream on their behalf of a day when they will know how much God loves them, and work with them towards that day, making their fulfilment and fruitfulness as driving an ambition as my own?

We have discovered over many years that people who want to save people but don't really love them tend to burn out quickly, damaging themselves and others. Our starting point must be love: the passion that sees the potential for fruitfulness in everyone we meet. How can we do mission among people we are not in love with; whose gifts and graces we are not committed to releasing?

I was once at a Christian conference with the American evangelist Tony Campolo. I was in charge of the youth venue, and had invited Dr Campolo in to speak. Eight hundred teenagers filled the room, sitting on the floor from the rear entrance right up to the edge of the speaker's platform. The meeting was already under way when Dr Campolo came in, so he had to pick his way over their bodies to get to the front. He had almost reached his goal when he spotted two girls a few rows into the crowd. They were African-Caribbean, among the very few non-white young people in the room. (This was a very middle-class, very "white-church" conference.) My sense is that Dr Campolo was acutely aware of the minority status of these girls, whether or not they sensed it for themselves. As he passed them he turned to fix his eyes on each of them in turn. "You are beautiful!" he said, in his best and loudest Sergeant Bilko voice. "You are so beautiful! You don't even know how beautiful you are. You are beautiful," and he turned and continued on his way to the platform to address his nonplussed majority-white audience.

I have never forgotten that moment. It was over in a few seconds. In the grand scheme of world history it didn't mean very much, but it struck me deeply. Why? Because Tony Campolo sensed that these two girls, in that context and at that moment, might need to be reminded of their worth. They needed to be told that they mattered; that their presence was valued and important. It was a spontaneous gesture, because they stood out from the crowd and caught his eye, and it was heartfelt, because he really was struck by their beauty. It was also deeply missional, because in a context in which there was a danger that they might not know their worth, he wanted them to know that they were *seen* and *valued*.

I learned three principles on that day that have come back to me many times in the intervening years. I learned the significance of eye contact – of letting people know, when I am with them, that they are seen and that they matter. I learned, too, that there are times when the value that I see in people should be spoken. Too often we think our compliments are trivial or obvious and that it's OK to think them without speaking them. I have left good things unsaid too many times, and I regret it. If I could live my life again one change I'd look for is to speak, more often, the good I see in people. Every human being has a value, set not by their choice or their behaviour, but by their maker. Where I see it, I should say it. Finally, I learned that like

Tony Campolo I should be a little bit obsessed with the value and worth of people. I should be as thrilled in the presence of humans as a trainspotter is at Clapham Junction; as excited to meet new people as a "belieber" is meeting Justin for the very first time.

God has a place for me in his purposes because he sees me as a valued child; because he knows my gifts; because he is committed to the fruitfulness and fulfilment of my potential. He made me. He called me to purpose. He has never given up on that call – and whatever place he has for me in his purposes will involve my seeing others as he has seen me. Mission means knowing that every person is his valued child; it means looking for and naming their gifts; it means committing myself to the fruitfulness and fulfilment of their potential. Mission begins when I know that God made each person. That he calls them to purpose. That he has never given up on that call.

Heirs and Graces

> The Bible starts out with a liturgy of abundance. Genesis 1 is a song of praise for God's generosity. It tells how well the world is ordered. It keeps saying, "It is good, it is good, it is good, it is very good." It declares that God blesses – that is, endows with vitality – the plants and the animals and the fish and the birds and humankind. And it pictures the creator as saying, "Be fruitful and multiply." In an orgy of fruitfulness, everything in its kind is to multiply the overflowing goodness that pours from God's creator spirit.
>
> WALTER BRUEGGEMANN[45]

Abandoned by their mother and out of touch with their father, Hungarian brothers Zsolt and Geza Peladi lived in poverty on the outskirts of Budapest. The only income they had came from the junk they scavenged from the streets. Both in their forties, neither brother had a girlfriend and the pair lived in a cave: until, that is, they were tracked down by charity workers to be told that their mother had died. They were joint beneficiaries of their grandmother's will – making them instant billionaires. Sergey Sudev, a journalism student, become one of the richest men in Moldova when an uncle he hadn't seen for ten years left him an estimated €950 million. Tomas Martinez, also homeless and destitute, tragically missed out on such a happy ending. When he was approached by two policemen in the town of Santa Cruz de la Sierra, Bolivia, he ran away, fearing that they would arrest him for alcohol and drug violations. What he didn't know was that they were looking for him for another reason altogether: to tell him that his ex-wife had bequeathed him a $6 million fortune.

These reports from the popular press illustrate the fascination we have with stories of unexpected inheritance. We are intrigued by the idea that a person can live in poverty unaware of or cut off from a family that is in fact worth millions, only to discover that a whole fortune is due to them. Inheritance does not depend on the condition or circumstances of the beneficiary, but is bestowed on the basis of their origin and the free decision of the benefactor. Your current condition can no more erase your inheritance than you can build a time machine to go back to the beginning of all things and alter your origins. No matter how shadowed the woods that you walk through; no matter what darkness you feel you have picked up on your journey; no matter how far you believe yourself to have fallen, your origin and the identity it guarantees *predate* it all. Origins anchor identity: identity dictates inheritance.

This is a powerful image in the story of God. The Bible leaves us in no doubt whatsoever as to our origins and God's intentions towards us. We are created beings, made to love and be loved by a personal, intentional, visionary creator. Over our origins is written the declaration "good, good, good". The astounding claim of the Christian faith is that this "litany of abundance" is our origin. This is the anchor of our identity. This is a picture of our inheritance. There are two good reasons for associating the language of inheritance with our understanding of God's mission.

The first is that it makes sense to do so. If our origins are so evidently found in God's abundance, then it is right and proper to link this goodness to our identity and thereby to our inheritance. Yes, there is a brokenness at the very heart of our experience; yes, our historic behaviour and current condition speak of other things apart from goodness, but neither of these realities changes our origins. Nor do they speak to our original condition. If inheritance is tied to identity and identity is anchored in origin then it is right for us to look for our inheritance right here, in the goodness of our maker.

The second reason we should place *inheritance* at the centre of our thinking on mission is that the Bible does so. A huge number of Old Testament stories revolve around the subject. Likewise the parables of the New. Citing the Psalms,[46] Jesus sums up the gospel of the kingdom in these words: "Blessed are the meek, for they will inherit the earth."[47] The apostle Paul twice describes the presence of the Holy Spirit in the life of the believer as a deposit guaranteeing our inheritance.[48]

In Romans 8 Paul expands on his vision of an inheritance that takes in not only the people of God but the whole creation:

> Yet what we suffer now is nothing compared to the glory he will reveal to us later. For all creation is waiting eagerly for that future day when God will reveal who his children really are. Against its will, all creation was subjected to God's curse. But with eager hope, the creation looks forward to the day when it will join God's children in glorious freedom from death and decay. For we know that all creation has been groaning as in the pains of childbirth right up to the present time. And we believers also groan, even though we have the Holy Spirit within us as a foretaste of future glory, for we long for our bodies to be released from sin and suffering. We, too, wait with eager hope for the day when God will give us our full rights as his adopted children, including the new bodies he has promised us.[49]

The theme runs through God's story, asserting that:

- There is a promise coming to us, an inheritance, in which all that has been destroyed and distorted by our brokenness will be put right. Not only will this future state transform us – it will change the whole creation.

- This promise – this inheritance – is strongly linked to our original condition. It is the fulfilment of the promise and potential we enjoyed before the world, not by its own choice but by ours, fell subject to God's curse.

The assumption is that if the curse can be broken – if that which robbed us of our participation in the life of God can be put right – then nothing stops us from receiving our inheritance. We will get what's coming to us just as soon as we can fully reconnect with our identity and origin. This is helpful language in our exploration of the mission of God because it tells us something of the scope of God's purposes – the breadth of the bounty he is determined to pour out – and because it allows us to personalize the promise. The world has an inheritance in the purposes of God *and so do I*. As his creature, I am included. Anchored in my origins in the abundance of God, based on my identity as his child, this is *my* inheritance.

Later on in our journey through the mission of God we will explore just what it is that he has done to make this possible – the precise drama of the breaking of the curse. For now, though, it is enough to hold before our eyes the image of all that will come to us, on account of our identity and origin, should the breaking of the curse prove efficacious. You have an inheritance in the purposes of God and its measure is the sheer exuberance of his creative joy.

You may be all too aware that you are broken, but you need to know that you are also beautiful, and that your beauty speaks of loving intention. To address the matter in the plainest of terms, beauty is more original than sin, and joy more final than judgment. Genesis 1 says of our past, "Good, good, good, good, good, good, very good!"[50] Revelation 21 says of our future, "He will wipe every tear from their eyes, and there will be no more death or sorrow or crying or pain. All these things are gone forever."[51] Stretched between the two is the adventure of God's mission, the journey from original goodness to final joy, passing through the valley of our brokenness and the glorious mountain of redemption. From beginning to end God's desires for us are good. Our birthright is the abundance of his love. Living in connection with God's purposes means knowing, acknowledging, and claiming our inheritance.

Breadboards and Horse Bells

> Taking all the words used of healing, health and salvation together, we begin to obtain a notion of "wholeness" as meaning completeness, all-round health and life and strength, entailing freedom from evil in all our relationships.
>
> JOHN BAKER[52]

It is significant that Paul, in the poetry of Romans 8, pinpoints the moment when the world, not by its own choice but by ours, fell under God's curse. The importance of this terminology is that it sets in opposition the two conditions human beings and the whole creation can exist in: the conditions of blessing and curse. The language of blessing, like that of inheritance, runs through the Bible's narrative from start to finish. The inheritance reserved for you on the basis of your origins is no less than the fullness of the blessing of God. Every time you read in Scripture any description of God's blessing; every time you see a picture of wholeness, of shalom, you need to know that this is what your Father wants for you. Actively, specifically, and continually, your maker desires for you all that he had in mind on the day he made you. A good place to start in understanding what the blessing of God might look like is Numbers 6:24–26, where Moses is told to give to Aaron and the priests of Israel these words with which to bless the people:

> May the Lord bless you
> and protect you.
> May the Lord smile on you
> and be gracious to you.
> May the Lord show you his favour
> and give you his peace.[53]

Peace in this prayer is *shalom,* which means health and wholeness; everything as it should be; the world and all within it functioning according to the will of its maker. Significantly, Moses is told that "[w]henever Aaron and his sons bless the people of Israel in my name, I myself will bless them". The priests are in effect appointed as God's co-workers to speak out and mediate his blessing. The words they are given to use tell us what it is that God wants. Deuteronomy 28:3–6 puts some flesh on the bare bones of this blessing. Here those who live in communion with their maker are promised:

> Your towns and your fields will be blessed.
> Your children and your crops will be blessed.
> The offspring of your herds and flocks will be blessed.
> Your fruit baskets and breadboards will be blessed.
> Wherever you go and whatever you do, you will be blessed.

The outcome of God's blessing is creational; visible in the physical world of matter. There's nothing quite as material and mundane as a blessed breadboard. This is a significant element of the Hebrew world view. Since God is honoured as the creator, it makes sense that his blessings will be evident in his creation. His initial act of moving from the non-material to the material, from a chaotic sea to the ordered beauty of the world, will flow through into his actions on behalf of those he loves. The suggestion that all God's blessings are spiritual – i.e. non-material – comes from the influence on the church of Greek thinkers for whom matter was by definition inferior to non-matter. To the ancient Greek mind, the reality we see and experience – the reality of the material world – was a mere shadow of an *ideal* that exists in the world beyond and is immaterial. It is not difficult to see the traces of this thinking in our churches. To the Hebrew mind, though, it is alien. The prophet Zechariah has a unique way of picturing the very physical blessings that the coming day of God will bring. "On that day," he writes, "even the harness bells of the horses will be inscribed with these words: Holy to the Lord. And the cooking pots in the Temple of the Lord will be as sacred as the basins used beside the altar. In fact, every cooking pot in Jerusalem and Judah will be holy to the Lord of Heaven's Armies."[54] Reality doesn't get much more physical than bells and saucepans, and yet it is on these, on the very fabric of the material world, that God's blessings are pronounced.

What do we learn from this Hebrew emphasis on God's visible and measurable blessings?

- That the blessings of God in your life will not be in some notional, virtual world but in the real world of your life and experience. The *shalom* God desires for you will be a peace you can touch and feel and see and experience – it will not be a distant mark on some heavenly account ledger where your savings are being held for some future time of bliss. *Shalom* means relationships healed, purposeful living, fears overcome. It is meat and drink for the hungry, shelter for the homeless, clothes for the naked – here and now.

- That the inheritance God has for you consists of the fulfilment of his plans for you: the actualization in your experience of all he promises. No one is suggesting that you can receive this blessing in its fullness by an instant and simple process, as if all you need for heaven on earth is a download code. What I am suggesting here, though, is that God's will for your future is rooted in God's intentions in your past. That which God desires for you tomorrow is that which he dreamed for you yesterday. You may shudder and stumble on the road to your inheritance; you may see it, claim it, and receive it one slice at a time, but the will of God will always be to move you towards the blessings you were born for.

- That this means that there is an inheritance with your name on it. Too often when we pray, "your kingdom come, your will be done, on earth as in heaven", we are thrown by the use of our planet's name. We dream big, and find ourselves praying for world peace. No bad thing – but what about the piece of earth you're standing on? What about the ground beneath your feet? What does it look like for the will of God to be done – for his kingdom to come – *in you*? It looks like blessing. It looks like *shalom*. Part of our growth and maturity in faith involves a move from praying for God's generic will to be done to discerning and welcoming his specific purposes.

- That the inheritance with your name on it therefore has a shape. It has substance and detail. It is not just the desire of God for you to be "blessed" in some general sense – even less for you to be "happy". It consists of the particular desires God has for your specific life. God has blessings in mind for you that he does not have in mind for me, in the sense that we have our own distinct fruit baskets and a different style of breadboard. The much-quoted admonition in Proverbs 22:6, "Train up a child in the way he should go, and when he is old he will not depart from it" can be read as a generic "teach your children to behave". Or it can be read more subtly: "Help each person to find the path that God wants for them, and then they can live it to the full."

There is something very powerful about moving in faith and prayer from the general to the specific. The child who prays, "God bless Mummy, God bless Daddy, and please, God, do look after yourself because if you go down we're all in trouble..." can be forgiven for being young and innocent. I can't. I have a responsibility as an intelligent adult to seek out more fully the particular contours of God's purposes for my life, so that I can pray with passion and conviction for the inheritance he has for me. The blessing may in essence be the same, but the way it lands, the shape it takes, will be different in each of our very different lives.

For all the passion of the promises of God for you, your inheritance is not only about your receiving God's blessing. It is also about passing it on. It is Zechariah, once again, who gives us words to capture this intention: "Among the other nations," he writes, "Judah and Israel became symbols of a cursed nation. But no longer! Now I will rescue you and make you *both a symbol and a source* of blessing."[55] The picture is of a people restored so that they can restore others; healed to bring healing; redeemed so that through them redemption can flow. It's only one chapter later that the prophet dreams of this promise being uniquely fulfilled – through a king riding into Jerusalem on the colt of a donkey.[56]

God's intention is to bless you and to bless others through you, and the two cannot be separated. Nor is there an intended time lapse between them, whereby you spend the best part of your life being blessed so that at its end you can pass something on. You are not an accumulator designed to suck in God's blessings until you're fit to burst and then think about passing them on. As Paul suggests very clearly to his friends in Corinth, there is a to-and-fro to giving and receiving. Provision provokes in us prodigality, and our first instinct on receiving from God is to give to others. Paul even suggests that this is the purpose of God's kindness to us – to harvest *in us* a crop of generosity.[57] Why is this so? Because inheritance denotes origins: God's blessing in your life is a sign of his Fatherhood, and his desire is for you not only to receive from him but to become like him. You were created to bear the image of a maker gracious in generosity and lavish in love.

Caution: Material is Not Monetary

The danger of speaking of God's blessings as material and measurable is that we will fall into the area of seeing them as monetary. We do this because of a human failing reaching back deep into our history. We love to measure things, and our favourite way of measuring is to count money. We say that things are "worth" this or that amount in monetary terms. This is a disease that has become endemic since the Industrial Revolution and has come to be known as "materialism". This is a serious misuse of language, since the value of money is entirely *immaterial*. Money is, in fact, the most virtual and non-material of all our measurements. Perhaps this is why the New Testament describes it both as a false god, *Mammon*,[58] and as a power the love of which can lure us into evil.[59] Counting money, as it turns out, is the very opposite of measuring God's blessings.

Perhaps it will help us to remember just who it was that the blessings of Numbers 6 and Deuteronomy 28 were addressed to. Material blessings did not mean for the Hebrew tribes anything remotely like the kinds of material comforts we seek today. These were a slave people, recently rescued from their captivity in Egypt, wandering now across a harsh wilderness where even the supply of food and drink was precarious. They would be closer, today, to a marching column of refugees fleeing the bombs and bullets of civil war than to a well-paid congregation hoping for new Porsches and a fat round of bonuses. Do refugees dream of flat-screen televisions and Jacuzzis? Perhaps they do, but only as a kind of light relief. What they long for is something far more basic. Daily bread. Shelter. Safety for their children. The opportunity to raise their family in peace. These are material desires, but they are not frivolous. Nor are they indulgent. The tribes of Israel, gathered on a dusty, wind-swept plain with the smell of goats and camels pungent on their clothing, did not hear promises of untold wealth and palatial comfort. They heard a promise of safety, of fruitfulness, of peace. They understood *shalom* as a woman who has fled with her children to escape a drunken and violent husband might understand *refuge*. A blessed breadboard speaks of essentials, not of excess.

We would do well to remember not only that this is the desire of God for us, but that it is so for *everyone*. When we pray

"Give us this day our daily bread", the *us* is as broad as God's family, and God's family is as wide as his love. Are you prepared to believe that the God who desires to bless you also desires to bless your neighbour, and the poor of your community? What about the stranger at your door? What about your worst enemy? Is there something that places them *outside* the scope of God's blessing, or do they, as God-made wonders, also share in his inheritance? Would that God would reignite our passion to pursue and pray not only for the inheritance he has for us but for all that he has for those around us.

Generations: Your Children's Children's Children

The late Hans Rookmaaker, Professor of Art History at the Free University of Amsterdam and author of *Modern Art and the Death of a Culture*,[60] was perhaps the twentieth century's most significant Christian commentator in his field. Having discovered in early adulthood the great truth that God's word had something to say to every area of life and culture, he "volunteered" to take on the world of art, because at the time he knew of no other Christians doing so. Known for his deep wisdom, his short temper, and his love of traditional American jazz, Rookmaaker discipled a whole generation of artists and art lovers across Europe, and was closely linked with Francis and Edith Schaeffer and the L'Abri movement. He was a man who would have an impact well beyond his own lifespan, and he knew it. Asked what motivated him to seek a Christian perspective on fine art, he would often give the same reply: "The work that I do, I do not do for my own generation, nor even for my children's generation: I do it for my children's children's children."

Rookmaaker understood that the Christian retreat from art in the nineteenth and twentieth centuries had been so extreme, and the ground to be made up was so vast, that it would take more than one professor and his students to turn it around. The work of bringing reformation to the arts would span the generations. He knew that God had called him to sow seeds whose fruit he would never himself see. His calling and passion made sense only in the wider perspective of God's work. He had to find his place, but leave the wider plan to God.

The same is true of the inheritance we seek through participation in the life of God. Some of the fruit is for us, and for now. We will see it. We can taste it. We will celebrate the "now reality" of the coming of God's kingdom. Some of the fruitfulness God calls us to, though, will not be so quickly realized. It will be the work of generations, a promise for our children and our children's children that we, nonetheless, have a part in seeing realized. The late Oscar Romero, Archbishop of El Salvador, expressed this need for perspective in addressing a group of priests for whom he was responsible. Ultimately martyred for speaking out for the poor and oppressed, Romero understood his own place in God's wider promise-plan. Speaking not long before his death, he said:

> It helps, now and then, to step back and take the long view. The kingdom is not only beyond our efforts, it is even beyond our vision. We accomplish in our lifetime only a tiny proportion of the magnificent enterprise that is God's work. Nothing we do is complete, which is another way of saying that the kingdom always lies

beyond us. No statement says all that could be said. No prayer fully expresses our faith. No confession brings perfection, no pastoral visit brings wholeness. No programme accomplishes the church's mission. No set of goals and objectives achieves everything. This is what we are about. We plant seeds that one day will grow. We water seeds already planted, knowing that they hold future promise. We lay foundations that will need further development. We provide yeast that produces effects far beyond our capabilities. We cannot do everything, and there is a sense of liberation in realizing this. It enables us to do something, and to do it well. It may be incomplete, but it is a beginning, a step along the way, an opportunity for the Lord's grace to enter and do the rest. We may never see the end results, but that is the difference between the master builder and the worker. We are workers, not master builders; ministers not messiahs. We are prophets of a future not our own.

This long-term perspective reflects a generational emphasis very common in Hebrew sacred writings. This is the context in which the law of God is given;[61] in which the stories of God are repeated, passed on from generation to generation;[62] in which daily life is woven through with the rhythm of God's word.[63] This is the core task of the community of faith, seeking God's blessing not only on their own heads but on the heads of future generations.[64] It is a measure of God's goodness, his kindness spread out over generations.[65] "Good people leave an inheritance to their grandchildren," the book of Proverbs tells us.[66] We are not called only to receive our inheritance, but to secure it for future generations.

The Fight: When an Inheritance is Stolen

One biblical story that highlights this responsibility is that of Naboth's vineyard, told in 1 Kings 21:1–19 and 2 Kings 9:23–26. This dramatic episode in the life of Elijah, in which he must confront the evil and corruption of a power-hungry king and queen, revolves around a stolen inheritance. Naboth, innocent of wrong, makes the mistake of owning a piece of land the king wants. He refuses to sell it, and the outraged queen arranges for his public humiliation and murder, accusing him of blasphemy and turning against him the very religion she herself rejects. Her actions bring God's judgment on her family – a judgment fulfilled not in her generation but in that of her children.

The language of the story could not be more stark. Just as blessing is the inheritance of the righteous, so those who abuse God's law and foster injustice bring on future generations a cursed legacy.

Many years ago when our eldest son was going through the rocky years of his late teens, Chrissie and I took a day out to pray for him. We were in Upper Arley, on the banks of the River Severn north of Worcester. A picturesque village, Arley is home to a stunning arboretum, with trees from around the world collected in the nineteenth century by Lord Valentia, one-time owner of the local manor. The beauty of the setting, however, hides a dark secret.

As we walked this beauty spot, praying for our son, we felt stirred to claim all that his maker had in mind for him. He was struggling with the issues teens so often face, and we sensed a danger that he could so easily miss the blessings God desired for him. We wanted him to live a life of blessing, not of cursing.

All these thoughts were running through our prayers as we discovered, part way through our walk, the local name given to the place in which we stood. It was known as "Naboth's" in reference to the Ahab and Jezebel story. Lord Valentia, it seems, was not as straight in his financial dealings as might be hoped. His plans for the arboretum were frustrated by the fact that one old lady lived in a tumbledown cottage in the very centre of the land he hoped to replant. He tried to buy her out but she refused, and when she died, her relatives unknown, he simply took her land, absorbing her small garden into his much bigger plans. To this day the outline of the stolen piece of land can still be seen. It is little more than a ripple in the sun-spotted splendour of the woods, but it is there all the same: a reminder of a stolen inheritance.

As soon as we saw this link, we read the passages in 1 and 2 Kings, and our prayers took on a deeper urgency and passion. We saw that the danger Joe was facing was that he would miss out on his inheritance – that the good things God had planned for him would be stolen from him. We couldn't let this happen, and our prayer was that nothing would be stolen, that he would receive all God had for him.

We have never forgotten that day because the story of Ahab and Jezebel, and its connection to our own local "Naboth's", was so dramatic. We think of this often when Joe, in a very different place now, comes to visit with his wife, Elin, and their gorgeous daughter, Seren. We pray for her now too, with an equal passion: that our children's children might receive every blessing God has for them.

The language of inheritance, on this occasion, helped us to understand God's purposes and to articulate just what it was we wanted for our son. Sometimes an inheritance is something we must fight for. Sometimes a blessing can be stolen. Might this language be of help to you as you pray and work for those you love?

Response: Walk with the Worldmaker

> Anyone investigating man to discover freedom finds nothing of it. Why? Because freedom is not a quality which can be revealed – it is not a possession, a presence, an object, nor is it a form of existence – but a relationship and nothing else. In truth, freedom is a relationship between two persons. Being free means "being free for the other", because the other has bound me to him. Only in relationship with the other am I free.
> DIETRICH BONHOEFFER[67]

Why is it important that our understanding of God's mission starts in Genesis?

- Because this is where divine intention is established. God lets us know, in Eve and Adam, what he wants – and what he wants, simply put, is this: to share his life in partnership with human beings so that through them he can pour out his wisdom, they and he together bringing out the fruitfulness of the earth.

- Because this is the basis of all mission. Mission is "what God is trying to achieve", and this has never changed. The garden tells us what the goal of mission is, and how we play our part in it.

- Because you have a creation story. You are not an accidental happening, any more than Venus is. You were planned; thought through; imagined. You were born as a result of God's intention and it is into God's intention you are being drawn.

- Because you are wired to be fruitful. You are designed for a purpose, and that purpose will bring blessing to the earth. You have value in yourself as God's creation but you have value, also, in the goodness you can bring out from the earth. God invites you to share in his life so that others can share in his blessings.

- Because you will not understand God's mission, or how he feels about your neighbour, until you understand how he feels about you. Mission is about God's reckless love for his creatures – even when they hurt him. How will you embrace that love from others unless you know that this is how you, too, are loved?

- Because our story begins in beauty, not in brokenness. We are broken, to be sure – Genesis wastes no time in telling us so – but we were beautiful before we were broken and even in our brokenness beauty persists. How will you engage in God's mission unless you know that he is looking for the beauty in you?

- Because God sees diamonds. He remembers how he made you, and each person. He remembers why. He sees their full potential, no matter how cracked the windows they hide behind. He is the hunter, searching for the beauty in each life.

- Because you have an inheritance in your maker's love. Your name means something. Your origin is proven. God's only desire is that you should get what's coming to you.

- Because you can begin, even today, to find your place in the purposes of God by:

    – Setting your identity as his creation,

    – Affirming that you have a purpose and that God wants you to find it,

    – Knowing that he loves you and can't wait to love others through you.

The splendour of a human heart that trusts it is loved unconditionally gives God more pleasure than Westminster Cathedral, the Sistine Chapel, Beethoven's "Ninth Symphony", Van Gogh's "Sunflowers", the sight of 10,000 butterflies in flight, or the scent of a million orchids in bloom. Trust is our gift back to God, and he finds it so enchanting that Jesus died for love of it.

BRENNAN MANNING[68]

CHAPTER 2

Vocation:
Depend on the Dreamgiver

You have a **VOCATION** story.
It is the story of your calling and purpose and
of a path uniquely fitted to your shape.
God's mission is a partnership:
your dreams for your life woven into
God's dream for his world.

Brother from Another Mother

Abraham and Sarah were both very old by this time, and
Sarah was long past the age of having children.

THE BOOK OF GENESIS[69]

People have different ways of responding to the promises of God. Some believe easily, others not at all. My favourite response is that of Sarah. When she hears what God has in mind, she laughs: and she laughs twice. The promise is of a child – to a man and woman who are both past it.[70] Sarah "laughed silently to herself", we're told, "and said, 'How could a worn-out woman like me enjoy such pleasure, especially when my master – my husband – is also so old?'"[71]

There's something sad and beautiful in Sarah's first laugh.

She's not mocking God. Rather, she can't believe what's being said. The text tells us that she laughed silently, to herself, and yet God heard. Did she know, at that moment, that God could eavesdrop even on the deepest of her feelings? Is that why she was afraid?

Perhaps as the days went on she wondered: if he can hear my private thoughts, perhaps he *can* do things I think impossible. Perhaps I could be visited by a miracle. She didn't find it easy to believe, to hope, but maybe… Could it be? And then the kick, and she knew.

When the baby comes, she laughs a second time. No attempt, this time, to hide it. A laugh of joy, that others will join in with.[72] An infectious laugh, because it *was* God. Because he *did* hear, and his promise was true. After three score years and ten of adult barrenness, Sarah is the mother of a son. Her testimony is simple: *God has brought me laughter.* In one year Sarah moves from laughing at her God to laughing with him.

Everything changes with the birth of Isaac. Not only because Sarah's days of loneliness and grief are over, but because all the promises of God are now made possible. Abraham has been told at the very outset of his faith adventure that from the child Sarah bears him kings will rise.[73] He struggles to believe it, as does she, even when she hears it from God's mouth. But with the birth of Isaac… well, it could be. What was impossible is now possible. If God can raise an heir from two spent pensioners, then he can raise up kings from homeless wanderers. It takes only one miracle to open up the door to all the rest.

I am moved by Sarah's faith because her struggle is so real. Abraham looks at the stars and dreams of becoming president. He's a big-picture thinker, bold in his ambitions. His conversations with God are about becoming great. Sarah, on the other hand, has simpler needs. She wants a child. The faith struggle for her is not political or historic. She's not thinking about the rise and fall of nations. What she is thinking about is that her body wants a child and her spirit wants a child and every fibre of her being wants a child. For what? For selfish ends? No. For completeness. For womanhood. For love of Abraham. Sarah's faith touches me because for her the stakes are personal. She has everything to lose if God is lying. She laughs because if she doesn't she might cry. Her longing is too deep to even talk about. Yet God has seen her heart. He knows her hunger. He is familiar with her deepest thoughts. And he will keep his promise to her. The letter to the Hebrew Christians tells us that, "it was by faith that even Sarah was able to have a child, though she was barren and was too old".[74] Even in her desperation, there is faith.

Abraham and Sarah are models of the way God calls his people into partnership. This is a faith journey, with many challenges along the way, but there is a tender beauty in the way it is completed. In the plans of God the dreams of all three dreamers are fulfilled. The dream of Abraham to seed a dynasty. The dream of Sarah to bear a child. The dream of God to find a man and woman he can partner with.

Some of us dream of nation-building, some of us dream of bearing just one child, and God takes all of our dreams seriously. The part you have in the mission of God is not the part that others have. It is the part that fits your heart, the role your maker has prepared for you. He sees you and knows you and hears the very longings of your soul. There is no one-size-fits-all proposal to this divine–human partnership. When God invites us to share in his life and be an agent of his wisdom in the world, he does it knowing who we are. Your vocation is as distinctive as your fingerprint. God calls humanity to work with him but he also calls each human.

God cares for Abraham but he also cares for Sarah, and his promise is specific. She, too, will be blessed richly.[75] She, for whom to bear one child is joy unspeakable, will be the mother of many nations.

Vocation, Vocation, Vocation

> There is more to God's call than simply sending us out – the commissioning, as calling is usually thought to be. Certainly, it ends by "sending us out," but it begins by "singling us out" – we are called by name – and it continues by "standing us up".
>
> OS GUINNESS[76]

Abraham and Sarah are paradigmatic because they enter into a self-conscious partnership with God to see his purposes fulfilled on the earth. They are in a sense the first missionaries, the first to dream God's impossible dream of a world made new. God's offer to them of a covenant agreement indicates that Adam's fall has not been final – that a rescue plan is already set in motion. By inviting Abraham into a modified version of the covenant of Eden, God demonstrates:

- That he hasn't given up his dream of seeing fruitfulness brought to the earth by human beings choosing, out of freedom, to obey.

- That the central dynamic of this process remains participation in the life of God. We are not yet speaking of the whole of humanity. We are at this stage speaking of one couple. But the implication is clear. God will start with them. They will become a family; the family a tribe. In due course nations will arise and the project of ruling and subduing will be theirs.

- That the brokenness of the creation requires that God's vision be presented in the "now but not yet" of deferred trust. The promise to Abraham and Sarah is just that: a promise. They will see its beginning, old as they are, in the birth of Isaac. They will not live to see its end. There are difficulties to overcome, but God has a plan, and in time its full expression will be seen. In the meantime faith is needed, to trust God in a half-formed present for the coming of a full-orbed future.

- That God's blessing is both personal and global. The promise is that Abraham and Sarah will parent many nations[77] and that ultimately "all the nations of the earth" will be blessed through them.[78] Abraham and Sarah and the family they create will be blessed to be a blessing.[79] They are chosen from among the peoples of the world *for the sake of the peoples of the world.*

To follow Abraham and Sarah into mission is to hear God's call to you to leave your limitations and strike out into his vision for your life. It is to choose a life of promise over certainty; a sky-wide future over the small ambitions of your narrow vision. It is to dream and to know that God dreams with you. From Abraham onwards, God's mission is expressed in partnership. He is always looking for the human representatives who are willing to walk at his side. The covenant with Abraham is a remarkable and perhaps surprising affirmation of God's determination not to act independently of us, but to seek partnership with us. He doesn't have to – any more than an elephant needs the friendship of a gnat – but he chooses to. Since Abraham and Sarah, and still today, God is looking for those willing to work with him.

The term traditionally used by Christians to describe this call to partnership with God is *vocation*. "Vocation" means *purpose* or *mission*. It can refer to my life's work or trade, to my chosen business or sphere of life, but it means more than all these things. Rooted in the Latin *vocare*, "to call", it is related to *vocem*, meaning "voice". Vocation does not refer to my sense of purpose per se. It describes a sense of purpose spoken over me. For there to be a call, there has to be a caller. Vocation finds its meaning in the voice of God.

This is the radical message of Abraham and Sarah's story. From all the people of the earth, God calls *them* to be partners in his purposes. The implication is not that they are special or unique, but that God's call to them is paradigmatic of the way he wants to partner with us all. To all who will listen, the call of God will come. To all who have ears to hear, God will speak. Vocation is not the preserve of the elite few who make it through God's high-octane selection programme. It is his desire for us all. God's invitation – to participate in his life and love; to be agents of his mission; to craft and complete the creation by his wisdom – is universal in scope. It comes to you not because you are unique but because you are human. You were made to hear the voice of God, and to respond.

Once you see the call of Abraham as a model of vocation – God's desire to call his people into partnership – you realize that this same pattern is repeated through the Bible. Our sacred writings could be called *A History of Vocation*. They tell the stories of hundreds, even thousands, of individuals as they have heard, in a thousand different places, the voice of God. Vocation, in these lives, has been a doorway into purpose. "Purpose is that deepest dimension within us – our central core or essence – where we have a profound sense of who we are, where we came from, and where we are going," Tom and Christine Sine write; "God is still inviting disciples to discover the difference their lives can make if they, like Jesus, make God's purposes their purposes."[80]

The call of Moses, which we will explore in a later section, is a powerful example. Here a very real voice plays a role, speaking from the centre of a bush that is aflame but not consumed. It isn't only the headliners like Abraham and Moses, though, who hear God's call. Others, perhaps lesser known, also find purpose. The true picture of the richness and diversity of God's mission will not emerge from singling out a few heroes, but from seeing the pattern spread across so many lives. Men and women, children, pensioners, the rich, the poor, the firmly established, and the tragically dispossessed – in every slice and sector of humanity examples can be found of individuals who have heard the voice of God.

Gideon, an unlikely hero: the lowliest member of an insignificant family in the nation's weakest tribe.[81] Hardly cut out for leadership, he hears the voice of God and one of Israel's greatest-ever champions is formed. How does God address this trembling coward, huddling for protection from his enemies?[82] "The angel of the Lord appears to him and says, 'Mighty hero, the Lord is with you!'"[83] God's call to Gideon is not to pretend he is stronger than he is, nor indeed to raise a great army. It is to "go with the strength you have".[84] The call is to start where you are, and trust God for the rest.

Samson, who achieved in death the conquering of an enemy he had failed, throughout his life, to overcome.[85] Struggling all his life to hear the voice of God, Samson was both immensely strong and entirely weak and foolish. In the end he understands that he will best serve God's purposes not by being clever *or* by being strong, but by accepting weakness as a gift from God.

Samuel,[86] honoured as the first of the prophets, who learned to hear the voice of God when very young.[87] From his long life we inherit perhaps the simplest, one-phrase guide to finding our vocation: "Speak, Lord, your servant is listening."[88]

To these we could add so many names – **Esther** and **Daniel**, who learned to trust God in the absence of God; **Jeremiah**, **Isaiah**, and the prophets, who knew how to listen and were unafraid to speak; **David**, who met God in battle, in worship, and in his most crushing failures; **Elizabeth** and **Mary**, who listened to the whisper of angels when others around them heard only silence; **Paul** and **Silas** and **Phoebe** and **Lydia**, pioneers all in the building of the church. There are so many. Some are so obscure we hardly know their names, and yet they teach us. **Micaiah**[89] and **Tychicus**,[90] faithful messengers of God in the Old and New Testaments respectively. **Jabez**, mentioned just once in all of Scripture,[91] and yet an influence on thousands.

These are not flawless heroes, deftly manoeuvring from one great victory to the next in some ballet of prosperity and triumph. They are complex characters, as familiar with failure as with favour, as likely to be found in prisons as in palaces. The pattern of their lives, though, is consistent. When the voice of God is heard – when purpose is found not in personal ambition but in his call – life has meaning. Vocation is a pathway to the fullness of the life of God.

One person whose story beautifully captures our need to hear God is **Deborah**,[92] a woman called to greatness in an age of men. Deborah's vocation is summed up in the words of a song: "Wake up, Deborah, wake up! Wake up, wake up, and sing a song! Arise, Barak! Lead your captives away, son of Abinoam!"[93]

The stories of the Judges are all stories of individuals taking a stand – choosing to rise up rather than lie down. This is a period that sees the people of Israel living in uneasy cohabitation with their pagan neighbours. Years later, in Babylon, they would name this experience "exile", and would contrast it with the joy and ease of living behind Jerusalem's safe walls, in the shadow of their own God's temple. In the time of the Judges this is a vocabulary they have not yet learned: all they know is that they are in an alien land, always under pressure and often under direct attack. Their wistful discomfort is captured in the repeated lament, "In those days Israel had no king; all the people did whatever seemed right in their own eyes".[94] They sense dark chaos around them, and wonder if it has perhaps seeped *into* them.

Deborah may well be the greatest and best of the Judges. In an era in which the people perish for lack of vision, she sees the future and moves towards it. And she does it all by singing her song, by being herself. In response to the voice of God she finds her own voice. This requires of her that she lead against the stereotypes of her culture. She has wisdom and authority; she shows courage and self-confidence; she is unafraid to make decisions on behalf of the nation. All these are traits more often associated, in her day, with men. Men hunt; women wait at home. Men fight; women stand on the sidelines, or are carried off as helpless victims. Men lead; women follow. Deborah bucks every one of these trends, and has God's backing for it. She leads out of who she is – who God has made her – not out of the expectations of others.

Vocation means hearing God's call to me to sing my song, to sound the one true note my lungs were made for. Interestingly, Deborah is not afraid, either, of teamwork and partnership. She forges a relationship with Barak which brings out the best in both of them: their two distinct songs artfully woven together. She senses that her vocation will complement the vocations of others, that God's mission will be a choral performance, not a solo recital. You are not called to sing my song and I am not called to sing yours, but if we will each find the note we were created to sound, the world will hear the song of its maker.

The Threedom Train...

> Knowing the Trinity is being involved in this circling movement: drawn by the Son towards the Father, drawn into the Father's breathing out of the Spirit so that the Son's life may again be made real in the world.
>
> ROWAN WILLIAMS[95]

I am suggesting that the call of Sarah and Abraham serves as a paradigm for the long parade of vocations that follow it through history. God is reaffirming, post-Eden, his intention to work in partnership with willing humans, and the decision has never been revoked. The story is foundational to our understanding of mission for a second intriguing reason, revealed powerfully in a fifteenth-century work of sacred art meditating on the Genesis texts.

Rublev's Trinity Icon, created in 1410 and often referred to as *The Hospitality of Abraham*, is one of the most sacred icons of all time. It is deeply revered in the Eastern Orthodox Church and well known throughout the world.[96] The work is based on the incident we have been looking at, in Genesis 18. Abraham receives three visitors – strangers to him – and fulfils his obligation to offer hospitality, creating for them a hearty meal. It is not clear in the text who Abraham's visitors are. They are first described as travellers,[97] but in the following chapter are revealed as angels.[98] The New Testament later affirms this description, citing them as angels in disguise.[99] When they speak, we are told it is with the voice of the Lord.[100] The promises Abraham and Sarah receive at this moment are foundational to their lives and mission. Whoever they believe their guests to be, there is no question as to their purpose. God has come to speak directly into Abraham and Sarah's lives, changing forever their trajectory – and that of all who will come after them.

Out of this mysterious event a tradition grew in the Christian community of reading Genesis 18 as an early appearance of the Trinity. The image of the three visitors at table sharing in the hospitality of Abraham was received and honoured as a picture of the God who is three-in-one. Nowhere is this connection more perfectly captured than in Rublev's icon. The icon is a meditation both on the nature of the Trinity and on the beauty of hospitality. The three figures are seen at table, Abraham's veal stew set out like a Eucharistic meal before them. Rich in symbolism, the icon uses colour and composition to explore the relationships of the members of the Trinity to one another and to us. Two aspects of this are particularly resonant.

The first is the perfect circle that can be drawn around the backs and shoulders of the three figures. There is no hierarchy implied among them, nor does any one figure demand or receive undue attention. Rather, there is an eerie balance of posture, as if each one has so perfectly deferred to the other two that they cannot but create an atmosphere of peace and harmony. A perfect circle of unconditional acceptance and love: this is the definition Rublev gives us, without words, of our God. The Trinity denotes our maker as "persons in relationship" and Rublev succeeds in telling us the nature of their love for one another.

The second remarkable aspect of Rublev's creation is what happens when you turn the circle, in imagination, through 90 degrees. When the circle you picture is placed not vertically, around the backs of the three figures, but horizontally around the table, so that it comes out from the image towards you, something unexpected occurs. The compositional circle of the image now extends towards you in 3D and you see at once something you did not at first notice. There is a space at the table. Facing you – inviting you – is a vacant place. The whole image is invitational. It establishes the table, the perfect community of love around it, and the central theme of hospitality: and it invites you to take your place.

There is a place for you at the table. This is the deep message of Rublev's icon, and the hidden truth of Abraham's encounter. God the Father, God the Son, and God the Spirit have not kept their inner life of unconditional acceptance and love as a closed circle, available only to themselves. They have opened up their love. They have invited human beings into the place of their communion, the ultimate table of acceptance and love. Hospitality, it seems, is more than an accidental theme in Abraham's encounter. It is a picture of the very nature of God.

Why is this image so important? Because it is the very foundation of mission. Before Jesus could come, before even Moses could arise to free the Hebrew slaves, God called Abraham. To Abraham God revealed the passions of his secret dream, to raise up in the earth a family and tribe that would know him and love him and walk in his ways: men and women who would take their place at his table. You might want to write this off as ancient history, as promises superseded by later events, but the Bible's narrative won't let you. The unfolding of the Old Testament story; the coming of Jesus; the birth of the church; even John's final great vision of the promised future: *all* link back to the dream revealed to Abraham. It is the city Abraham believed in that descends at last from heaven at the consummation of all things.[101] By "placing" the Trinity at the very centre of this founding moment, *The Hospitality of Abraham* raises for us the question, what does it mean that the mission of God in the world *is* the mission of the Father, Son, and Spirit?

Trinitarian theology has been more deeply revered in the Eastern than the Western church, but in recent decades there has been a significant and very fruitful convergence.[102] Western theologians have become aware, in both modernity and post-modernity, of questions and issues their received ideas have struggled to do business with. In a return to the ancient roots of the faith, and to Trinity, many have found a bubbling source of renewed inspiration. Some of the most creative and fruitful theology of the past fifty years has come from engagement with Trinity, and has brought together Eastern and Western sources separated for almost a millennium. A second process, of applying this renewed appreciation of Trinity to the study of mission, is only just beginning, and shows enormous promise. Might the missional crisis of the Western church – expressed in its bluntest form as *people don't believe or belong any more, and most of our solutions aren't working* – find some kind of resolution in a fresh appreciation of God's "threeness"?

How might such an appreciation change our view of mission? There are several ways:

- It gives substance to the assertion we have made, from the Genesis account of creation, that the goal of mission is human participation in the life of God. The image of the Trinity inviting each of us and all of us into the open circle of an unconditional love is a powerful picture of what participation might mean.

- It gives context and substance to the incarnation of Jesus and the sending of the Holy Spirit, both of which we will explore more deeply in later chapters of this book. If we see incarnation as the opening out of the Trinity to draw us in and Pentecost as the complement and completion of that process, we begin to see that these events are not novel additions to the plan of God. He didn't wait around in splendid isolation for centuries and then suddenly come up with an idea. Rather, from the first moments of the Eden crisis, he began the process of opening himself to us, and, in that long, slow movement of embrace, Bethlehem, Calvary, resurrection and Pentecost are visible, measurable events.

- It enables us to grasp more deeply just how it is that "what happens to us must be done by us".[103] The message and the medium of God's mission are the same because both involve a "yes" to the embrace of the Trinity. My engagement with God's mission is my participation in his life – I am taking my place at the table. At the same time my conviction is that you too are invited. I know that this embrace is what you need because it is so deeply what I need. In being embraced, I embrace. In receiving unconditional acceptance, I learn to offer it.

- It offers us a model for the community of the church, and of human society, that has no equal. The startling image of three persons living as one; of a perpetual outpouring and exchange of unconditional devotion; of hospitality and welcome as the very fabric of the universe, tells us *exactly* what it is that God is doing in the world. "Because the Christian God is not a lonely God, but rather a communion of three persons," Miroslav Volf writes, "Faith leads human beings into the divine communion. One cannot, however, have a self-enclosed communion with the triune God – a 'foursome', as it were – for the Christian God is not a private deity. Communion with this God is at once also communion with those others who have entrusted themselves in faith to the same God."[104]

I love the way my good friend Thierry Eudeline describes the Trinity as "like a family in which no one person is afraid to speak their mind for fear that the other two might reject or ridicule them". It is this kind of security, of unconditional acceptance and embrace, that makes mission possible.

Rublev's instinctive desire to see Trinity in Genesis 18 is consistent with the way the early Christian church came to see God as three-in-one. They didn't embrace Trinity as something God had *become* since Jesus, but as that which God had always been. They looked back and saw that creation was an act of the Trinity, as was the call of Abraham; of Moses; of Gideon and Deborah; of Daniel and Esther. The Father, Son, and Spirit had been at work throughout their history, bringing them deeper and deeper into the revelation of his plans for them and for their world. The creeds of the Christian church are not founded on the invention of the Trinity, but on its revelation. Jesus shows us who God truly is, and always has been. That, at least, is the faith we confess.

All of this allows us to say, from our vantage point twenty centuries beyond the coming of Christ, that our purpose is to discover our lives inside the communion of Father, Son, and Spirit. We are invited not only to take our place at the table but in doing so to realize that *this is where we belong*. This is where we have always belonged. This is what it means to be human. Mission begins with the invitation of the Father, Son, and Spirit: the call to every human being to take their place in intimate communion with their God. This is what it means to come to full participation in the life of our maker. This is the invitation into the inner circle of God's love, to a place at the table of his fellowship.

> The table or altar lies at the centre of the picture. It is at once the place of Abraham's hospitality to the angels, and God's place of hospitality to us. That ambiguity lies at the heart of communion, at the heart of worship. As soon as we open a sacred place for God to enter, for

> God to be welcomed and adored, it becomes his place. It is we who are welcomed, it is we who must "take off our shoes" because of the holiness of the ground... For the space at this table is on our side. We are invited to join the group at the table and receive the heart of their being for ourselves. We are invited to complete the circle, to join the dance, to complete the movements of God in the world by our own response. Below the altar a rectangle marks the holy place where the relics of the martyrs were kept in a church. It lies before us. It invites us to come into the depth and intimacy of all that is represented here. Come, follow the Spirit up the hill of prayer. Come, live in the shadow of the Son of God, rest yourself beneath his tree of life. Come, journey to the home, prepared for you in the house of your Father. The table is spread, the door is open. Come.[105]

The historical process by which the early Christian church, over its first three hundred years of existence, came to the point of being able to articulate the Trinity as doctrine is a hugely important aspect of our faith. Without it the Christian faith, like a model without glue, simply collapses to be a jumble of oddly-shaped fragments piled on the floor.

So how did we come to see that God was Father, Son, and Spirit?

The answer is that we experienced God in this way before we knew how to explain it. The worship life of the early disciple-making community was Trinitarian before ever the doctrine was formalized. The formalizing process begins in the pages of the New Testament but was taken on by the Church Fathers, and essentially involves recognizing or affirming three realities:

The first is the experience of knowing and worshipping Yahweh, the God of the Hebrews and creator of heaven and earth. Yahweh is the God of Jesus, the deity he himself addresses as Father. Without this heritage, the pre-existence of this one true God, the ministry of Jesus falls to nothing. The first followers of Jesus were committed monotheists who believed that they had a maker who loved them. Unless Jesus was in some way connected to Yahweh, he had neither authority nor credibility. You can't get to the God who is three-in-one unless you first affirm that there is only one God.

The second affirmation is that in Jesus this same God Yahweh has come to meet us. The incarnation is the cornerstone of all Christian faith, so that John can say repeatedly in his letters that the confession that Jesus is both man and God is the single, non-negotiable, and indispensable qualifier of the word "Christian".[106] Those who worshipped the One God affirmed, after the resurrection, that the Jesus they had walked with in the flesh was the-one-God-incarnate, equal in nature and authority to the Father.

They were still pondering this puzzle when the Holy Spirit, the promise of the Father spoken of by Jesus, came upon them. Now in their own existential reality they know that God is with them. Not with them as he was with them in Jesus, tied to a physically contingent presence, but with them *everywhere* and, stranger still, with *each of them*. The fragmentation of the Spirit into tongues of fire resting on each head is the single most explosive innovation in faith since the resurrection of Jesus. Not only is the one God present both in Yahweh and in Jesus, he is now present by his Spirit in each person.

These experiences were embodied in the worship of the Christian community from the very beginning, so that Paul is able to commit his friends to "the grace of the Lord Jesus Christ, the love of God, and the fellowship of the Holy Spirit".[107] Only later did it become necessary to explain how this can work. The affirmation that Father, Son, and Spirit were all divine – one God in three persons – was already fully established at the very heart of the church's worship. It had to be, because without that acknowledgment the ministry of Jesus and the growth of his church made no sense at all. Exodus, Bethlehem, and Pentecost were fixed points in the world view and heritage of the first Christians – they could not but be Trinitarian in their worship.

The Trinity of Father, Son, and Spirit, then, is the foundation of all our faith. If we are to truly know God, love ourselves, and live for others, it will only be as we surrender to the reality of this communion of love. Our faith becomes emaciated and lifeless when we strip it of the complex mystery of Trinity. When we trade God's three-ness for simpler formulas, we begin immediately to drift away from the shores of orthodoxy – and the oceans we drift onto are wide and wild.

It is significant that it is in Genesis 18 that Rublev finds the Old Testament's most thrilling image of Trinity, because the chapter is foundational to the unfolding picture of God's mission. This is the birthplace of the divine–human partnership that will grow into a global movement and, in time, deliver Jesus to us. It is right and fitting to see the Father, Son, and Spirit working here. The mission of God is the mission of the Trinity. The invitation is into the perfect circle of love that constitutes the life of God. The "sending" aspect of mission begins not in our sending, but in God's self-sending: the extraordinary journey of Jesus that has inspired the church's worship from its earliest days,[108] and the explosive sending of the promised Holy Spirit so that individual believers and the church as a whole can genuinely have "fellowship" with God. Church Father Irenaeus of Lyons, in the third century, used the image of the "two hands of God" to describe the actions of the Son and Spirit in the world. The metaphor is not a perfect one, but it serves us well in picturing God's "sending" as the opening of his embrace. All of mission, in this view, consists of God the Father stretching wide his arms in the form of God the Son and God the Spirit to invite the whole creation into his reconciling embrace. God is missional because he is the sender and the sent – all mission finds its meaning in the mission of the triune God.

Intermission – A Pause Between Acts 1 and 2

In case you're worried that Rublev's meditation on a relatively obscure passage in Genesis might be a little shaky as a foundation for a theology of mission, there is a second passage in Scripture that also places Trinity at the centre of all missional engagement. We are not this time in an ancient story of the patriarchs. We are at the very pinnacle of the ministry of Jesus.

In Acts 1:6–11 Jesus gathers his followers to explain what life will be like for them after his ascension. His life, death, and resurrection are now part of their history. Everything he came to do has been done and the baton is about to pass to them with the pouring out of God's gift, the Holy Spirit. The age of the Spirit will be the age of the church, when the purposes of God will rest not on the one man, Jesus, but on the many – men and women who have surrendered their lives to God's purposes and are living in the power and presence of his Spirit.

This will not merely be an event to shake Jerusalem; it will be a movement that changes the world.

Jesus tells his friends – at this stage still a small group – that they will be the agents of this movement; that something will begin in them that will reach to the very edges of the world. In the course of telling them this, though, he includes another, unexpected, instruction. He tells them not to go anywhere. They are to wait for the outpouring of the Spirit, after which nothing stands between them and the very ends of the earth. They are to go nowhere until the Spirit comes, and then to go everywhere. Don't start until God fills you, but when he's filled you, don't stop!

Surely the words to his friends at this moment qualify, if anything does, as the core commissioning of the church to its life and mission. This is how the conversation plays out:

> ...when the apostles were with Jesus, they kept asking him, "Lord, has the time come for you to free Israel and restore our kingdom?"
>
> He replied, *"The Father alone has the authority to set those dates and times, and they are not for you to know. But you will receive power when the Holy Spirit comes upon you. And you will be my witnesses, telling people about me everywhere – in Jerusalem, throughout Judea, in Samaria, and to the ends of the earth."*[109]

These are the last words Jesus speaks before ascending to heaven. If he hadn't already died and come back, you might call them his Last Will and Testament. It is on the basis of these words that the entire project of the church is built. The age of the Spirit – the age we have lived in since Jesus ascended and will live in until his return – is shaped by this commission: and the commission is Trinitarian to its core.

Jesus asks his followers to do three distinct things: to leave it to the Father to decide when and how the kingdom will reach its final consummation; to be open to the empowerment of the Holy Spirit; and to tell everyone, everywhere his story – that is, the story of Jesus. You might summarize this Trinitarian framework for mission as:

- Trust the Father
- Receive the Spirit
- Tell the story of the Son.

And if you did, you would have a missional theology that could carry you to every sphere of culture, through every season of your life, and to every sector of the world: a story sufficient to sustain you to the very ends of the earth. The importance of this framework is the recognition that our mission is not Jesus-centred but Trinitarian. The Father, Son, *and* Spirit are involved, each with a particular role or perspective to bring. These three actions – the choice we make to trust, to receive, and to tell – can be applied to every circumstance we face and in every setting God takes us into.

We **trust the Father**, because there will always be aspects of our life and mission that are too big for us to grasp. We do not see the whole picture, and we must learn to trust the voice that shows us our part in it. Our engagement with God's mission must be anchored in this father-love that predates our existence by an unimaginable margin and is too broad and deep and long and high to be shaken or dented by our troubles, no matter how intense they are. Without this knowledge of a parent beyond and outside our existential experience, we will fluctuate with the wind. Only by throwing our anchor into the heart of the Father whose life is established beyond the very boundaries of time and space can we be fully secure. Writing to his friends in the church of Ephesus, the apostle Paul prays that they will *"have the power to understand, as all God's people should, how wide, how long, how high, and how deep his love is"*.[110] This is the Father from whom all parenthood is derived,[111] the God who can do more for us than we can even imagine.[112] Only by being anchored in this ocean beyond ourselves can we hope that we will *"no longer be immature like children. We won't be tossed and blown about by every wind of new teaching. We will not be influenced when people try to trick us with lies so clever they sound like the truth. Instead, we will speak the truth in love, growing in every way more and more like Christ, who is the head of his body, the church."*[113]

The picture is of stability that is derived not from our inner sense of control but from its opposite. By relinquishing control to the higher power of our loving maker, we find ourselves anchored in a rock that cannot be moved. We tend to move towards being *in control*, but only by *losing control* can we find life – and the opposite of control is trust. Can we trust our Father to look after the big picture while we faithfully pursue the small part of it he has revealed to us?

We **receive the Spirit**, because it is only by God's dwelling in us by his Spirit that we can embrace the tasks and purposes he calls us to. If the Father is the one by whom we know, from the deepest past to the furthest future, that we are secure, the Spirit is the one by whom we know right now what it is to do the will of God. The Holy Spirit is God the present tense, our maker present in our present circumstance. To speak of trusting the Father, or of worshipping Jesus, without the existential reality of his Spirit with us is to tell only a small part of the story. Without the presence of the Spirit, the first disciples couldn't even get out of the room they were meeting in. They prayed behind closed doors, locked behind the tight walls of their human limitations. They weren't growing in any way and they weren't going anywhere, even though they had been witnesses of the resurrection. Only when the Spirit came did their horizons widen. By the Spirit they broke out of their small room; they stirred the whole of Jerusalem; they received gifts beyond their expectations – and within weeks they began to see that this church would indeed go to the ends of the earth. There are only two sets of walls that can contain you: your own, which are narrow and tight and confine you to the tiniest corner of your God-given potential, or God's, which are wider than the universe. Once the Holy Spirit has broken you out of your small selfdom, there is no limit to where he might take you. This act of receiving, of being open to God's presence in your present, is deeply connected to your first act of trusting the Father. *Because* you trust the Father, Jesus says, *wait for his gift*. Don't jump into your own plans; let him shape you in his. The Holy Spirit is the one by whom the purposes of God are actualized within you. There is nothing God wants to do in you or through you that will not be done through his Spirit. As often as you pray "your will be done on earth as in heaven" you are praying, by implication, "Come, Holy Spirit".

We **tell the story of the Son**, because it is the story of Jesus – the specific and particular account of the incarnation – that unlocks the purposes of God in every life. It is highly instructive that, having given such honour to the Father and the Spirit, Jesus says "You will be *my* witnesses," not "*our*".

The framework is triune but the story is singular: it is that of Jesus. Why? Because the story of our maker taking on flesh and becoming one *of* us and one *with* us is the unique, game-changing reality at the heart of all mission. "Of our flesh and of our bone," the hymn-writer Charles Wesley wrote, "Jesus is our brother now, and God is all our own."[114] The biography of God is Trinitarian, and there are truths we need to learn about Father, Son, and Spirit, but our way into that biography, the on-ramp that will take us to those truths, is the story of Jesus. This is true for a number of reasons, but two stand out at this point in history. The first is that the truth of the incarnation cannot be arrived at by a process of logic or intuition: we perceive it by revelation and its counterpart, confession. There is so much about God that *makes sense*. He is our maker; the power at the heart of the universe. All those sunsets and mountaintops must point us to *something*. But the confession that Jesus is both God and man is an irreducible minimum that we arrive at by faith and confess in trust. It takes us somewhere our reason will never carry us. The second reason this matters so much now is that post-modern sensitivities struggle intensely with this level of *particularity*. We are ready to say that God *might* exist and *can* speak and *could* even be a lot like the God the Bible describes; but to say that God *has* spoken, and that he has done so definitively in the historic, human life of the man Jesus, requires a different level of commitment. It shatters the misty numinousness of our wandering imaginations and asks us to give assent to a concrete, non-negotiable truth. It is this assertion that allows us to attach the adjective *Christian* to our faith and experience. This is not an easy step to take in our age, but it is the very challenge of taking it that makes it worthwhile. For the record, it wasn't all that easy the first time round. The notion of an incarnation, particularly an incarnation that submitted to death, was scandalous to a Jewish audience and foolishness to the Greeks. Our struggle to believe is not all that new after all.

The setting of the challenge to tell the story of Jesus in the context of trusting (the Father) and receiving (the Spirit) gives us a clear sense of how this struggle to believe can be surmounted. Those sunsets and mountaintops can help us after all, because they raise our eyes to a far horizon, where we can begin to believe that a loving creator might after all be watching over us. The short step of confessing our creator to be personal gives us courage, perhaps, to pursue the journey a little further. We open our hearts to the possibility of God. How then do we find the faith to confess his reality? Because he comes to us, by his Holy Spirit. The message from above, "*I am here*", is met by the message rising in us, "I am *here*, too", and the two together give us faith to believe. Because we trust the Father and receive the Spirit, we have faith to embrace the story of the Son.

This is very much the pattern we see rolled out through the book of Acts, even though the era of modernity has asked us to work the other way. The Christianity of the modern age, perhaps especially in its Evangelical expression, has asked us to embrace and understand the story of the gospel and *as a result* to meet the Father and receive the Spirit, but the pattern in Acts is often the reverse. Consider Cornelius and his household in Acts 10. Even though he is a Roman officer, Cornelius has a devotion to Yahweh. He is looking to that far horizon, reaching towards the God who is Father to us all.[115] God sends Peter to him, and Peter sets out to explain to the gathered household how they might be saved. Even as he's speaking, though, they receive the Holy Spirit.[116] Only after this event – according to the text, *because* of this event – are they baptized into the name of Jesus.[117] The new converts are baptized into the church because they have received the Spirit, rather than being invited to receive the Spirit because they have been baptized into the church. This order of things deeply challenges the mentality that has dominated the church in the Christendom era. No more so, though, than it challenged Peter's mentality at the time, which is why the story was included in the book of Acts in the first place.

The apostle Paul follows a similar pattern in his groundbreaking address to the pagan intellectuals of Athens. He affirms both the Fatherhood of God over all of them and the dynamic presence of the Spirit, God's breath, in them[118] before narrowing down his vision to the very specific and particular role of Jesus.[119] His presentation is both radically inclusive and concretely exclusive. You are all included in the parenthood of God, and the specific way he has chosen to love you is through the incarnation of his Son. Paul's address is an extended challenge to trust the Father, receive the Spirit, and embrace the story of the Son.

These three actions underpin the adventure of Christian mission. Whoever we are, wherever we go, and whatever God asks us to do, it will be framed by this threefold challenge.

The Earth Beneath My Faith

> It is vital to insist that although the belief in their election could be (and was) distorted into a narrow doctrine of national superiority, that move was resisted in Israel's own literature (e.g. Deut. 7:7ff.). The affirmation is that

> Yahweh, the God who had chosen Israel, was also the creator, owner and Lord of the whole world (Deut. 10:14f.), and that Yahweh had chosen Israel in relation to his purpose for the world, not just for Israel. The election of Israel was not tantamount to a rejection of the nations, but explicitly for their ultimate benefit.
>
> CHRISTOPHER WRIGHT[120]

Not only does the call of Abraham and Sarah tell us where mission comes from – it is an outworking of the invitational love of the Trinity – it also tells us where mission is going. Vocation, as it turns out, says a lot about *location*. The writer to the Hebrews takes significant time to highlight Abraham and Sarah as pioneers of faith, and says of Abraham that:

> ... even when he reached the land God promised him, he lived there by faith – for he was like a foreigner, living in tents. And so did Isaac and Jacob, who inherited the same promise. Abraham was confidently looking forward to a city with eternal foundations, a city designed and built by God.[121]

Even those of no faith must recognize the profound impact of these adventures on the unfolding of the human story. There is something about this man who left his home and journeyed for a better life that speaks to the very core of human aspiration. We sense that his quest is our quest. We find ourselves, like Abraham, longing for a land of promise and prosperity. And yet we often miss the core of the old man's commitment. When his story is told retrospectively by the writer to the Hebrews, it is his faith that is highlighted, and nowhere more so than in the dramatic phrase in verse 9. Even when he reached the land of promise, he lived by faith. The assertion made in the letter to the Hebrews couldn't be more graphic. The tent at its centre is as bright as a billboard. Abraham believed the ground on which he walked was promised to him, when he didn't own a scrap of it.

Might this be the very definition of faith: to make a home in a land that has been promised without holding a title deed to one piece of it? Abraham didn't own soil enough to bury his wife in. He lived, so the letter tells us, as a stranger in a foreign country. He lived in tents, as did his sons. As do nomadic peoples with no home base. As do refugees. As do displaced people. The whole experience is a paradox: living in a place that represents the very promise of God, yet never seeing the promise realized. This is deferred gratification of the most extreme kind: knowing every day that the promise is true, yet seeing every day the proof that it has not yet been fulfilled. Abraham's experience is the very opposite of the consumer culture his legacy has become. Our culture is more or less constructed on a foundation of the great patriarch's aspirations. We have inherited his longing – for a better life; for home and hearth; for safety and security for those we love; for a place of our own. What we haven't inherited is the patience that goes with it. We want it all, and we want it now. And our out-of-control, advertising-driven culture is the result: an insanity we all secretly despise but few of us have the courage to challenge. We have Abraham's dream. What we need is Abraham's faith.

What gave this adventurous old man the capacity to wait in this way? How could he wake up each day on someone else's land, confronted with the overwhelming evidence of non-ownership, and yet persist in the belief that it was his to inherit? To ever believe while never seeing? In a word, God. Abraham believed that his future was in the gift of a being outside himself: a divine person who could be trusted. The promise had not come from a random universe, but from a loving creator. Abraham and his sons were not waiting for "things to take a turn in their favour". They were not, week-on-week, buying lottery tickets. It was not fate, or circumstance, or their own ingenuity and effort that would bring them home. The word of promise had come from a God who loved them and had spoken to them. You cannot trust history, or destiny, or the market in such a way. Trust is personal. The key to Abraham's story, so much the foundation of our own, is the I–Thou relationship at its heart: his journey is a spiritual quest. Perhaps it's not Abraham's aspirations that our culture needs as much as trust in Abraham's God. The faith modelled here is adventurous, aspirational, future-focused – but it is above all personal. It is belief not in something but some*one*.

Approximately one-third of the world's population – Christians, Muslims, and Jews – trace their heritage to Abraham's adventurous disposition. Whole cultures have come into being because of one man's courageous camping. Too many Christians, though, while staking a claim to be counted in the children-of-Abraham crowd, have badly misinterpreted the temporary nature of their patriarch's accommodation. They read into this passage in Hebrews an earth-vs-heaven paradigm. A temporary sojourner on earth, Abraham was waiting / anticipating / moving towards the joys of heaven. The city he was looking for was elsewhere, a promise held for him beyond the blue horizon. Living in a tent was inconvenient, but one day he would have a mansion in the sky. We picture the family packing up their belongings yet again, to move yet again to a new location. They are tired; dusty. The children are fractious. It's all so tedious. But they are singing as they work, with joy in their hearts. The words float across the burning desert: "I've got a home in glory-land that outshines the sun..."

It's a compelling picture: but it's the opposite of what actually happened. Abraham didn't live under canvas because he was in transition, waiting for a permanent home elsewhere. He lived a camper's life because he was waiting to inherit the campsite. Every tent peg the old man and his family drove into the ground reminded them that this very soil had been promised to them. This is a story about earth and heaven, but the punchline is about inheriting the earth. Which is why Jesus, centuries later, embodied the faith of Abraham in a simple prayer. God's kingdom come here. His will be done on earth as in heaven. There is no "elsewhere" in the faith of Abraham. If anything, there is an "elsewhen".

The Christian hope that the writer to the Hebrews finds anticipated in the legend of Abraham is not the hope of heaven. It is the hope of an earth transformed. Our future is only "in heaven" in the sense that it is being prepared for us, now, in the very presence of God: prepared not to await our arrival but to await its due delivery date.

As well as changing the locus of his hopes, this understanding switches the polarity of Abraham's engagement with his culture. He isn't thinking, "This life is tough but it's OK because I won't be here for much longer" – he is actually thinking, or muttering under his breath, "This life is tough but it's OK because YOU won't be here for much longer." For all his political incorrectness, Abraham is waiting to see the current owners of the land evicted. It is they who are temporary residents. He's not "just passing through", they are, though they don't know it yet. This is faith audacious almost beyond imagining. Abraham isn't dreaming of a destination somewhere else – he dares to dream of the total transformation of the ground on which he stands. At the risk of repetition, the phrase "going to heaven" has no place in this description of faith. The expectation is expressed in other words altogether. Heaven is coming here. This means that when an Abrahamic faith confronts addiction and child abuse, pornography, violence, poverty and injustice, it doesn't respond by saying, "It's hard to live with these things, but, thank God, my days here are numbered". Faith looks in the face of evil and says boldly, "YOUR days here are numbered."

God's eviction notice has been served on all that does not conform to his will; on all that is not the full expression of love. We are not waiting to escape planet earth, but to inherit it. What a difference it makes to know that it is not rescue you have been promised. It is redemption.

Are you looking for the location of your inheritance? The placement of your promised land? Bang your foot three times on the ground. You're standing in it. The promise of God to you is the ground beneath your feet. Your engagement with the mission of God will not be a simple set of instructions for the completion of a time-delineated task. There is no a+b=x formula for mission. Rather, to enter into the mission of God, to sense his call on your life, is to choose to dream his dream. It is to claim your small stake in his commitment to the transformation of the universe.

I recently came across a contemporary example of an Abrahamic call to mission that has a lot to teach us about sharing in the dream of God for the ground beneath our feet. The story of Dave King, and Salford Docks, is a paradigm, for me, of missional engagement.

The closure of the docks in 1982 plunged Salford into decline and despair. The port had served for a century as the main access point for Manchester, linked by a ship canal to Liverpool and the sea. The advent of super-sized container ships had rendered the canal unusable and with its closure the local economy collapsed. Fast-forward thirty years and a different story is emerging. Salford Quays is now home to Media City UK, with over 100 companies, including large sections of the BBC and ITV. An area that was for many years the very picture of dereliction and deprivation has become a prime location for UK media industries. Salford is buzzing with energy and life.

Local pastor David King grew up in Salford and has pioneered a movement to unite its churches. His father, a pastor before him, prayed for forty-five years for the renewal of the area – one of the most deprived in the UK. Dave took up the same challenge, regularly tramping the streets to pray. One of his habitual walks took him through the wasteland where the thriving docks had once been. At one stage during this process, David and those praying with him received an extraordinary promise. They felt God saying to them that a day would come when "the nations would again come to Salford and Salford would again go to the nations – from this very place". They believed that God had called their city to be a "home of creativity". They held on to this word as in all weathers they trudged the deserted roads among the rusted cranes. Imagine their excitement when, in 2006, the BBC announced the move of 1,800 jobs to Salford. Others followed suit and the area the team walked, calling out to God, is now the very epicentre of UK broadcasting.

Sound familiar? It may be difficult to spot the tents and goatherds among the newsreaders and *Coronation Street* cast members, but this is a twenty-first-century parable of the story of Abraham. Hebrews tells us that Abraham lived as a foreigner *in the very land that God had promised him.*[122] He was not hoping for some other destination; he was driving his tent pegs into the soil of the land he walked. He trusted in God's promise: that a new city would be built on this very ground. Abraham didn't own the land he camped on, but he fully owned the promise of God. This is the faith, we are told in the letter to the Galatians,[123] that was credited to him as righteousness.

I love David's story of transformation in Salford because I've engaged in this kind of prayer over three decades in cities and towns across Europe, standing with local believers to declare God's promises over their town. We have so much to learn about turning prayer from a tedious activity in a cold church hall to an adventure of hope and creativity. At its most basic, prayer is a bridge between heaven and earth – between a realm where the will of God is done and a location where it isn't. As Jeff Fountain of the Schuman Centre says, *"it is always the will of God for the will of God to be done"*. If you don't know what that might be, go to Scripture. Locate the promises of God in the Bible and *apply* them to your areas of concern. What does God want for your city or village? For your region? For the people you are bringing before him? God's kingdom is an aeroplane looking for a place to land. Maybe your prayers can build him a runway. Alan Platt from Doxa Deo in South Africa says, "We have a saying, 'It takes a village to raise a child', but who takes responsibility to raise the village?"[124] At times

God may call you to pray for the growth or success of your church. This is good, but it is not enough. If we are praying for God's will to be done, then there is no limit to what we can pray for. What does God want for your local schools? For hospitals? For business life and the media? Start to ask God for more imagination, and he will take you further. What issues in culture and civic life is God asking you to carry in prayer?

Our missionary engagement with the city of Caen, in Normandy, has been shaped by this same brand of Abrahamic faith. It has had to be. We are working with a group of local believers to plant a church in the city, with a vision of transformation guiding us from the very start. We are small in number, with scant resources, yet we have enormous confidence in God's plans for Caen. Why? Because over twenty years ago God spoke specifically to us about this place. In September 1991 we were sailing into Ouistreham, the sea port linked to the heart of the city by a ship canal. Praying on deck at dawn, we read Psalm 107:7: "He led them by a straight way to a city where they could settle." It's hard to explain how deep our conviction was that God had spoken. We had good reason to take this scripture verse seriously, and once we acknowledged the voice of God, we were unmovable. Since that morning we have lived in Rouen and Paris, in the UK and in Amsterdam – until recently everywhere *but* Caen – yet we have always known that we would one day be established in the city. When we moved in 2009 to establish a missional training base just 45 km outside the city, could we even doubt that God intended to fulfil the promise? What are the places and people you are holding in your heart for the promises of God to be fulfilled in them?

Response: Depend on the Dreamgiver

Do you have a reason for being, a focused sense of purpose in your life? Or is your life the product of shifting resolutions and the myriad pulls of forces outside yourself? Do you want to go beyond success to significance?... Listen to Jesus of Nazareth; answer his call.

OS GUINNESS[125]

How does the picture of *vocation* given through the Bible encourage you to think about God's mission?

- It tells you that the divine human partnership is the substance of the mission of God. He is always looking for the men and women who will share their life with him, share his life, and find their purpose in his purposes.

- It tells you that the ways that God can work with people are as varied as the people that he works with. His call is different for each person. Diversity is fundamental to the plan.

- It tells you that true purpose doesn't rise entirely from within you but is spoken over you by God. To hear his voice is to know that you are moving towards the purpose you were made for.

- It tells you that the basis of vocation is relationship. The Father, Son, and Spirit invite you to share in their life, and from that place of divine hospitality to learn to serve. Your service will always be a reflection of God's love for you. Out of his life you are empowered to share your life with others.

- It tells you that the earth that God desires to bless includes the earth beneath your feet. God has a dream for every place he sends you, and in every place can use you to bring blessing.

- It tells you that you, too, can find your purpose in the purposes of God, if you will:

    – Make space to hear his voice

    – Take time to listen to your heart. What are the dreams that God might want to blend with his?

    – Surrender to participation in his life. Know that the time you take to give yourself to the life of God is not time away from his mission but the key to finding your place in it.

"I believe that Christianity happens," Brennan Manning writes, "when men and women experience the reckless, raging confidence that comes from knowing the God of Jesus Christ."[126]

CHAPTER 3

Liberation: Be Changed by the Chainbreaker

You have a **LIBERATION** story.
It is the story of the prison cell God brings you out from
and the promise he is leading you into.
God's mission is a journey
from slavery to freedom.

Midwives to the Purposes of God

The woman we honored today held no public office, she wasn't a wealthy woman, didn't appear in the society pages. And yet when the history of this country is written, it is this small, quiet woman whose name will be remembered long after the names of senators and presidents have been forgotten.

BARACK OBAMA, AT THE FUNERAL OF ROSA PARKS[127]

These words were spoken in 2005 by the then Senator Barack Obama, at the Detroit funeral of Rosa Parks. Fifty years earlier, a forty-two-year-old Parks had altered the course of American history through a single act of civil disobedience: refusing to give up her seat to a white man on a city bus in Montgomery, Alabama. Her arrest triggered a 381-day boycott of the bus system led by the Revd Martin Luther King Jr. This may not have been the birth of the Civil Rights Movement, but it was its coming-out party. "The world knows of Rosa Parks", former President Bill Clinton said, also at the funeral, "because of a single, simple act of dignity and courage that struck a lethal blow to the foundations of legal bigotry."[128]

History books are written in honour of those (often men) who stand on the world's stage. They all too easily forget those (often women) who got them there. Witness, for example, the story of Shiphrah and Puah. These two women are among the least known on the Bible's long cast list, and yet their role is crucial. Shiphrah and Puah were midwives, in charge of births across the Hebrew slave community. Their story is told in the first chapter of the book of Exodus and centres on a single verse: "Because the midwives feared God, they refused to obey the king's orders."[129] Their act of disobedience ushered in a whole new chapter in God's mission. They are midwives to the plans of their maker.

A power-hungry Egyptian king, determined to limit the number of Hebrews born in his country,[130] commanded the midwives to murder at birth all the male children.[131] They chose to disobey this law of terror,[132] tricking Pharaoh into believing that they couldn't get to the mothers in time.[133] As a result of their courage three things happened: the Hebrew race grew;[134] Moses was born safely;[135] and God blessed his two faithful midwives.[136]

Like Parks and King centuries later, Shiphrah and Puah engaged in a sustained plan of civil disobedience that struck, in their own context, *"a lethal blow to the foundations of legal bigotry."* They played a vital part in the unfolding plans of God, not by taking centre stage but by carrying out their day job with diligence and justice and by finding the courage to defy an unjust law. They are an abiding model for all who see life not as a journey into fame and fortune but as an opportunity for faithfulness to the purposes of God. Here are three key principles active in the lives of these lionhearted women.

1. The Midwifery Principle – In Exodus 1 the story of God's mission in the world is taking a new turn. Moses is about to come to prominence, and with him a whole new chapter of God's purposes will be written. There will be a shift from family to nation; a new emphasis on justice; an unfolding of God's plans for community and worship. All these things, though, depend on the turn being made – and the hinge is in the faithfulness of these two women. In pursuing a path of obedience (to God) matched with disobedience (to injustice), Shiphrah and Puah take their place in history. They are used by God to usher in a whole new era. By their breadth of vision and submission to the ways of God, they "deliver the deliverer" of Israel. What higher calling could there be?

2. The Principle of Long-Haul Blessings – We know very little about Shiphrah and Puah beyond this one courageous decision, but we are told that the blessing of God went with them. "Because the midwives feared God," Exodus tells us, "he gave them families of their own" (verse 21, NLT). One interpretation of this draws on the traditional view that midwives in the ancient world were often women who could not themselves have children. Their act of supporting young mothers was a kindness extended at the cost of great personal pain. Whether this is true or not, the clear implication here is that for these women there was blessing to be found in serving others. A literal translation would be that God "gave them households". He established them, extending to them the very blessings they were helping others to enjoy.

3. The Unexpected Joys of Obscurity – Do you love others in the hope that you'll get a good blog post out of the experience? Are you hoping to be noticed, building your own career on the backs of those you "serve"? I know you want to say "no" – but I know, too, that the answer is too often "yes". It has been for me, on many occasions. You and I share a tendency to practise righteousness "in front of others, to be seen by them".[137] How insightful of Jesus to warn us of such a danger two thousand years before Facebook even existed. Grace calls us to a deeper way. It is the way of hiddenness, a road on which, away from any spotlight, we act out our love for our maker and for our neighbour before the eyes of God alone. Our reward is the good that it does us; the growth we experience; the joy of intimacy with God – and the vicarious pleasure of holding someone else's baby and knowing that "I helped bring *this* into the world…" Do you sense the call of God to embrace such obscurity?

Women in both Egyptian and Hebrew families were socially powerless. They had no property rights, and in effect *were* property. They had no political clout, and were not taken seriously in either religious or societal debate. Their place was in the home with the children, while their men met at the City Gate, or in the Temple, or at the royal court to transact the really important deals. But God is not fazed by human convention. Our notions of who is significant mean nothing to him. He slips under the fences of our self-importance and sows seeds of redemption. While we look for the spotlight, he works at the margins. While our eyes are fixed centre stage, he hovers gently in the wings. The exodus is a narrative set in patriarchal times and with a generally patriarchal spin to its story. The good guys and the bad guys are for the most part just that: guys. The God of Abraham, Isaac, and Jacob, who called Moses and Aaron to lead the people in a confrontation with Pharaoh, his magicians, and his army shows little sign of running an equal opportunities policy, and the Hebrew culture created post-exodus was male-dominated to a fault. But look again. The very fact that Moses is available as a masculine hero role model is down to the bravery, tenacity, kindness, and faith of a whole series of women. The Hebrew midwives are the first to subvert Pharaoh's regime, risking their own lives in disobedience, but they are just the start. Moses' mother, unnamed in the text, applies courage and creativity in a complex plot to preserve her son's life. A sister – presumably Miriam – is then recruited to oversee the plan. And finally Pharaoh's daughter herself becomes involved, showing compassion and mercy and risking the wrath of her father. In a time when the prophets are silent and no man speaks for the slave people, it is women who keep the dream of God alive. The same pattern is repeated in the New Testament, where it is the receptive faith of Elizabeth and her young cousin Mary that opens the way for the incarnation. If we rush too quickly past these miracles, past these women of faith risking their very lives, we will end up with a story of salvation that is not only male-dominated but is also incomplete and skewed. The fact that just such a narrative holds sway in some of our churches goes to show how poorly we read our own history.

What this group of women provides is a vital transition between two stages in the unfolding plan of God. They are the bridge between the time of the patriarchs, when the purposes of God are centred on individuals, families, and – at their widest – tribes, to the era of Israel and the building of a nation. This is important because so much of what we need to know about God's mission will be revealed through the exodus, and specifically through the call of Moses. It is fitting that it should be Shiphrah and Puah who get us to this point, because much of what we learn from here on in will be about a God who hears the cry of the unheard; who cares about injustice and oppression; whose heart is stirred with compassion for those in slavery. Exodus will give us a clearer view of what it is that the God of Abraham and Adam is working towards. It will show us in much greater detail what it means to connect with his purposes. And it will demonstrate, above all, the nature of the freedom our maker desires for us. God is an artist who lets us see his workings, and in the book of Exodus we are invited – at a crucial time in the human and divine adventure – to look over his shoulder as he works.

> And so the scene is set. The determination of Yahweh, the Creator God, to continue in his plan to redeem humankind has been established. So has the terrible plight of his much-loved people, pushed now into the very depths of slavery and suffering. Will the river of God's plans find its way around these obstacles? Will the people be set free? Much will depend on the one man chosen by God to be a go-between – going between the people and Pharaoh and going between the people

and God.[138]

Liberation: The Story So Far

In Jewish culture stories are received not as soulless means of transferring information, but as a vital legacy. The past is very much alive in its capacity to shape our present. Nowhere is this more true than in the story of the exodus. The *Haggadah*, the book that retells the story of the exodus, from which the Passover Seder is conducted, uses intentionally ambiguous language:

> We were slaves to Pharaoh in Egypt, and the Lord, our God, took us out from there with a strong hand and with an outstretched forearm…

Citing Deuteronomy,[140] this "we", every time it is used, raises the question, "Who are we talking about?" Is this the "we" who crossed the sea? The "we" who later settled the land? Or is it the "we" around the table now, millennia further on; this family reclining to remember? The answer is yes to all three. The "we" includes all Jews, of every generation. Even those separated by centuries from the stories of the Bible are encouraged, year on year, to see themselves within them. The acts of God in freeing a slave people are so powerful, so dramatic, so foundational to the Jewish identity that their repetition reconnects each new generation with their past. This reflects an ancient view of anthropology in which a people group are considered to be "in" their ancestors as seed. We were in Adam, in Abraham, in the tribes that crossed the sea. The early Christians took the same view of the cross to say that we were *in* Christ in his death and resurrection. We don't read these stories merely to remember; we read them to proclaim our own participation. In terms of the Old Testament, the exodus is the greatest such event. For Jewish and Christian believers alike, this story is the ancient world's most stark and significant window into the mission of God. The *Haggadah* continues:

> And if the Holy One, blessed be He, had not taken our ancestors from Egypt, behold we and our children and our children's children would [all] be enslaved to Pharaoh in Egypt. And even if we were all sages, all discerning, all elders, all knowledgeable about the Torah, it would be a commandment upon us to tell the story of the exodus from Egypt.[141]

We tell this story time and time again because *this is who God is* and because *this is who we are*. This is where we see God's character and learn of his intentions in the world. To try to understand God's mission without spending time here would be futile. Equally, the story of the incarnation loses meaning if it is divorced from this, its Hebrew antecedent. The God who comes to save an enslaved people, breaking on the cross the power of all that holds them captive, has already shown us who he is. The exodus has much to teach us, even today, about the purposes of God in our world.

Extraction; exit; excavation; exclusion; export; expedition: "ex" words speak of a "moving out from", a change from being in one place or condition to being in another. There is a hint of freedom, of coming from a restricted to an open space. The tooth that is extracted was blocked in, held tight; now that it is out, you are free of pain. The expedition moves out from a small place – home – to discover the open landscapes of a wider world. Exports follow much the same path, with goods instead of people.

To be "ex", then, is to be "out", and exodus, the outward movement of God's people, is a foundational theme of the biblical narrative. Mission is the movement of men and women from slavery to freedom. The Bible's story establishes this priority early on. Of its first five books, known as the Pentateuch, one deals with the important subject of creation. The rest are all about the journey of God's people, from slave tribes to free nation. Hebrew self-identity is entirely wrapped up in this narrative.

Because a Christian understanding of mission is built on Jewish foundations, and because the ministry of Jesus draws directly on exodus language, it is clear that this theme is also crucial for the worldwide Christian. Ever since the burning bush, and the call of Moses to "set my people free", Christian mission has been linked to freedom: personal, social, economic, emotional, spiritual. If mission is not a movement out of oppression and slavery and into flourishing and freedom, then it can hardly be called Christian mission at all. "Let My People Go," writes Harvey Perkins. "With this cry, Moses demanded that his people be released from slavery. 'Let Go' is a call for liberation. From that time on, liberation has been the central theme of God's redeeming work."[142]

It is important, for our purposes here, to establish just how strongly the book of Exodus shows continuity with Genesis. The saving God of Exodus is the creator God of Genesis. The God who prepares and calls Moses is the God who created Adam, saved Noah, chose Abraham, and preserved Joseph. The story of salvation does not begin with Exodus – it is rooted in the very first moment of the fall, when God went looking in the garden for his human friends. Moses will be called to be one link in the great chain of mercy that stretches from the garden of Eden itself to the eternal throne of God. The story – God's story – has already been under way for generations. The freedom won for the slaves is, in one sense, theirs alone. Had you been among them you would not lightly have offered up your freedom as a metaphor for someone else's: in your experience, ending Hebrew slavery would have been enough. In a different sense, though, this is one expression, a footprint, of a much larger freedom. This is the creator, working towards the ultimate freedom of his world. This is an imprint of the whole creation's movement from captivity to liberty. The final freedom God is moving us towards is the freedom we first lost in Eden: the freedom to love and serve him, by choice: our full participation in his life.

What can we learn from the Exodus narrative about the nature of God's mission in the world?

Firstly, that mission is not ours, but God's. It is God who sees the suffering of his people, and God who comes himself to rescue them. Moses may be his spokesperson, his chosen deputy, but the action is all God's. All mission is God's mission. Anything we do is but a reflection of what he is doing. He hears, he acts, he rescues. Where Christianity becomes a movement of activists, it loses this foundation entirely. We are a movement, rather, clinging to the shirt tails of an active God. Philip Greenslade has written, "The God of our story is not woodenly acting out a pre-determined script. He is living out a passion for His people and for the world's redemption. ... This is a God who is passionately aroused by injustice, and plunges into emotional involvement with His people. ...God hears and feels, sees and knows, remembers and acts to save

His people."[143] Exodus tells us that mission is fuelled by the passion of God. If we seek to change the world through our own passions, we will fail. Worse still, we will be burned by the experience. Our calling, rather, is to discover God's passion; to feel what he feels. To know that however much you love your neighbour, God loves them more.

"Israel's deliverance from Egypt was not based on human resources," Gailyn Van Rheenen writes. "The Israelites had no army; they had no weapons with which to fight; they had no expertise in guerrilla warfare. God was the sole power behind this mission of deliverance."[144]

Secondly, that the mission of God is inextricably tied in with freedom. We have already said that the first prohibition ever given by God to humanity begins with the words "You are free..."[145] The freeing of the Hebrew slaves should tell us, if nothing else does, just how deep and uncompromising God's commitment to our freedom is. To seek freedom; to ask God for it; to promise it to others in God's name: all this is legitimate if our missional theology is rooted in the Exodus account. Oliver Cromwell, during the English Civil War, described the exodus as "the only parallel of God's dealing with us that I know in the world".[146] Martin Luther King Jr frequently spoke of the Civil Rights Movement in 1960s America in the language of the exodus. On the day before he was shot by an assassin in 1968, he said, "I've been to the mountaintop. And I've looked over, and I've seen the Promised Land. I may not get there with you, but I want you to know tonight that we as a people will get to the Promised Land. So I'm happy tonight. I'm not worried about anything. I'm not fearing any man. Mine eyes have seen the glory of the coming of the Lord."[147] Our call is not to harness God's passion to a particular political agenda;

it is to hear God's call to "let my people go" and understand its implications for our world. Were these men wrong to see, in their own quest for freedom, the overtones of Yahweh's promise? Is this model available to us as a means by which to grasp the movement of God in our lives and cultures? An overview of the biblical narrative would suggest that it is – though an overview of what so many of us mean by "mission" might say otherwise.

Thirdly, that freedom calls for courage. The journey of the Hebrew slaves was not a Sunday-school picnic. There was conflict along the way, and danger. Long before they reached their promise they were scared enough and tired enough to long for a return to slave conditions. Freedom is hardwon, and, until we rediscover the essential role of courage in connecting with God's mission, we will in all likelihood miss its most important benefits. Freedom, peace, justice – these are not prizes won easily, like soft toys at a funfair. They take effort and work and the passage of time, and they demand that we accept a life of risk.

"There is no way to peace along the way of safety," Dietrich Bonhoeffer writes. "For peace must be dared, it is itself the great venture and can never be safe. Peace is the opposite of security. To demand guarantees is to want to protect oneself. Peace means giving oneself completely to God's commandment, wanting no security, but in faith and obedience laying the destiny of the nations in the hand of Almighty God, not trying to direct it for selfish purposes. Battles are won, not with weapons, but with God. They are won when the way leads to the cross."[148]

Fourthly, that freedom is never exclusively external. The often untold story of the exodus is the time it took for the slaves, freed from their external masters, to even begin to appropriate inner freedom. Even in the days and weeks following God's Red Sea victory, there are incidents in which the wandering Hebrews demonstrate their slave mentality. They are fearful, struggling to trust even God their rescuer. They are angry, convinced that freedom is a worse lifestyle than slavery. They want to go back. They worship other gods. The chapters of Exodus that tell us how God got the slaves out of Egypt are vastly outnumbered by the chapters that chronicle his efforts to get Egypt out of the slaves. The commitment of God's mission is to our full freedom, to the true freedom that changes not only our outer circumstances but our inner lives.

"The Exodus story highlights the holistic and relational nature of God's redemptive work", writes Bryant L. Myers. Liberation, the journey out of slavery and into God's promise, serves in Scripture both as a metaphor and as a real outcome of mission. It is metaphor in the sense that we are slaves to so many oppressions and impulses: our own habits; our longing for comfort; our rituals of God-pleasing. There are many, many things invisible inside us from which God wants to set us free. But liberation is also a real outcome in that mission also addresses visible, political, and economic situations of oppression. Poverty, violence, trafficking, addictions, and crime: these forces weigh on the backs of the poor as surely as any slave-driver's whip. And the God of Exodus is against such weights. It is impossible, if we are to take the Bible seriously, to conceive of God's mission in the world without this dimension of freedom.

God at War

> For biblical authors, to wage war against such things as injustice, oppression, greed and apathy toward the needy was to participate directly or indirectly in a cosmic war that had engulfed the earth. ...God's good creation has been seized by hostile, evil, cosmic forces that are seeking to destroy God's beneficent plan for the cosmos. God wages war against these forces, however, and through the person of Jesus Christ has now secured the overthrow of this evil cosmic army.
>
> GREGORY BOYD[149]

There's a lot of violent language in the Old Testament, not least in the unfolding of the exodus. It is a huge challenge to understand how to read this violence, particularly when set against the peaceful ministry of Jesus. Scholars have struggled to relate a narrative of violent conquest and the utter destruction of God's "enemies" to the very narrative of liberation they are reading. Is God violent? Is he consumed by wrath, his heart set on vengeance? If he is, then the mission of God is a mission of *anger*. It seems important that this question be settled early on in our attempt to understand God's purposes. Violence and non-violence are not complementary disciplines, where you can mix and match mercy and vengeance according to your context. They are a choice you have to make right from the start.

Two overriding considerations about how we read sacred texts are helpful here.

The first is that we place each story in its proper setting in the wider narrative of God's intentions. We ask on the macro scale, "What does God want?" and apply those priorities to the micro. The most important story God is telling us is the Genesis-to-Revelation arc, the majestic movement from original goodness to final blessing. Everything we meet along the way must be read against the backdrop of this story.

The second is that, as followers of Christ, we read these texts through a Jesus-shaped window. Jesus is, in Christian belief, the ultimate and final revelation of God. He shows us things that previously have been obscured. He opens our eyes to see what we've been missing. The radical claim of the New Testament is not that Jesus is like God. It is that God is like Jesus.

Given these two hermeneutic strategies, the Exodus narrative itself gives us some clues to the nature of God's anger. It shows us:

- **That the creator rails against all that corrupts, destroys, and harms his creation.**

God's emotions are stirred against the evil that he sees oppressing the earth's people. He hates the slavery, not the slaves. Both the Old and New Testaments, Vinoth Ramachandra writes, are "filled with descriptions of how Yahweh-Adonai, the covenant God of Israel, is waging war against those forces which try to thwart and subvert his plans for his creation. He battles against those false gods which human beings have fashioned from the created world, idolized and used for their own purpose. … He contends against every form of social injustice and pulls off every cloak under which it seeks to hide."[150]

If I meet a young cancer doctor, a woman who spends her days reassuring dying children, and I ask her how she *feels* about the disease, what is she likely to say? It might depend on what kind of day she's had. I'm sure it is possible, at times, to be dispassionate and scientific and view the sickness she fights as a professional challenge – but there will be other days. There will be days when her only response will be to say that she *hates* cancer; that she wants not just to cure it but to crush it; that she longs for a world with no place for it to hide. She might say that she dreams of a day when there isn't a single cell in a single body in all the world that is marred by this destructive presence. She might call cancer her *enemy*, and she might just be a little *angry*... If she said all this, would you assume that she was angry with the children she treats? You wouldn't. You would know that she is angry *for* those children, on their behalf. The more passionate she became, the more you'd see it. The sickness is her enemy, not the patient. Setting Exodus in the context of Genesis enables us to see this same process at work. The God who meets Moses is the God of the garden. Whatever he needs Moses to do, it is something to do with recovering original intention.

- **That the evil God sees may manifest in physical reality, but is rooted in spiritual power.**

The process by which Pharaoh is persuaded, in time, to free the slaves is much more than a political conflict. The story of the plagues of Egypt, long and complex as it is, shows that behind the political pressure there is a deeper spiritual reality. It is with the magicians of Egypt that Moses must do battle, and in the end it is the superior strength of Yahweh in the spiritual dimension that brings about a political reversal. "The contest between Egypt and Israel, Pharaoh and Moses, was a contest not only of strength but of spiritual power."[151]

Fuller Professor of Transformational Development, Bryant L. Myers, has for many years worked with the NGO World Vision to forge an understanding of poverty that makes sense in terms both of the world we live in and of biblical theology. He has access to some of the most innovative projects in transformational development, working in some of the world's most challenging settings. Aware as he is of the human and political roots of the poverty many people face, he warns that we must also see its spiritual roots. "Any account of poverty that ignores the reality of an Evil One," he says, "lacks the full explanatory power that the Bible offers."[152]

Many would argue that for centuries the churches of the West saw the exodus *only* in spiritual terms, missing entirely its radical political message. The liberation theologians of Latin America and the Civil Rights Movement in the USA made just this claim, and they were right to do so. If the exodus is no more than a metaphor, the narrative entirely loses its dynamic power. We lose the passion of God for the poor and oppressed, and there is no Good News for slaves. If, however, we see only a political emancipation here – if there is no spiritual dynamic at work – our picture of God's mission is equally diminished. The power of this story – the very reason it has been so long an inspiration to so many – is precisely that it shows to us the overlap between a spiritual and a social reality. God's mission will always touch on both these dimensions.

- **That evil is personified in a being who is the enemy not only of God, but also of humanity and of the whole creation.**

It isn't popular, in the twenty-first century, to talk about the devil, except in comic books and comedy, but the clear assumption of the Bible is that our enemy is personal. The Old Testament makes the claim and Jesus more than endorses it. Just as our maker has good intentions for the created world, intentions that are intelligible, which we can grasp and be drawn into, so there is both intentionality and intelligence at the root of evil. There is an *alternative narrative* to the future of our world that looks to death instead of life; that brings not fruitfulness but barrenness; that seeks sickness and hates healing. Everything that God wants for our world, in every detail, is "unwanted" by his enemy and ours. "The Evil One is in the world working actively against life and shalom," Myers writes. "This evil works through the sin in human beings, encouraging bad choices by promoting a web of lies."[153]

Four of the New Testament names given to the enemy of God help us to understand his modus operandi.

He is the "Father of Lies"[154] – where God speaks truth into our lives, he comes to whisper untruths, always asking, "Did God *really* say...?"[155]

He is the "accuser of our brothers and sisters... who accuses them before our God day and night."[156] Where God speaks grace to us, our enemy speaks shame, and God must ask again, "Who told you that you were naked?"[157]

He is our "great enemy",[158] a predator determined to destroy all that God is seeking to achieve in us. The mission of God has an end in view, but it also has an enemy. The prowling lion, like the slithering snake, is both shrewd and wild.[159]

He is the "ruler of this world".[160] This does not mean ruler in any legitimate sense; more in the sense that Hitler was the ruler of France from 1940 to 1944. The time has now come for him to be cast out.[161]

- **That God's final victory against all evil is already assured.**

Implicit in the exodus victory is the promise of a greater freedom, a final liberation when the whole creation, like Hebrew children tramping through the mud, will take its long walk to freedom. Because the liberator *is* the creator, nothing short of this complete emancipation will ever be enough. The exodus serves in the biblical narrative not as the climax of God's work but as his calling card. It is a promise of the freedom still to come. This is how Paul, writing to the Christians of Rome, can invoke the language of exodus to say that "with eager hope, the creation looks forward to the day when it will join God's children in glorious freedom from death and decay".[162] Like Paul, we know this to be true through the revelation of Jesus, but even in the Exodus text itself the seeds of this promise are present. The Red Sea is not the end of Israel's journey but its beginning. The triumph of Yahweh is ultimately seen as a victory *for* the creation against all that enslaves it. "The good news", Walter Brueggemann writes, "is that with the victory of Yahweh, all creation is now freed (as it had been groaning in travail like slaves in Egypt); all creation is now authorised, to be its best true self, functioning as intended by the creator..."[163]

What do these realities tell us about our own journey into the mission of God?

They assure us that God's mission will have both a spiritual and a socio-political dimension. Its results will be both seen and unseen, registered both on earth and in the heavens.

They tell us, too, that all true mission will face opposition. If we are doing something God wants done, we will face the force that doesn't want it done. You can help an addict to find freedom, but the dealers won't give the neighbourhood up without a fight. God is at war, not with his creatures but with the evil that stalks them like a lion.

They tell us that our struggles all take place within the story of God. Our maker still has good intentions for our world and his enemy still seeks to resist them, but the story's end is already written (spoiler alert: God wins).

Free at Last

> Roll the stone aside.
>
> JESUS[164]

Franklin D. Roosevelt is a towering figure of the twentieth century, often cited as one of the greatest of all US leaders. He is the only president to have served for more than eight years, remaining in the White House from 1933 to his death in 1945. He came to power in a society devastated by the Great Depression, with unemployment at an all-time high of 25 per cent and poverty on every side. His first inaugural address galvanized the nation. "The only thing we have to fear is fear itself," he said, "nameless, unreasoning, unjustified, terror which paralyses needed efforts to convert retreat into advance."[165] FDR understood that we are oppressed not by the things we fear, but by our fear of them. We are terrorized not by death itself but by the shadow of death. Yann Martel writes in *The Life of Pi*:

> Only fear can defeat life. It is a clever, treacherous adversary, how well I know. It has no decency, respects no law or convention, shows no mercy. It goes for your

> weakest spot, which it finds with unnerving ease. It begins in your mind, always ... so you must fight hard to express it. You must fight hard to shine the light of words upon it.[166]

A lot of fears are faced on the exodus journey. When we first meet Moses he is afraid of all that is happening in his life;[167] when Moses first meets God his response is fear;[168] and yet when he confronts the armies of Pharaoh, in a final showdown, he can say to the people "Don't be afraid".[169] Even when his own sister is stricken with leprosy, quite possibly as a judgment from God, he calms her fears.[170] The exodus is, for Moses, a deliverance from the slavery of fear. This resonates with God's intentions throughout the sacred texts: the phrase most often used by angels when they appear to men and women is "Don't be afraid".

This is an important insight, and resonates with the Bible's view of the relationship of fear to freedom. It is fear, in Genesis 3, that keeps Adam from communion with God. Centuries later, the apostle John would write that "there is no fear in love. But perfect love drives out fear, because fear has to do with punishment. The one who fears is not made perfect in love".[171] If this is true then freedom from fear may well be the greatest freedom of all: the full freedom God is drawing us towards.

A New Testament account of Jesus facing human fear head-on is given in John's Gospel. It is *fear* that Jesus confronts when he stands before the tomb of Lazarus[172] – not his own but that of those he loves. This is the FDR moment of his ministry. Jesus stands before the tomb of his old friend, the fear of those around him so strong that he can taste it in the air.

It is left to Martha to voice their terror: "He has been dead for four days. The smell will be terrible."[173]

Will it? Too terrible to risk for the sake of resurrection? Too terrible even for Jesus? Martha's protest is neither rational nor balanced. It is a visceral, instinctive submission to fear. The stone rolled across the tomb of her brother represents the most important boundary in her culture: that between the living and the dead. Death is her greatest fear – a fear so deep she calls it by other names. Hunger, sickness, poverty, shame, embarrassment – all these small fears are ultimately expressions of our greatest fear. It's not only sheep that don't want to walk through the valley of death's shadow. The Walking Dead have been the stuff of horror across the world for multiple generations. "Most people would rather face the light of a real enemy than the darkness of their imagined fears," says Max Brooks, their modern-day spokesman, in *World War Z: An Oral History of the Zombie War*.[174]

And here Jesus stands. He is three metres from the horror most feared in all the world and three minutes away from finding out whether zombies are real. What does he do? Does he respect Martha's boundaries and out of compassion let her remain in her fear? Does he leave the thing she is so frightened of in its hiding place, safe in its stone-lidded box? No. He does something different altogether. He says, "Open up!"

We are told that a deep anger has risen in Jesus. It is anger at death, and the power death has over people. Anger at the way fear reduces them; oppresses them; deprives them of their full humanity. Jesus is not angry with Martha, or with Lazarus, or with the crowd. He is angry with death itself. He is angry on behalf of Martha and the crowd. So he looks straight at the tomb, looks into the darkness they most fear, and says "Open up! Let's see what this thing you so fear actually looks like. Let's open up the tomb and call death's bluff. Is it really something to be so afraid of?"

"Let's open the box and look at the things you most fear," Jesus says to us. "Let's see what power they really hold."

Can you see how this applies to your fear of poverty; of shame; of humiliation; of social embarrassment; of exposure? Every day you are surrounded by people imprisoned by their fears. Lazarus is the one in the tomb, but we, the crowd who mourn him, are the ones shut in by fear. We hold back from the fullness of trust in God because of our fear. What if I don't have enough money? What if I lose my home, my friends, my position? There are so many things we find security in. The fear of losing them dents and distorts our behaviour. More people are held hostage by the enemy of their souls through fear than through any other means. "Voldemort is playing a very clever game," J. K. Rowling says. "Declaring himself might have provoked open rebellion. Remaining masked has created confusion, uncertainty, and fear."[175]

The Bible tells us two things about such fears.

First, that God wants to take us to the very end of our fears. Love cannot leave us entombed by fear, because it wants all of us. If you allow him, God will stand with you to look into the eye of that which you most fear and call you to "open up". Fear is the enemy of your faith. When the disciples wake Jesus for fear of the storm, he asks them, "Where is your faith?" The presence of fear in your life does not exclude faith, but listening to your fears does. Fear is the Alsatian in your next-door neighbour's garden. He may be chained up and kept behind a fence, but you still give his snarling a wide berth. Fear is the anchorage of slavery in your soul. This is what the mission of God will free you from.

Second, that fear evaporates when love breaks us open. When it is the love of God that asks you to confront your fear, you will discover what a shadow it was. We fear the worst happening but fail to see that, if it did, we would still be loved. We would still be held in the unbroken embrace of God. Darkness cannot stay where light shines, and fear flees when love shines on it. When we open our hearts to love, we both risk fear and take a step towards its end. God does not want to overcome your fears with courage, or determination, or strength, but with love. It is love that he offers in place of terror.

It isn't only Lazarus that Jesus wants free of death. It is Mary, and Martha, and the great crowd lost in their grief and confusion. It is us. God wants to open you up where fear has kept you in the tomb. Are there areas of your life where you know it is fear that has limited you, depriving you of full humanity? Ask God to come and speak his word of resurrection over you. What about those you love? Are there places where their rebellion, their destructive patterns of behaviour, their rejection of your friendship, are signs of fear? Can you help them to the place where God will open them up? Where they are Martha, kept in thrall to fear, will you let the compassion and the anger of Jesus rise in you? Will you trust this Jesus, who looks death in the eye, to take both you and those you love beyond fear and into his freedom?

Wholly Grounded

> Here we see God at work; silently at first, equipping Moses with those skills and abilities which will later be required of him and will help make him the great deliverer

of God's people. It will nevertheless be nearly 80 years before God is ready to act. God's time-scale is rarely ours and we can often be deceived into thinking that He is inactive, even unconcerned. Yet God is working all the time, unseen by us.

STEPHEN DRAY[176]

From *Changing Rooms* and *Escape to the Country* to *What Not to Wear* and *A Place in the Sun*, TV makeover shows have been all the rage for some time. Whether they involve redecorating your home, reinventing your wardrobe, or relocating your whole life, these shows, watched by millions, have one thing in common: they speak to our longing to make changes. In every show there is a *before* and an *after*: and where possible a gasping audience to appreciate the difference.

The story of God's liberating acts to bring the Hebrew slaves out of Egypt is told at two levels in the book of Exodus. At one level it is the story of the people, a chapter in the history of Israel. Tracing their roots to Abraham, they have become a large tribe, a subsection of the Egyptian population. By the end of the story they will be a nation, beginning the journey of learning how to live in freedom. Exodus is a huge part of their story. At another level, though, this is the biography of Moses. It opens in effect with his birth and much of it is told from his perspective. His encounter with God on Mount Sinai sets the whole adventure in motion, and the promises made there hold true right through the story. Just as the vocation of Abraham and Sarah have been paradigmatic of the era of the patriarchs, so that of Moses is central to this new phase in God's mission.

"Do not come any closer," the Lord warned. "Take off your sandals, for you are standing on holy ground."[177]

The burning bush encounter[178] is one of history's great "before and after" stories and as good a picture of the workings of calling and purpose as any given to us. We meet Moses as a confused and fearful man, struggling to find his identity. He makes mistakes, brings trouble down on his own head, and is forced to flee the country. Forty years on he is living a quiet and anonymous life, afraid even to think of going back. Yet just a short while later he stands before the most powerful dictator in the known world and speaks with confidence and conviction. Something has moved him from cowardice to confidence, from fear to freedom. What is the mysterious makeover that accounts for the "before" and "after" of Moses' story? It is that he has connected with the mission of God. God has invited Moses to play a part in his unfolding plan of salvation, and in that participation Moses has found passion, purpose, and power. A connection to God's mission becomes, for the old Hebrew shepherd, a personal journey of liberation.

It took Moses eighty years to even begin to see the significance God had always seen in him. He spent another forty wrestling with it, working out the role God had for him. Calling is a lifetime's work, rooted in the dreams of God before your life began. All the same, there can be little doubt that this encounter moment, when he stands before the very presence of God, is foundational to his life's calling. Like Abraham before him, he hears God speak in a way that resonates deeply with his history and aspirations. For all its wider historical significance, this is very much a personal encounter. The call of Moses has been seen for centuries as a model of God's dealings with humanity, and for good reason. There is much we can learn here about connection with the purposes of God.

What must it have meant to Moses to be told that he

stood on holy ground? He was, in effect, grounded. A wanted murderer in Egypt; a profound embarrassment to his adopted (royal) family; living in a country he didn't want to live in; doing a job he didn't want to do: Moses had no way out. And all the time he fumed that the Hebrew slaves didn't, either. His efforts to help his people had failed. He was wracked with guilt, overwhelmed by the sense of his own powerlessness. Apart from the relative compensation of an apparently good marriage and a supportive father-in-law, on most other indicators Moses was down and out. Until he hears the voice of God declaring that the ground on which he stands is holy. The very ground of his grounding – the place he doesn't love but can't escape – is pronounced blessed. This awareness of "place" or "ground" in the conversation between Yahweh and Moses is exceptional. On the surface, there is a call to the land of promise. This is a place far away where the Hebrew people can be truly free: a land flowing with milk and honey. The promised land, later called the Holy Land, is the very embodiment of the blessing of God. It will be a place of peace, of *shalom*, where the freed slaves will be built into a nation. But it isn't this land God calls holy. It is the ground on which Moses stands. "I'm calling you to a new place far away," God says. "But I'm calling the place you are standing holy."

How are we to understand this double call? What does it mean for Moses to be both called to a new land of promise and affirmed in the sacredness of the land he's now in?

- It means that Yahweh is not local. In the age in which Moses lived, all gods were geographically contingent. They had places in which they were powerful and other places in which their power faded. The most powerful god was still little more than a neighbourhood warlord. Not so Yahweh: he is God here and he is God there. He has power to give us territory far away, but he has power also to make our current territory holy.

- It means failure is not terminal. The ground of Moses' shepherd pathways was, for a thousand reasons, the ground of his failure, but this is where God meets him. He doesn't have to go anywhere to encounter Yahweh, even if the encounter calls him to go. The shortest distance in the universe is the distance between where you are right now and where you need to be for God to call you.

- It means that Moses is called *now*. God is not waiting until they all get somewhere else before instructing Moses to act. The work starts now, in present-day reality. The promised land is the fulfilment of a dream, but it won't be found by dreamers. This is not a fantasy of freedom but real, hard-won freedom, and the work of gaining it starts now, in slavery. The longest journey has a first step, and the burning bush is Moses' wake-up call. Your calling may take you somewhere you have never been, but its first requirement of you will be to act in the place where you are.

Whatever happened in Moses' head and heart at this moment, it gave him courage to face a challenge he had been running from for forty years. Like the alcoholic who at last signs up for AA; the prodigal who turns towards home; the unsigned songwriter who finally presses "record", Moses turns to face his fears and breaks the deadlock of his grounding. What makes the difference? The discovery that God is with him in his exile; that God is never "over there" but always "right here"; that there is not some distant holy ground waiting for Moses to reach it. Quietly, consistently, under the surface of exile, God has been preparing one of the greatest religious and political leaders in the history of humanity, whose bold imagination will in time not only free the Hebrew slaves but set a template for human societies across the world for generations to come. Through forty years of apparent exile, God has been sowing in Moses the gifts and experiences he needs for the remarkable journey ahead. With the burning-bush encounter, that preparation breaks the surface, and Moses comes to see that God is with him, has always been with him, and will be with him in all the adventures to come. Old, tired, guilty, flawed, washed-up, and burnt-out: Moses becomes the beginning of a global revolution.

God's call to Moses not only offers him liberation, but at the same time shows us what kind of freedom it is that we are offered. This is not freedom from all constraint but freedom within the constraints of relationship. There is a sense in which Moses is even more "grounded" than he was before his fiery encounter. He is fixed not to a place but to a person. Whether he stays or goes, whether the promise comes quickly or comes slowly, whether he even lives to possess the promised land (spoiler alert: he didn't), he is now glued to his God. It is not his location that is consistent but his orientation. From this point on he will live a Godward life, and it is to this that he will call those he leads. Why does this matter? Because it helps us get the foundation right. The mistake is to think that Yahweh called his people to a land, and that this is their foundation. The truth is that he called them to himself. For the most part they got this wrong, and it took the later pain of exile to correct them. God is interested in *who* you are and only then in *where* you are. Freedom comes when we are grounded in relationship, glued to God. In such a grounding, every place is holy, every land a land of promise.

Centuries later the apostles Paul and Peter would each describe the true freedom of the believer as a form of slavery. Emancipated by the liberating God, we become slaves of Christ.[179] The freedom we are offered is the freedom to respond to God, obeying him not out of coercion but by choice. This is the condition established, and then lost, in Eden. Its recovery is the goal of all mission.

The Shepherd's Bush Triangle

> As Christians we have learned much about sharing the love of Christ with people all over the world who have never heard the gospel. We continue to see the salvation message preached in the far corners of the earth and to see indigenous Christian churches vigorously extending Christ's kingdom on every continent. We have learned how to feed the hungry, heal the sick, and shelter the homeless. But there is one thing we haven't learned to do, even though God's Word repeatedly calls us to the task. We haven't learned how to rescue the oppressed…
>
> GARY HAUGEN[180]

Because we read the Bible from the vantage point of later history, we know how this story will end. We have the privilege of knowing that Pharaoh will eventually agree to let the people go; that, even though he changes his mind, God will intervene and miraculously deliver them. We know that they will, over time, become a nation and that, though they have their ups and downs, they will never again be forced to manufacture bricks without straw. To grasp the full drama of the story, however, it is important that we recognize that Moses knew none of these things. Before his wilderness encounter he didn't even know if Yahweh cared, one way or the other, what happened to the slaves. As the story begins he doesn't know if God wants to free the slaves; if he's powerful enough to do so; if Pharaoh can be beaten. As is clear from the conversation, he doesn't know if any of the slaves will even follow him.

Moses doesn't know these things because, at this point in history, no one does. We tend to assume that the attributes of God – his power, love, faithfulness, and beauty – are all obvious. Surely *everyone* knows what God is like? We need to remember that in Moses' lifetime no one knew what God was like. The God of the Bible is a God of revelation: we come to know him because he shows himself to us. There is a popular saying among theologians, "Only God knows God". The aspects of God we do know, we know because he chooses that we should.

The Exodus narrative, then, and specifically the conversation Moses has with God, is a revealing of the divine nature. The shape of the mission of God emerges not on the basis of some formula or theory, but directly from the actions of God in our world.

Three aspects of God's character and purpose implicit in the burning-bush encounter, and proved by the events unfolding from it, are:

1. That God has a plan.

2. That God knows the heart of Moses, and has dreams for him.

3. That God cares about the plight of the slaves.

Underlying the vocation of Moses, these three distinct histories are in formation. The first is the history of God, the second that of Moses, and the third that of the Hebrew slaves. The confluence of these three histories provides a kind of vocational triangulation by which Moses is able to know, with little room for doubt, what he should do. It is the meeting of these histories, in this moment, that takes Moses forward. The Exodus narrative is the unfolding story of the love triangle between Yahweh, Moses, and the Hebrew slaves.

If we accept the call of Moses as a paradigm of mission, then the pattern here, represented in the conversation he has with Yahweh and worked out later in his dealings with Pharaoh and the slaves, can help each one of us to find our place. I do not have the same vocation as Moses, just as you do not have the same vocation as me, but I suspect that for both of us the elements of the burning-bush conversation will be present in our call.

This "triangle of purpose" means that, as a result of Moses' saying yes to Yahweh's call, three things will happen. In each of our three histories, fruit will be borne.

In the history of the mission of God, **plans to establish God's rule on the earth will move forward**. A "yes" from Moses means progress in God's purposes. The things that God is trying to do – in the vernacular, *what God wants* – will come to pass. In the immediate this is to do with the freeing of the slaves, but we've already seen – and it is evident in any case from both the setting and the unfolding of the Exodus narrative – that this is only one step in a much larger plan. The God who walked with Adam, who chose Abraham and Sarah, who prospered Joseph precisely in order to bring his people into Egypt, is up to something. He is working towards an end goal – a vision sparked, as we have seen, by the events in Eden. God presents himself to Moses as the God of Abraham, his identity and nature buried in the deep past, and he lifts his servant's eyes to the horizon, the promise of his faithfulness thrown into the far future. The scale of his thinking is panoramic. There is a bigger picture – a longer, wider, deeper story – and he is inviting Moses in, to play a part in it. A test of the efficacy of Moses' call will be to ask, a few years down the line, "Did the purposes of God move forward because of what we did together?" The same question can be asked whenever any one of us says "yes" to our place in God's mission.

In the life history of Moses, mission will have done its work if the shepherd **finds himself engaged in tasks that he is fit for, that make sense of his past, and that usher in a future of meaning and significance.** Moses doesn't come to his bush-fire as a blank slate. He has form. There are aspects of his life that cause him grief, and nothing he has done so far has helped him fix them. Paramount among his concerns are his problems with identity. Raised as an Egyptian prince, his discovery of his adoptive status has thrown him into confusion, pushing him to seek out Hebrew company. But slaves don't tend to go out drinking with their owners, and Moses is as uncomfortable with them as back at court. Related to this, he has a temper problem. He is passionate about justice, and deeply moved by the slavery of his birth family, but his attempts to intervene lead him to violence. God's picture of a bush that burns but is not consumed may be a coded message: Moses needs to find a passion that will not destroy him. Lastly, as the culmination of his existential crisis, he is a fugitive, living in exile. He calls his first son "Foreigner". He takes a job despised by those of his rank. He accepts defeat and settles to a life of smouldering regret. The test of God's call in this area will be to ask, "Did the things God called me to resolve these issues? Does my participation in God's mission make sense of my life?" It is difficult to see a call as fruitful if it only leads its subject into deeper dilemmas.

Lastly, in the history of the Hebrew slaves, **the only fruit that matters will be freedom**. Their problem is slavery, and no peripheral solution that doesn't address that central point will mean much to them. They are oppressed, and their oppression is increasing.[181] Pharaoh's instruction to the midwives smacks of eugenics.[182] Motivated by fear and hatred, he is paddling at the shallow end of genocide. Moses knows that things are bad, and getting worse. He also knows his adopted family: knows already, perhaps, how hard their hearts are; how far they are likely to go. The Hebrew story doesn't look set to end well, and the clock is ticking. Enter Yahweh, and a bush on fire. Moses discovers, perhaps to his surprise, the passion in the heart of God for his slave people. There is a meeting of minds as God's swirling emotions resonate with those of Moses' own heart, offering some kind of redirection. All it needs for this common affection to be translated into action is the third wheel on the wagon: the "outward focus" of the plight of the slaves. The story could not be told if it involved only God and Moses. Thrilling as that narrative might be, it would not be the great adventure we have before us. In every encounter between Moses and God, in every prayer and conversation, there is this third party – sometimes physically present, sometimes absent, but always remembered. The zeal shared by Yahweh and Moses has a goal – it is a directed zeal. It does not float unconnectedly between them, but flows towards a shared objective: the liberation of the people God has chosen.

Moses discovers that God has an inner compass, pulled inexorably towards the magnetic north of his people's need, and that he, too, is drawn by this same goal. He has been confused by this force in the past and has never known what to do with it, but it has been the defining force of his adult life. This is why he couldn't enjoy the long-term benefits of royal adoption. This is why he couldn't "let things lie". This is the root and source of his exile and dislocation. It is when he sees that the flow of his own heart and life and the arrows of the passion of God are pointing to the same goal that he steps into purpose. "God is the champion of the poor and those pushed to the margins of life," Terence Fretheim writes. "God is one who liberates them from the pharaohs of this world."[183]

The importance of this hillside conversation is that it sets the tone for all that is to follow. As the Exodus adventure unfolds, we see that these three factors are, indeed, fulfilled:

- The purposes of God do move forward, and not just with the parting of the sea. There is a land of promise, a Law to live by. There is a nation to be shaped. Once the wheels of the mission of God get rolling through the Red

Sea mud, there is no stopping him. The train has left the station and it is speeding towards its goal.

- The life of Moses does begin to take on deeper meaning. He is uniquely qualified, it turns out, for the job God wants him for. Who else has Hebrew blood *and* Pharaoh's private line on speed dial? Moses' past and passions, his strengths and weakness are all taken up into the plans God has for him. Mission makes sense of who he is, as no other career choice could.

- The slaves are freed. This is the objective, measurable reality resulting from the "yes" of Moses' call. People who were struggling under a great burden of forced labour, their very survival threatened by a genocidal despot, are now free. In a literal foreshadowing of a much later prophecy,[184] "Good News has come to the poor. Captives have been released and the oppressed set free." For the Hebrew slaves, the time of the Lord's favour has very definitely come.

Perhaps the experience of Moses can tell us what it means to find our place in the mission of God. Might purposeful living be defined by the triangle of these three conditions?

A forward movement in the plans and purposes of God.

A resolution of my past, making sense of all the longings of my heart.

Slaves are freed, and succour brought to the evident need of the human family.

Religion assumes that we can be consumed by the first in isolation. It even encourages us to leave all else aside. To pursue the perfect will of God, at any cost. Humanism assumes that the second is enough. If I am satisfied and happy, what else matters? A secular political agenda holds us to the third. Only God's mission insists that all three voices must be heard. This is the triangle of purpose: a zone in which it is possible to identify and engage with the intentions of God, to find personal growth and fulfilment, and to love and serve your fellow human beings. It doesn't ask that any one of the three be withered or distorted by an excess of attention to another.

The experience of Moses tells us at the very least which road to take if we want to know more fully our vocation. Move towards the centre of the triangle. How can we do this? By giving attention to all three dimensions: understanding the will of God and hearing his voice; understanding your own journey and listening to your heart; understanding the needs of the oppressed and letting their cry reach you.

Vocation, as it turns out, isn't all about one voice. It is a choir of three. Once you recognize this triangle you realize it is implicit in the Scriptures. Jesus was sketching out the boundaries of this zone when he summed up the Law of God: "Love the Lord your God with all your heart and with all your soul and with all your mind. This is the first and greatest commandment. And the second is like it: 'Love your neighbour as yourself.' All the Law and the Prophets hang on these two commandments."[185]

You, God, Your Neighbour: The Perfect Love Triangle

Whatever purpose God has prepared for your life, you can be sure that it will draw you into this triangle. God's purpose for you will serve three goals at once:

It will contribute to the fulfilment of God's purposes for the whole earth. The call of God is born in the character of God. Mission is an expression of *who God is*.

It will bring fulfilment to the passion and potential that God has invested in your personality. The call of God gives ultimate expression to your identity. Mission throws light on *who you are*.

It will move towards the liberation and salvation of humanity, meeting the needs of those on whom the love of God is focused. Mission releases human beings to be *who they were created to be*.

Understanding, exploring, enjoying, and fulfilling the call of God implied, for Moses, stepping into this three-way adventure. He was called, in effect, to know God, to know himself, and to know the needs of the people. Clues to finding the purpose of God for your life can be gleaned from all three of these dimensions, and a sure sign that you are on the right track is that a balance is established among the three: when you discover that the things you are doing fit into God's plan, make sense of who you are, and meet the needs of others. As Moses stepped into God's purposes, he discovered that he was stepping into his true identity, moving on in the love and service of others, and engaging with God's plans for the world. Are you?

The Core of the Core

The triangle of purpose is more than simply a technique to find your calling. In a very real sense it is the end result of this whole journey into the promises of God. If there is a single, attainable goal at the heart of these seven stories, this is it. The holy grail of your quest is this: to love God, to know yourself, and to live for others.

- *To love God* because without that love the essence of your quest is lost. Connection with your maker is the very substance of these stories. Participation in the life of God is the primary goal of your life.

- *To know yourself* because self-rejection is the enemy of every achievement. We hide in shame, in guilt, in self-loathing, but until we know ourselves as the beloved of God we cannot begin to embrace his intentions for us. God's desire for us is that we know ourselves as loved, and from that security learn to love others. "Self-rejection is the greatest enemy of the spiritual life because it contradicts the sacred voice that calls us the 'Beloved'. Being the beloved is the core truth of our existence."[186]

- *To live for others* because my capacity to love and be loved by my fellow human beings is the acid test of whether the first two conditions are met in me. Knowing God frees me to serve others, knowing myself as loved frees me to love them, and living for the blessing of others becomes the measure of my freedom.

Response: Be Changed by the Chainbreaker

> The God of Israel is a relentless opponent of human oppression, even when the oppression is undertaken and sponsored by what appear to be legitimate powers.
> WALTER BRUEGGEMANN[187]

Liberation is a key category in understanding the mission of God because:

- All that God is doing *in* us and all that he wants to do *through* us is characterized by freedom. He frees us from our inner slavery and sets us up as those who can bring freedom to others.

- Our life with God is a journey deeper and deeper into his freedom: a freedom born not of independence but of relationship.

- Freedom is the original condition of humanity. We are free to run from God, but we are free to know him, and his desire is that we would learn, in freedom, to obey him.

- In our hearts and in our world, the slavery God opposes will always have a spiritual dimension. We may experience captivity in physical, emotional, social, or economic terms, but all captivity is rooted in spiritual realities. The enemy of God is also the enemy of our freedom.

- God's freedom "from" is always at the same time freedom "to". We are freed from oppression and selfishness – our own and those of others – and we are freed to trust, to love, and to serve.

- The place of greatest freedom we can live in is the centre of the triangle of purpose, where the will of God is done, the longings of our hearts are satisfied, and the poor are delivered into freedom. This is the triple goal of mission.

- It is only those who will let God set them free who are able to bring others into freedom. This is the nature of the mission of God: changed people change people, and the people they change change the world.

> The salvation we enjoy now includes that redeemed community of transformed disciples challenging all status quos in the name of their risen conquering Lord. And even when the raging powers of darkness gain temporary victories, we know that the day of cosmic salvation will surely come when the kingdoms of this world will become the kingdom of our Lord and even the groaning creation will be at peace. With such a hope ablaze in our hearts, how can we fail to erect signs of that coming salvation throughout the created order?
>
> RON SIDER[188]

CHAPTER 4

Formation:
Hold on to the Heartseeker

You have a **FORMATION** story.
It is the story of your affections,
the things that matter most to you,
and God's desire to win your heart through worship.
God's mission comes to birth
in a life abandoned to his love and mercy.

A Song for Miriam...

We don't just hear truth. We taste it, smell it, touch it, wrestle with it, argue with it, confront it, turn away from it, hide from it, hold it, and fall in love with it. It is more than intellectual – it is sensual. The mystics memorised the Scriptures, said them aloud over and over again, until the words of God became a part of them, flowed through them like water, soaking into their skin and bones – until Scripture became like an old friend.

DUFFY ROBBINS[189]

The quickest way to trace the progress of the mission of God through Scripture is to chart the lives of its headline heroes. We've already done this with Abraham and with Moses. We could carry on with Joshua and Samuel; with David and Solomon. This is the quickest way, but it is not the best. Giving attention only to the "rock stars" of the story means we miss important lessons taught by lesser-known players.

One of these is Miriam, the sister of Moses. Miriam is an intriguing character because we know so little about her. She is first mentioned in Exodus 15, shortly after the crossing of the Red Sea. She surfaces again in Numbers, when an unexpected conflict with Moses and a subsequent case of leprosy mar her life. This incident is mentioned again in Deuteronomy, in a section giving guidelines on dealing with disease.

Apart from these few mentions, Miriam is silent and invisible: but she is not unimportant. Three details show this. The first is in the argument Miriam has with Moses. Both she and Aaron make the claim that God has spoken not only through Moses, but through them as well.[190] The text presents this to us as an act of pride, and the argument is settled when God explains how special Moses is and Miriam is distracted by a skin condition.[191] The intriguing aspect of this episode is that Miriam and Aaron are portrayed as equals, and that their claim to hear from God must surely have at least some basis in experience. Miriam, it seems, was not so insignificant.

The second detail comes in Numbers 20, where a note is made of Miriam's death in the wilderness of Zin.[192] No detail is given, but the very fact that her death is noted gives her status. How many others have the time and place of their birth or death recorded in the pages of the Bible?

The third affirmation of Miriam's role comes much later, in the prophecies of Micah. Centuries after the events of the exodus, the prophet is reminding the people of Israel of God's love for them. He reaches for a single incident or image to sum up the care and passion Yahweh shows his people. The exodus is an obvious example, and this is how he describes it:

> For I brought you out of Egypt and redeemed you
> > from slavery.
> I sent Moses, Aaron, and Miriam to help you.[193]

At so great a distance from the events themselves, Micah's naming of Miriam alongside her two brothers must reflect the traditions of his day. Despite her non-involvement in the initial events of the exodus, despite so little being known about her, Miriam is one-third of the leaders God has sent to free his people. We hardly remember her name, but she matters.

There is one last example of Miriam's engagement with God's purposes that I have left until this point. Covered by just two verses, this incident tells us everything we need to know about Miriam's role. After the crossing of the Red Sea, with the armies of Egypt drowned and the slaves at last truly free, Moses leads the people in a long and complex praise song.[194] When he's done with singing, an odd thing happens. We meet his sister for the first time. We are told:

> Then Miriam the prophet, Aaron's sister, took a tambourine and led all the women as they played their tambourines and danced. And Miriam sang this song:
>
> "Sing to the Lord, for he has triumphed gloriously;
> he has hurled both horse and rider into the sea."[195]

We've never before been introduced to Miriam – her very existence is unacknowledged to this point. Yet here she is, a prophet leading the people of God in a high-spirited dance. Moses' act of worship is wordy and complicated; Miriam's is stripped back and spontaneous. She picks up her tambourine, leads a merry dance, and repeats, over and over, in exuberant abandon, a simple statement of the victory of God. You can't dance to such words sung once – the repetition is implied, and important. This is a rehearsing of the victory of God. It is a dance because exuberance is needed. It is not so much an intellectual engagement with the acts of God as a sensual celebration. Miriam is doing more than describing God's victory. She is revelling in it.

Why does this incident matter? Because it tells us something of the role that Miriam will take. She is a worshipper, a prophet with a passion to lead God's people into praise. Until the crossing of the Sea, she has no role. There is no corporate worship, because there is no community. What there is is a power struggle. Political action is needed; high-level decision- making; courageous negotiation. For all these Moses is uniquely qualified. His only flaw – a nervousness in public speaking – is made up for by his brother, Aaron. The two men form a team, and take the pressure. When it comes to worship, though, Miriam outshines them both. She is the dancer, the leader, the enthusiast who can stir others into praise. In worship, Moses is happy to give way to her.

Like Shiphrah and Puah before her, Miriam is a hinge leader. Her presence at the head of the procession indicates transition. The phase of political action is not entirely over – nation-building is a long, slow road – but politics alone is no longer enough. The new nation of Israel needs a heart, and its heart will be found in worship. For this, the erstwhile silent Miriam is needed.

The hinge is so tiny that you could easily miss it. In just two verses Moses steps aside for Miriam, and the people move from politics to worship. I wondered if this hinge idea might be an exaggeration. Could the direction of the nation really change in just two verses? So I looked up "tambourine" in my concordance. There is only one previous mention in the Bible. The context is a family party, in Genesis.[196] Apart from that, Miriam's is the first tambourine mentioned in Israel's history. It is definitely the first played in worship. Exaggeration? Do you know how central tambourines are to Jewish life? Miriam's dance is not a minor detail in the narrative. It is the birth of Hebrew worship.

Formation: The Story So Far

> The organ for seeing God is the heart. The intellect alone is not enough.
>
> JOSEPH RATZINGER[197]

Miriam's "hinge moment" of exuberance is more than just a fleeting incident. It is a vital punctuation mark preparing us for perhaps the most significant transition in the story the Old Testament is telling. We have seen how *creation* anchors the mission of God in his original intention. He has not abandoned his first plan, to bring the earth to fruitfulness by drawing into partnership the men and women who will make the choice, in freedom, to obey him. We have seen that in Abraham and Sarah he finds two such people, and the idea of *vocation* is born: human beings invited by the voice of God to share in his life and find purpose in his dream for the world. Further, we have seen the plans of God grow, his ambitions stretching from a couple to a family, to tribes, to a nation. We have seen that *liberation* must become his first priority. A nation held in slavery can never, out of freedom, choose to serve him.

And now we reach a point where that liberation has been achieved. The people stand on the threshold of nationhood, ready to become the family God longs for. What tone will the next phase of the journey take? What is God's priority now?

The answer is *formation*. God must take the wandering slaves and *form* them into nationhood. They must be shaped into community; built together as a people. And not just any people. They will be a people who reflect the heart of God. The slaves are free, but they must learn to live in freedom. Their external slavery is ended. Their inner journey into total freedom now begins.

The mistake many readers make is to assume that the basis of this journey is the Law. So high-profile is the giving of the Law to Moses that it is easy to see how the mistake is made. The assumption is that it is by following God's moral law that the new nation will reflect his character. Their moral perfection will mirror God's perfection, and the world will know how truly wonderful he is. The language of the Law lends itself to this, as does Moses' way of communicating. He is, after all, trying to save their lives. Hygiene laws are not optional when you're guiding thousands of refugees through the desert, and these are a slave people – they're not used to any kind of obedience that is not forced on them. Having said all that, though, it is *not* the purpose of the Law to shape the heart of Israel. That job will be tackled in a very different way. It will be the goal of worship, not of law.

There are three pieces of evidence that support this assertion.

- The first is that the major part of Exodus is given over not to Law but to worship. It is the building of the tabernacle, the people's mobile worship centre, that occupies the larger part of Exodus.

- The second is that much of the Old Testament then follows suit. The major obsession of the Old Testament narrative is not moral perfection; it is worship. It is the hearts of the people God is after. He wants their affection, and affection, in the sphere of divine–human contact, is the fabric worship is woven from.

- The third, which follows from the other two, is that the sin of which the people are most often accused – the failing that dogs their steps at every turn – is not their failure to keep the moral law, important as this is. It is idolatry: false worship. The first commandment is not a moral commandment at all. It is a call to worship. The accusation God must bring against his people, time and time again, is not that they have failed to meet his highest moral standard. It is that they have withheld from him their hearts. Worse still, they have been romanced by other gods. Worship, not law-keeping, is the goal towards which God's acts of nation-building move.

Does this mean that the Law doesn't matter? Far from it. In order for there even to be worship there has to be a community, and communities need laws to live by. It's a cliché, but you do need to decide which side of the road you'll drive on – not for the sake of moral perfection or to win God's approval, but for the sake of not causing a pile-up. The absence of law is anarchy, and anarchy, especially in a community under pressure, leads to death. Laws are given for the sake of justice, to protect the weak. They champion fairness. They provide a framework within which trade and relationships, family life and neighbourhoods can all continue. Laws save lives. They promote peace. They are about the health of a community – they are not about its standing before God.

I've often been intrigued by the preponderance, in Jewish laws, of diet rules. Kosher eating – clean and unclean – is probably the single most recognizable expression of Jewish practice to this day. I used to wonder where this emphasis had come from; why food was so important in the Jewish story. Until I spent some time with Moses and watched him try hard to keep alive a chaotic gaggle of families and tribes with zero governance experience travelling through a hostile, barren wilderness. How do you care for such people? How do you ensure their safety? It's a pretty complicated task, I'm sure, but "Don't eat the scorpions" would be a good place to start. If I were Moses, I'd nail that one right away. And don't kill your neighbour. Or steal his wife. If there were ever two activities that don't contribute to a peaceful travelling band, adultery and murder would be them. And I'd make sure that anyone with signs of infectious disease was moved – for their own recovery and the health of those near to them – to a place outside the camp. This is not a population with ready access to hand sanitizers. Is it naïve to see in these laws the seeds of civilization; an early, rudimentary attempt to create order? Is Moses not the first sheriff of a frontier town, reeling from the excess of the gold rush: a one-badge judiciary trying to get agreement on at least a handful of basic regulations?

I'm aware that this doesn't explain all the laws, but I remain convinced it explains many of them, and it leaves me wondering how we ever thought God gave the law to make us perfect, or to guarantee his approval.

If obedience to the Law is not what shapes us after God, what does? What is it that Yahweh wants from his people? The answer is worship. He wants the affection of their hearts. This is not because he's selfish and likes to be told how great he is. It is because worship shapes us. Where our hearts direct our affections, there will be the source of our behaviour. We become that which we gaze upon. It is through worship – the directing of our affections towards the one who sets us free – that the work of our formation will be done.

Present to the Presence

> I'm not one for sunbathing. Too much lying around and I get fidgety and a bit guilty. But there is something about sunbathing that tells us more about what prayer is like than any amount of religious jargon… You're not going to get a better tan by screwing up your eyes and concentrating. You simply have to be there where the light can get at you.
>
> ROWAN WILLIAMS[198]

The Jungle in Calais is not a refugee camp in any normal sense. There are no neat lines of matching tents; no UNHCR teams holding it all together. Instead this was, in 2015 and early 2016, a thrown-up shanty town of rutted muddy tracks and wind-blown tents, where a pallet-and-tarpaulin lash-up was the most permanent structure available. There is garbage everywhere, including tents flattened by wind and rain, abandoned where they fell.

In the midst of this transient chaos, the Orthodox Church of St Michael is an oasis of peace and beauty. Solomon Gatachow, its guardian, sleeps in a hut beside it to ensure twenty-four-hour security, and fights for the funds to run its generator and gas fire for daily morning and evening prayer and crowded Sunday services.

When Solomon and his friends built the church in 2015, it was in a clearing away from the camp. Starting with a frame made from fresh-cut branches, they scavenged for plastic sheeting, paced out a church shape on the ground, and made their masterpiece. In time the camp grew around it, engulfing it in the very chaos it was designed to overcome. A head-high fence of recovered timber patched with corrugated iron was thrown up around a makeshift courtyard. The doorway to the church itself is narrow, topped with two brightly painted angels. A small lobby area allows just enough space to take off your shoes before you stepped into the sanctuary itself.

Inside, nothing has changed. No matter how crowded and chaotic the Jungle becomes, this will always be a place of peace. The floor is carpeted, the tarpaulin walls fabric-lined. Brightly coloured icons of Jesus, Mary, and the angels guide the prayers of the faithful. Michael, muscular and angelic in equal measure, battles Lucifer on their behalf. A cluster of hand-made walking sticks are made available for the old and infirm, who find it hard to stand for services lasting three to four hours. Part circus tent, part art gallery, part cathedral, this holy space gives rich meaning to the term "sanctuary". Its daily visitors are people in desperate need, people whose lives are in free fall. Fleeing poverty and war, their way into the UK is blocked. Increasing violence marrs the nights when hundreds try to outrun a growing police presence to grab a life-threatening slot on the undercarriage of a train. Others give up the fight, but where should they go? Home is not an option; France hardly more so. They stay, and try as best they can to build some kind of life in the wilderness.

Those who spend precious moments in this tabernacle are able, even briefly, to believe that they are part of a story bigger than themselves. Bigger even than war, than slavery, than violence. The late Robert Webber once wrote that "[t]he very narrative of faith which we seek to know is symbolically expressed in our space... Space becomes the visual image of the connection between the known and the unknown".[199]

He would have liked Solomon Gatachow. The label "place of worship" is too often used for redundant buildings that are no such thing. Here, in the most unlikely of settings, is a structure worthy of the name.

The parallels with Exodus could not be stronger. A refugee people, fleeing oppression, wrestling with the harsh realities of a wilderness environment; living in tents; unsure, for the moment, what their final destination will be. Will they ever reach their promised land? It was for this people, at the very heart of their hard journey, that God designed a place of worship. Why? Because that is exactly where worship belongs. The Hebrew people, to this point, had never had a life of worship. They had their heritage – the legends of their patriarchs told and retold as fireside stories. They had a sense of their God – a hunch that somehow, in the call of Abraham, the character of their maker was shown. They linked the God of their fathers to words like "promise" and "inheritance". They were still waiting for the dream of Abraham and Sarah to come true.

What they didn't have was any ritual means of embodying these hopes. They didn't have liturgies: songs and words to tell them who God is. They had a deep, visceral longing for this God – but they had no way of expressing it. Now, in the wilderness, they are halfway to becoming a nation. The land is not yet theirs, but they are moving towards it. They are free, and learning how to live with freedom. They need worship. Worship will remind them of the God who has effected their rescue, of the people he is calling them to be, of the promises that he has set before them. Through worship they will know *who they are* because they will remember *whose they are*.

The primary vehicle for the establishment of worship at the heart of the wilderness community is the tabernacle. The transition, in Exodus 15, from a narrative of liberation to a narrative of worship is confirmed in the fact that "Nearly one-third of the book of Exodus is devoted to considerations regarding the tabernacle, Israel's wilderness sanctuary."[200] Worship is to be the focus of the life of the freed Hebrew slaves. Detailed instructions are given for the completion of a movable feast of worship, a mobile home for God in the midst of his people.[201] The rhythms of this place of worship are to be central to the life of the nation. Centuries later, the people of Israel would still be living in the rhythms established for the tabernacle. In many ways Jews today still are, and Christians too. The tabernacle establishes that worship:

- **is intentional**. There is a determination here to place prayer and worship at the heart of the community. The structure of the book of Exodus reflects the understanding that has shaped the Jewish faith and still does, and which gave birth in turn to the Christian understanding that in the midst of secular life we should make space for worship. Sabbath speaks of a rhythm of sacred *time* woven through our lives. The tabernacle speaks of sacred *space*. "At this small, lonely place in the midst of the chaos of the wilderness", Terence Fretheim writes, "a new creation comes into being."[202]

- **is related to God's presence**. The tabernacle is a space for meeting face to face with God. The defining characteristic of the people of Israel was that God was with them. Their strength, identity, and purpose all came from this one fact, and the tabernacle was the vehicle by which the Lord would make his presence known. It took the idea that "God is with us" and gave it roots and reality. It asked, "How can we celebrate this idea? How can we be reminded that God is with us? How can we let the fact that God is with us shape our lives? How can we live all our lives in the light of God's presence with us?" This is not to say that God is present only in the tabernacle. The underlying implication of the exodus is that God is everywhere. He is the Lord of all creation, as sovereign over Pharaoh as over Moses.[203] Like Jesus centuries later, he is the one whom the wind and waves obey.[204] In what sense, then, is the tabernacle the vehicle of his presence? The answer is that it creates, for the people, a place set apart, where they can be *present to the presence*. The holiness of this one space does not render the other places we live in less sacred. Rather, it establishes the basis on which all of life is sacred – because God dwells in the midst of us. Worship is the space that we create, in the midst of our own chaos, to be truly present to our God.

- **is a place of singular beauty**. I am in awe of Solomon Gatachow and his friends for the sheer beauty of the church that they built, without resources, in a place of tragic ugliness. God calls Moses to harness all the creativity of the slave community to create a space that is not only set apart but in every way special. It is to be an ordered place, reflecting the creativity of Yahweh. Bezalel and Oholiab, leaders of a community of artists and craftspeople, are recruited and financed to make God's mobile home magnificent:

- "The Spirit of God with which the craftsmen are filled is a sign of the living, breathing force that lies behind the completing of the project just as it lies behind the creation".[205]

- The tabernacle is not a thrown-together jumble sale of spirituality; it is finely crafted, beautifully conceived and made: a canvas cathedral worthy of the God in whose name it stands. Like a room at the Tate Modern converted to a 24/7 prayer room and inspired by Westminster Abbey, the tabernacle is a place of beauty and stillness; of peace and prayer; of spiritual encounter and aesthetic celebration. This is to be a rich experience of prayer: resourceful, intentional, creative, and heartfelt. Unlike many of our experiences of prayer and worship, the one thing it won't be is dull.

The tabernacle is a facility uniquely adapted to the Hebrew slaves' desert journey. Its purpose is not to tell us that there should always be a meeting tent at the centre of our campsite. It is, however, to tell us there should always be worship at the centre of our lives. Why? Because it is through worship that God wins our hearts.

The greatest danger facing the Hebrew people as they crossed the desert was that they would forget who God is. They would, and did, forget how terrible their slave conditions were.[206] They would forget the magnificence of the miracles by which God had freed them.[207] They would let fear overtake them, and forget that God was urging them to trust him.[208] They would forget his promises and settle for the sand and dust.[209] They would forget the love he had for them, and give their hearts to other gods.[210] All these threats were real. All, in fact, came true.

God's answer to these dangers was not more rules, but more worship. In worship the people would remember who God was, and he would win their hearts. It is in the place of worship that God forms us for his purposes. Present to his presence, we align our hearts and lives with his. Our behaviour changes because our hearts are drawn, like a compass needle to magnetic north, to the goodness and blessing of God. The purpose of the tabernacle, a template for all that would follow in the worship of the Jewish nation, was to place this compass at the very centre of the people's lives. The formation of God's people – the shaping of their hearts to display his character – will happen through their life of worship.

The New Testament appropriates this tabernacle language in two ways. In the first, John's Gospel borrows from the imagery of exodus to explore the incarnation of Jesus. When he describes Jesus as the one who "became human and made his home among us",[211] scholars suggest he is deliberately invoking the idea of tabernacle. Jesus "tabernacles among us" and incarnation becomes the model for our worship. It is in Jesus that we are able to be "present to the presence" of our God.

In the second, this same "tabernacling" becomes true of

FORMATION: HOLD ON TO THE HEARTSEEKER

each surrendered heart: so Paul is able to claim Christians are a "temple of the Holy Spirit"[212] and Peter calls us "living stones" to be built into God's dwelling place.[213] The Spirit is given to each one of us so that the presence of Jesus goes where we go. The risen Christ is present in the world through his presence in the church and in each believer. Whatever craft and intentionality went into the making of the tabernacle and then the temple now goes into the shaping of our lives, alone and together. You are the meeting place of heaven and earth; the arena of encounter with God; the sacred space wherein his presence dwells. This means that the order and beauty that come to the wilderness through the work of Bezalel and his colleagues come to your desert world every time you, too, worship.

Our worship and the surrender of our gifts to God's anointing become the means by which the desert places reconnect with the fruitfulness and rest intended for them at creation. Every heart that bows the knee to Christ becomes a tabernacle in the world. The truly abundant life is not a life of high expenditure but a life lived gracefully; each day spent in optimal openness to the presence and participation of God. And whether worship is expressed in the assembly of God's people or in the tabernacle of the heart, it is intended to be beautiful and artful: colourful, imaginative devotion that draws the very best out of our lives.

In Matters of the Heart, the Heart Matters

> I may be saved by grace, but I still have years of habitual anger, materialism, lust, and many other things to be dealt with. They're not just going to go away. Like someone who has a bad golf swing and always slices off

to the right, I'm going to have to practice hitting the ball in a different way to make it go straight. The slice is in my body; it's how I have been formed. The disciplines help transform my habitual actions. The disciplines are not a substitute for grace, but receptacles for it.

DALLAS WILLARD[214]

A much later incident in the life of Israel illustrates this principle that formation is established through worship. In 1 Kings 18 the prophet Elijah is caught up in a protracted conflict with King Ahab and his scheming wife, Queen Jezebel. The contest, ultimately, is for the devotion of the people, whose dedication to Yahweh has been displaced, throughout the land, by the worship of Baal.

The episode involves fire and rain and an epic mountaintop showdown, but it turns on two key moments: the first in the question Elijah puts before the people; the second in the prayer he prays.

With the people gathered on Mount Carmel, Elijah stands before them to ask, "How long will you waver between two opinions? If the Lord is God, follow him; but if Baal is God, follow him!"[215] Later, when the prophet prays, he says, "Lord, the God of Abraham, Isaac and Israel, let it be known today that you are God in Israel and that I am your servant and have done all these things at your command. Answer me, Lord, answer me, so these people will know that you, Lord, are God, and that you are *turning their hearts back again*."[216]

The implication here is twofold. Firstly, that the central problem of the Jewish nation is idolatry. This is a theme that runs the length of the Old Testament. The core failure of God's people is misdirected worship. Obedience matters, but obedience flows out of worship. Worship sets the direction of our lives; it draws us forward. To a large extent it shapes our values, telling us what is or is not important. God's desire is for his people to be firmly rooted in his love – to know without doubt who they are – and worship is the only way this rootedness arrives. In the Old Testament, Daniel Block writes, "[i]dolatrous practices are treated as spiritual harlotry,[217] an abomination,[218] detestable,[219] foolishness,[220] and utterly disgusting.[221] According to the orthodox Yahwist, the God of Israel would brook no rivals. In this respect the Hebrew view of Israel's relationship to its patron deity differed fundamentally from the perceptions of all the other nations around."[222]

Secondly, this problem of idolatry is a question of the heart. It is the heart of the people God is seeking. This does not mean that he requires a sentimental allegiance. The heart in the ancient world is not seen as the seat of the emotions (this privilege is generally reserved for the bowels!). Rather, the heart is the centre of the will. It is the place of our intentions and affections, the place where we decide what matters; who we care about; what values and outcomes we are committed to. The heart is about who we love, because who we love is more than just a a sentimental choice. The father who dives into an icy river, risking his own life to save a child, doesn't do it out of sentimental stirrings, but he does do it for reasons of the heart.

Hearts, in the Old Testament can love; can fear. They can harbour hate. They can harden against God's ways. They can remember and reflect. They can incline towards God. They are the seat of hope, as of despair. They can be yielded, just as they can turn away. They are the place of our intentions, as of our secret failings. The image is of the heart as a single, inner organ whose affections set the tone for all we do. Like a central navigational device, the heart steers the mind and body. The one truth that is evident throughout the Bible in its treatment of the heart is this: whatever the hearts decides to do, the life will quickly follow. "The mouth speaks what the heart is full of," Jesus said.[223] The heart is our inner compass. Where its needle points is where we go. And God wants the hearts of his people.

Jesuit priest Pedro Arrupe writes in a meditation called "Fall in Love":

> Nothing is more practical than finding God, that is, than falling in love in a quite absolute, final way. What you are in love with, what seizes your imagination, will affect everything. It will decide what will get you out of bed in the morning, what you do with your evenings, how you spend your weekends, what you read, who you know, what breaks your heart, and what amazes you with joy and gratitude. Fall in love, stay in love, and it will decide everything.[224]

The understanding of worship proposed by the Bible revolves around these questions of the heart. In essence, from the tabernacle onwards, God wants us to know:

- That the heart is the key place of our decision-making. It is here that we choose to participate in the life of God, or not to. From that decision, all else – obedience and disobedience; fruitfulness and barrenness; life and death – will flow.

- That the language of worship is a language of the heart. To worship God, put simply, is to give him our hearts. It is to lean towards him to set our affections on him. It is to point the inner compass of our lives to his true north, and let all else be shaped by that choice.

- That worship is a process, not an event. I cannot once surrender to God and think the job complete. The inclining of my heart towards him is a daily act, a rhythm of affection running like a river through my life. Worship is a thread, a pattern woven into my activities and actions. It is a tabernacle in the midst of my wilderness journey.

- That the affection we withhold from God will be given to another. There is no question of a human being choosing not to worship. The only question is what we will worship. Idolatry exists because that inner compass always needs a north to point to.

- That he desires to be our true north because he is our maker, because he knows us, and because he has abundant good intentions for us. Worship is not a duty or an obligation and it is not there so that he feels good. It is God's chosen way of getting us to where we need to be.

- Lastly, that worship is a fruitful occupation. God's intention for us is that we should participate in his life, so as to pour his wisdom out into the world and see good fruits grow up in it. The participation he desires for us, without which none of the rest can truly happen, is worship. It is as we share in intimacy with him, taking our place at the table of his inexhaustible love, that we become all he intends for us to be, and start to do all he intends for us to do.

It is evident that the Old Testament understanding of the heart is consistent with the New – the ministry of Jesus gives it a central place. He tackles head-on the confusion of law with worship, telling his disciples just why he is at odds with the Pharisees and their strict laws of diet and behaviour:

> Anything you eat passes through the stomach and then goes into the sewer. But the words you speak come from the heart – that's what defiles you. For from the heart come evil thoughts, murder, adultery, all sexual immorality, theft, lying, and slander. These are what defile you. Eating with unwashed hands will never defile you.[225]

The theme surfaces often in the Gospels, not least in the Sermon on the Mount, arguably a treatise on the heart's affections.[226] The message is clear: it is your heart that God is after, and it's in worship that he'll win it. "God only has one ultimate goal for us all," Matt Redman writes, "the goal of being conformed to the image of His Son.[227] To be conformed is a tough and arduous task, a journey that leads us to the anvil and the altar, moment by moment. It's a process of transformation that results from consistently renewing our minds by God's truth."[228]

Some will raise the question of what we mean by worship. Is it singing? Dancing? Playing tambourines? It was all three for Miriam; does it need to be for us? The only way to answer that question is to ask another. What most causes you to surrender your affections to God? I don't mean theoretically – *I love him because he first loved me*, etc. – I mean actually, in your life. What are the activities that most allow you to surrender to his love, to hear his voice, and to see your life aligned to his purposes? In my own journey both corporate and private worship play this role, including singing (and silence), reading the Bible (and sometimes other books), retreating to the prayer room (or going for a walk). I can point to several different episodes in which God has in a quite specific way won my heart, and I can show you the decisions that were made, and the fruit they led to. I realized several years ago that my approach to worship needed to be less cynical and more simple: I decided that whatever activities enabled me to give my heart to God, I would increase. So I do pray more than I used to, and I do spend time alone in the prayer room. I do give myself to public worship, and to singing when that's the environment I'm in. I don't allow myself the privilege of sitting on the sidelines, like some coach or critic, when someone else is working hard to bring God's people into worship. I'm not there to decide if the chords are right, or whether I would have said it with just *those* words. I am there to find, with the help of Bezalel and Oholiab, a space in my own life to be present to the presence. Not because God needs my praise, but because I need his presence.

Worship: It's No Sacrifice

> The God of the Bible, and above all the God of Jesus, is not our rival or our examiner or our prosecutor but our lover. There is nothing we can do to impress him or put him in our debt. If we start from the assumption that we have to do these things, we shall become either deludedly arrogant or despairing.
>
> ROWAN WILLIAMS[229]

When the late Christopher Hitchens published his 2008 book *God Is Not Great: How Religion Poisons Everything*, I was deeply drawn to the title. I think that as a person of faith I was supposed to be annoyed, perhaps even shocked. Truth be told, there was much in the book that did annoy me. I remain unconvinced by many of Hitchens's arguments, even if he was always an intriguing and enlightening arguer. On his title, though, I am 100 per cent sold. To the extent that his book set out to divest God of his greatness, and to prove that the human instinct for religion has done more harm than good in our world, I stand with him, and I do so as a follower of Jesus. Why? Because these are precisely the two goals that Jesus came into our world to pursue.

If the Christian narrative, and especially its cross, says nothing else to us, it says that our creator no longer wishes to be "great". The *deity formerly known as great* has chosen in Christ henceforth to be known as love. Greatness – power, strength, victory, omnipotence, dominance – are attributes of a God perceived by the people of Israel through the haze of their own limited experience and education. All gods, surely, carry greatness as their calling card? The bigger the god – and the stature of a god was often tied, like an index-linked pension, to the geographical spread of the territory he ruled over – the greater we can assume him to be. I say "he" inclusively, though in reality most of them were. The newly freed Hebrew slaves were surrounded by tribes playing a deadly and constant game of "my god's bigger than your god". Joining in was a no-brainer. No matter how hard Yahweh might try to tell them otherwise, they couldn't talk about him in any other language. Until Jesus. For victory, Jesus substitutes defeat. For greatness, love. For dominance, a bruised body incapable of even taking a drink.

Jesus didn't come to win. He came to lose, and, by losing, to change the game. I wonder whether a review copy of *God Is Not Great* was sent heavenward, and, if so, if it was greeted with a deep sigh of "At last, someone gets it"?

The danger is that our worship will borrow too much from the "my god's bigger than your god" school of thought, and not enough from Jesus. The religion Jesus came to put an end to is the religion of pleasing the gods; making sacrifices; bringing offerings. Religion is behavioural adjustment; sin management; living on the knife edge of our maker's wrath. In religion the gods reject us until we pay them off. Our performance – of worship, of morality, of alms-giving – is a necessary precursor to their changed mood. In religion, if you do nothing you get nothing. In Christ, you do nothing and get everything. There's no irony here: everything about Jesus suggests that he, too, believed this kind of religion poisons everything.

So how do I respond to God's invitation to worship him without falling into the pagan trap of placing greatness over love and bringing him my offerings in place of the fullness of my heart?

Banal as it might seem, a lot of this is about the language we use. When we pass around a basket to ask for contributions to our church's expenses, do we call it an *offering*? Is this because we secretly want God to like us more than he does and are making him a gift to ease his mood? Offerings to God or the gods are part of a pagan economy in which human contribution is required to maintain balance. Without our offerings, the gods will become disaffected; our lives will no longer be bathed in the benevolent glow of their patronage. It is only our offerings – regularly and satisfactorily supplied

– that keep them on our side. The gods of an offering culture are by nature your enemies – it is only by sacrifice that they become your friend, and even then this is a temporary arrangement.

The same applies, sadly, to offerings of praise – a concept all too easily adopted in our churches. The act of worship is transformed into an act of sacrifice and God, we hope, is cheered up by our singing, like an unhappy grandparent in the local home who didn't really want us to visit in the first place but at last relents when he sees how much trouble we have taken to entertain him. If worship is our *sacrifice*, no matter how attractive it might seem, we are in danger of recasting God in idol's clothes.

Should we not want to please God, then? Is it wrong to give him gifts? No it isn't, but whatever gifts we give him must come from the realization that he is pleased with us already. Overwhelmingly pleased. Dancing-In-The-Streets pleased. Pleased to the extent that the pagan gods might justifiably call him soft. To give out of a sense of fear, of duty, of shame – out of a sense that we are dealing with a being who will not find us acceptable until we have given – is to reduce our God to the scope and scale of the capricious idols he has so comprehensively displaced. To think of this in terms of the dynamics of distance, we often describe our acts of worship as a process of drawing close to God. The irony, then, is that our language of sacrifice and offerings places God at a distance from us that he has neither chosen nor imposed. In our shame we suggest that there is some ground to cover, a minefield to cross, before we can be intimate with him, but this is our invention, not his. Time and time again we recreate this journey – the supplicant crossing a great chasm to reach the throne – when God himself has declared, in Christ, this distance covered. The barriers are ours, not his.

God says to us, "Come close: there is nothing stopping you" and we say, "Oh but there is. If you only knew what I'd been doing these past days, or thinking these past minutes, you wouldn't find me so acceptable. I couldn't possibly come into your presence in these rags. Let me go and change, or here, accept this offering. It's just a token, but maybe it can cover my nakedness, so I can stand in your presence." And God says to us, as he has always said, as he said within seconds of our shame, as he has never stopped saying: "Who told you you were naked?"

This is the revolution Jesus brings into the Hebrew faith – the play that changes the game. This is the return to the beginning, to rediscover the grace that has always been God's heart. Pleasing God is not a goal you move towards; it is the place you start out from. You are not a disappointing child who has let your perfect parent down, failing in every area in which he held such hopes for you. You are not a problem that he needs to solve, a nagging need he wishes he could do without. You are not a burden to him. Far from it. You are his beloved; the one he can't wait to see. He can hardly breathe as you approach. So in love is he that his heart beats double time. His palms are sweaty. The very idea of seeing you draws from him a song of such joy, of such exuberance, that his neighbours the angels are concerned for his soundness of mind.

He loves you. Do you get it? As a thunderstruck young man loves his bride. As a mother loves her newborn child. As a trainer loves a stallion he has poured his life and talent into. Whatever reluctance there is to the proposition of intimacy with God, whatever resistance you experience, it does not come from him. There is nothing that stands between you and the fullness of his embrace.

Worship is never an attempt to win God's love. It is a celebration of the love he freely gives us.

Worship: Born Again, Again

> I tried to place myself, naked, poor and alone, in the presence of God's eternal majesty.
>
> CARLO CARRETTO[230]

If worship calls us to encounter God, to meet him in the deepest of intimacy in the nakedness of a surrendered heart, then it will ask of us at times to set aside the clutter of our lives. Even our religious jumble, gathered over years of trying to worship, can get in the way. What we need, in Jesus' words, is to be born again.

There is a story told of Mahatma Gandhi meeting for the first time King George V of England. Gandhi had spent much of his adult life resisting British rule in India, so his trip to London in 1931 was significant. He visited 10 Downing Street before being taken to Buckingham Palace to be presented to His Majesty. The king, as might be expected, was decked out in the formality and finery of his office. Gandhi, by contrast, wore only his habitual loincloth and shawl – he was dressed no differently from how he would be for a walk through the poorest district of Calcutta. After the meeting a journalist asked the exotic visitor if he had been embarrassed to be so underdressed in the presence of the king.

"Not at all", Gandhi replied with a smile. "His Majesty was wearing quite enough for both of us."[231]

We don't know very much about Nicodemus, but we do know that he enjoyed a high social status. He was wealthy, powerful, and well-educated. He held a position of respect in the religious and political establishment of his day. We also know that he was conscious enough of his rank to require a secret, night-time meeting in order to speak to Jesus. This is a man who wore his status like a uniform: an instantly recognizable minor celebrity. Jesus, by contrast, was poor and had little formal education. At this stage in his public ministry he was almost certainly homeless, relying on the charity of friends like Lazarus and Joanna, whose husband worked in the household of King Herod. Nicodemus the professor meets with Jesus the couch-surfer, and guess who turns out to be cleverer?

The conversation centres on two linked themes: new birth and the ministry of the Holy Spirit. This is the passage that has given us the phrase "born again" and spawned a whole movement of twentieth-century evangelists. It is highly unlikely, of course, that "born again" when Jesus introduces the idea to Nicodemus has anything at all to do with "born again" in the way our TV evangelists suggest. For a start, there were no evangelicals in Jesus' day and the concept of conversion as we know it simply didn't exist. Using "born-again Christian" as a label for a particular way of pursuing the faith may have some sociological usefulness, but it bears little relation to this passage.

What, then, is Jesus talking about? Like Gandhi before King George, he is talking about the sheer weight of the clothing Nicodemus has allowed his faith to be buried under, and the nakedness that is the prerequisite for worship. The religion of Nicodemus; his education; his prosperity; his social standing – all these have become fashion accessories, badges, and medals to be worn for all the world to see. Jesus is interested in what's underneath. Who is Nicodemus without all these things? Stripped of his sophistication and cleverness, who might this old man really turn out to be? To truly experience the presence of God, Jesus says, we must come to him as a newborn baby – naked, uneducated, carrying neither wealth nor status. We must set aside the tools and tricks we have spent so long acquiring, and simply let God love us as we are.

Three aspects of the sacred journey Jesus calls his new friend to can help us as we, too, travel down the birth canal of worship:

- This is a challenge born of the most perfect compassion. Jesus is not angry with Nicodemus for having gathered all his props. On the contrary, he feels such a love for the old man that he longs for him to be free of these entrapments; to experience, as Foy Vance recommends, "The Joy of Nothing".[232] This conversation illustrates the most stirring aspect of Jesus' encounters with different individuals. He is never swayed by their status – low or high – and always responds with compassion. As capable of sipping champagne with the rich as of sifting garbage with the poor, Jesus sees each person for who they are, beneath the masks of both power and poverty, and finds a way to move them "further up and deeper in" to love.

- The idea of being "born again", as Jesus suggests it here, is strongly linked to the ministry of the Holy Spirit. Nicodemus, a student of Israel's history, knows that as a nation they have been the beneficiaries of the Spirit's power. The wind that "blows where it wants to" once blew over the chaos of an unformed sea to shape their paradise, and blew against a sea's high waves to bring them out of slavery and into God's promise. Nicodemus knows what it is for the Spirit to be at work. But what has he done, what has Israel done, with this raw blessing? They have wrapped it up in ritual and the workings of religion; they have smothered it in social convention and judgmentalism. The Spirit longs again to fill their sails, but their sails are tightly lashed to the masts of their religion, to structures so unbending it will take a hurricane to shift them. Nicodemus, for his part, is heavily invested in these structures. His whole identity comes from them. Will he be the one, fond as he is of Jesus, to break the mould? Will he have the courage to loosen the locks of the Temple and seek again the wild winds of the Spirit?

- The third key aspect of this conversation is its most intriguing. In urging Nicodemus to be born again, Jesus is describing a journey he himself has taken. "How can a man re-enter the womb?" Nicodemus asks, unaware that he is asking the only man alive who has actually done so. Only Jesus, from a position of maturity and power, has made the choice to re-inhabit infancy and experience birth. He is not asking his friend to do anything he has not himself done. The earliest creeds of the Christian community describe this journey.[233] Jesus sets aside prestige and power to enter the world poor and naked. This, Paul tells us, is the attitude that we should have. We too are called to give up adult securities and trust God as helpless infants. This is the birth canal we are being asked to move through, to follow Jesus in kenosis, the chosen path of radical self-emptying.

How can we respond, so many generations after Nicodemus, to this challenge? The answer is self-evident: we can be born again. All of us, even those as established in our faith as Nicodemus was in his, need God to make us small again. Even those of us who use the label "born again" – perhaps especially those who use such labels – need to be born again.

- We need to set aside the very clothing of power and prestige, of status and self-satisfaction, and come to faith, and to the love of God, in our birthday suit.

- We need to be ruthless in seeing where our religion has become the very prison that prevents us from embracing God's ferocious mercy.

- We need to loosen the ropes of our rituals and practices and seek again the wild winds of the Spirit.

What does this mean for our worship? It means we will seek once again a place of naked vulnerability before God. To stand on the clifftop of his love, the wind in our faces. To know, holding nothing in our hands, that we are valued. Worship is not the culmination of a complex religious ritual, where God is not impressed unless a choir *and* a rock band both join in and the readings are just so, delivered by the voice of Richard Burton. Worship isn't theatre. It is not in any sense performance. It is, rather, the naked soul exposed before its maker, trembling in its weakness. Being loved. Only as we do these things will we discover the inestimable joy that Jesus had in mind for Nicodemus. It is the joy of owning nothing, of bringing nothing to the party. The joy of being stripped of all the things we thought were so important, and discovering, without them, that we matter. It is the joy of being held as newborns in the arms of our Father, as he beams with pride and giggles over us the words, "Welcome to my world…"

Worship: Shadows and Light

> Then David confessed to Nathan, "I have sinned against the Lord."
>
> THE BOOK OF SAMUEL[234]

The Florentine artist Michelangelo was just twenty-six years old when he received a commission to rescue and complete an abandoned marble sculpture provisionally called "The Giant". He worked tirelessly for two years, unveiling in 1504 what is probably the most famous sculpture in history. The six-ton statue of David quickly became recognized as symbolic of the whole Renaissance period. It was remarkable in that David had previously always been portrayed as the victor holding the head of Goliath. Here, he is shown before the battle, an intriguing contrast established between his intense facial expression and his relaxed posture.

Alongside its unique place in art history, the statue is often remarked upon for the figure's nakedness. An homage to the Greek ideal of the hero, David's state of undress also speaks of vulnerability, of transparency. This is a man with, literally, nothing to hide: so much so that a plaster copy installed in the Victoria and Albert Museum featured, out of respect for Queen Victoria, a detachable fig leaf, strategically hooked into place during royal visits. The combination of David's ambiguous expression and naked state is remarkably artful, but it is also theologically insightful. Few biblical characters are portrayed in as much detail as David, and the portrayal strips him bare. We meet David as a teenager and stay with him to his death at nearly seventy. We see him in his moments of triumph, but also when his own rebellion against God's ways leads to multiple tragedies. And we see him in recovery, when repentance brings him back to full communion with God. David's life is the original prototype of naked spirituality. The book of Psalms, which carries some of David's own words and deeply reflects his world view, insists on showing us both the light and the darkness of the human heart.

No one has contributed more to the worship life of Israel than King David, and yet he, too, discovered what it means to be found naked in God's presence.

Honesty is the hallmark of David's journey. His biographers gleefully record his triumphs, and with equal enthusiasm share his failures with us. His own prayers reflect this same combination. Nowhere is this more true than in Psalm 51, in which David repents of lust, covetousness, adultery, and murder. The events that have brought David to this point are reported elsewhere.[235] What the psalm records for us is his response. This is how, in the place of worship, David does business with the darkest aspects of his heart. His crimes against God's law have not been committed when he is desperate; when he is a hungry fugitive, cruelly pursued by an unjust regime. They are committed when he *is* the regime: powerful; successful; with everything he's ever wanted now at his fingertips. It is not poverty that drives David into sin, but wealth: not weakness, but power. So significant is David's confession that the apostle Paul, centuries later, employs it as a central plank in his unpacking of the gospel:

> Even if everyone else is a liar, God is true. As the Scriptures say about him, "You will be proved right in what you say, and you will win your case in court."[236]

Paul hears the great Hebrew hero say to his God, "Your assessment of me is true", and knows that such naked candour is a vital part of grace. The journey to the dawn of forgiveness passes through the dark night of confession. How can David's searing honesty help us to live our worship life more deeply?

It brings into the place of worship both our beauty and our brokenness. The poet who declares that he is God's "marvellous workmanship", "knit together in his mother's womb",[237] here tells us he was "born a sinner", "from the moment my mother conceived me."[238] Incredibly, David dates both his beauty and his brokenness to his origins. He recognizes that as a human being he carries deep within himself both the image of his maker and the capacity to do incredible harm. He reminds us that no one is so beautiful that nothing in them is broken, and no one is so broken that they bear no beauty, and that the place of worship, of nakedness before God, is the place for doing business with both.

It tells us that worship is a lifetime's journey. Though we grow older, our challenges don't diminish. David is honest enough as a leader and father, an established politician, and a nationally loved figure, to admit that he has done wrong. His mistakes do not all belong to his youth, and neither does the need to repent. The more we grow in age and perhaps social stature, the harder it is to admit that we are wrong, but we need to be prepared to do it. Nothing will encourage honest self-assessment in those around you as much as their experience of your honest self-assessment. Honesty breeds honesty, even more so when you're old enough to run from it.

It tells us that we need grace and forgiveness, and God's transforming power. David not only asks for absolution; he asks for transformation. "Create in me," he says, "a clean heart."[239] He knows he cannot change himself. He cries out to God for renewal. In a poem worthy of a Twelve Steps meeting, David admits his powerlessness (Step 1) even as he undertakes a "searching and fearless moral inventory" (Step 4). As millions have discovered in recent years in battling addiction, David comes into the freedom of admitting his need of God. His prayer acknowledges two truths: that he can't change himself and that God can change him. Without the second, the first is a long road to hopelessness. With the acknowledgment that God can change us, the recognition of our failings becomes good news. True confession is, in this sense, the doorway to unlimited grace. Like Moses before him, and Elijah who will follow, David knows that serving God is a matter of the heart. Only when his heart is changed can he expect to change his patterns of behaviour.

Lastly, it tells us that if we won't repent for our own sake, we should repent for the sake of others.[240] David's focus shifts from his own heart to the city of Jerusalem. It is an unexpected change of gear – until you realize what it is that David is saying. He is admitting to the connection between his own inner life and the health of the city. As king, he knows that if he harbours secret sins in his heart he is not the only one who will suffer. His family, his entourage, the very nation itself will be held back by his refusal to confess. Honesty unlocks freedom in those David leads. Sometimes our repentance is triggered by our own sense of need, but there are times when it can and should be triggered by the sufferings of others. If your secret behaviour is having an evident impact on those you lead, the place of prayer is waiting for your honesty.

The lesson of Psalm 51 is that I need the place of worship because without it I will not do business with the deepest, darkest parts of me. "When I confront God's word, I am confronted," Mike Yaconelli writes. "When I read God's word, it reads me; when I seek God's presence, he seeks me."[241] This is not a morbid fascination with the depths of sin. It is an honest recognition that in all our lives there are dark shadows and that we need a place where they can come to light. David's journey is not about inventing or embellishing false guilt. It is not about confession for its own sake. It is about honestly facing up to our real guilt, dealing with the secrets of our hearts – and knowing that the God we love offers forgiveness joyful enough to sing about.[242] Our life of worship is in part about this process of discovering the truth about ourselves, and finding healing. The presence of God is the safest place on earth to bring the truth about ourselves. In the face of his grace, no secret we tell can hold power over us.

Let Justice Roll

> It is true that the most drastic social reform, the most complete dethronement of privilege, cannot of themselves bring the kingdom; for peace and joy in the Holy Spirit can only come to us by the free gift of the Transcendent. But at least these can clear the ground, prepare the highway of God; and here each act of love, each sacrifice, each conquest of prejudice, each generous impulse carried through into action counts: and each

> unloving gesture, hard judgement, pessimistic thought or utterance opposes the coming of the kingdom and falsifies the life of prayer.
>
> EVELYN UNDERHILL[243]

Is the place of worship disconnected from the world we live in from day to day? Are we asked to choose between an active and a passive life; between engaging with our culture and spending time with God? The prophets would reject a choice between the cloister and the culture. They call us to invest passionately in both. They would tell us, in fact, that true worship leads to action and true action drives us to the place of worship. To make the case we need only spend time with perhaps the most active, and most worshipful, of them all.

Amos was a shepherd who became a prophet to both Israel and Judah. The first prophet to lend his name to a book of Scripture, Amos was an early contemporary of Isaiah. He lived in the era when Jeroboam ruled Israel's Northern Kingdom and the much-loved Uzziah was king in Judah, the Southern Kingdom. This was a time of relative calm for God's people. Enemies who in the past had threatened and harassed them, notably Syria and Assyria, were locked in a protracted war, too busy fighting each other to bother with the Jews. Peace brought prosperity, and the people of both Israel and Judah were more comfortable than they had been for generations.

You might think that the result would be a stirring period of praise and gratitude to God, a season of passion for Yahweh that recognized his goodness. Far from it. This was an era of complacency and laziness, when God's people "lived at ease".[244] They "recline on beds of ivory and sprawl on their couches".[245] The people are living in safety and security, feasting on fine meats,[246] drinking good wines,[247] and anointing themselves with expensive oils.[248] They are so self-satisfied that they are even writing worship songs to praise themselves![249] The picture is of an indolent self-satisfaction. God's people have forgotten their God. Two glaring symptoms shout loudly that the people are no longer devoted to their God: their worship of idols and their crass mistreatment of the poor. Such is their heart-betrayal of Yahweh that the worship they do offer him is poisoned. "Away with your noisy hymns of praise!" God says through Amos. "I will not listen to the music of your harps. Instead, I want to see a mighty flood of justice, an endless river of righteous living."[250]

Amos is uniquely qualified to point out these twin failings for two reasons. Firstly, because he is himself a poor farmer,[251] detached entirely from the ruling classes and their priestly collaborators.[252] Amos sees the world from the underside. He is Katniss Everdeen to Jeroboam's Coriolanus Snow. Secondly, Amos is devoted to Yahweh. His is a simple faith of worship and obedience. He speaks because God has called him.[253] Prophecy, for Amos, flows out from a relationship with God – the very relationship so many of his contemporaries have left behind. He too is a man of the heart. When he denounces the public festivals of Israel,[254] you can hear in his words the passion of a true worshipper. Worship, for Amos, reflects the character of God. It includes justice and mercy because God is just and merciful. To annex the name of Yahweh to anything short of this is in itself a form of idolatry.

What can we learn from the life and words of this outspoken peasant?

We learn that God can and will use your background – your experiences and insights and the things that by their nature make you angry – as part of your prophetic calling. They can never be all of it, because anger unrefined becomes petulance, not prophecy; but if you will let your God, in worship, shape you, he can bring the best out from your history. Moses tasted life on both sides of the tracks. David was a simple shepherd. Jesus served a long apprenticeship in woodwork. Mary was a poor, uneducated teenager. What threads of justice, passion, and righteousness lie dormant in your story waiting for God's fire to give them life? Even what has hurt you in the past can be refined by grace to become a vital aspect of your calling. The formation God is forging in your life will not replace you with some new, efficient super-worshipper. Rather, it will take the threads of who you are and weave them into something beautiful. The "you" to emerge from God's transformation process will always be recognizable as the you who first said "yes". He will change you: he will not destroy you.

We learn that comfort is the enemy, not the friend, of conviction. Do you pray more when you're broke, or when you have money in the bank? Does sickness compel you to seek God, or health; conflict or harmony? In my own experience it is need – painful, personal need – that most drives me to the place of prayer. The things I so often pray for – provision, comfort, healing, safety – are, ironically, the very things that cause me to pray less. Blessed are those who hunger and thirst, Jesus said, but how many of us want to be hungry and thirsty? Amos shows us that, in our personal as in our national life, it is in times of peace and prosperity that we should most give attention to our devotion to God. Where circumstances don't drive us to the place of prayer, we need another motor, and only personal commitment will do it. There are motivations that are thrust upon us, and there are motivations we must choose.

The second type is harder, by a long stretch, to maintain.

We learn that very little changes in the real landscape of human interactions. The judgments of Amos are delivered to a people who by today's standards lived in poverty and privation. Only Uzziah and Jeroboam, as kings, would have had a lifestyle that comes remotely close to the comforts we now enjoy. We are so much better off than the people of the eighth century BC – but have our flush toilets and flat-screen TVs made us more or less devoted to God? Have we too forgotten our maker, and all he has done for us? Does the worship in our churches sometimes sound like a series of songs composed in our own honour? And what of the poor in our midst? Are we mindful of their needs? We are in reality no different from the people Amos spoke against, and his challenge to them works equally for us – to return to our God,[255] to root out our idolatry,[256] and to care for the poor in our midst.[257] The parallel with Isaiah 58 is unmissable: only through "true fasting" can we find the true blessings God has for us.

We learn, lastly, that no judgment of God is purely bad news. Beyond the admonition, the naming of our sins, there is the hope of redemption – the promise of a nation restored. Amos is a stunning poet, and he ends his book with one of the most beautiful descriptions in all history of the promise of God's kingdom. In our exploration of the purposes of God, we have seen that his original intention still applies to us. He desires that we should participate in his life, so that his wisdom pours through us into the world and his creation yields its fruits as a response. In worship he longs for our heart so he can form us to be like him, seeping through us into the very ground we stand on. Hear, then, this promise in the words of the shepherd–prophet:

> "The time will come," says the Lord,
> "when the grain and grapes will grow faster
> than they can be harvested.
> Then the terraced vineyards on the hills
> of Israel
> will drip with sweet wine!
> I will bring my exiled people of Israel
> back from distant lands,
> and they will rebuild their ruined cities
> and live in them again.
> They will plant vineyards and gardens;
> they will eat their crops and drink their wine.
> I will firmly plant them there
> in their own land.
> They will never again be uprooted
> from the land I have given them,"
> says the Lord your God.[258]

This is the promise of our maker to all who give their hearts to him. This is the goal of our worship.

Response: Hold on to the Heartseeker

> To discover God in the smallest and most ordinary things, as well as in the greatest, is to possess a rare and sublime faith. To find contentment in the present moment is to relish and adore the divine will in the succession of all the things to be done and suffered which make up the duty to the present moment. ... A living faith is nothing else than a steadfast pursuit of God through all that disguises, disfigures, demolishes, and seeks, so to speak, to abolish him.
>
> JEAN-PIERRE DE CAUSSADE[259]

Worship and mission are inseparable partners in the life of God because:

- It is in worship that God wins my heart, and through my heart he shapes my life and guides my steps.

- To engage in God's mission is to want what God wants, and only in the place of full surrender can I begin to know this.

- Serving God's purposes is a journey of becoming all that God wants me to be. Worship is the rhythm allowing this to happen.

- Worship is the space we set aside that allows us to be present to his presence. It is not God who has a short attention span, but us.

- Worship is not the sacrifice I bring to make God happy. We are not mood-enhancers for the heavenly courts. Rather, worship changes me, aligning my heart with the heart of God.

- Worship is remembering. I need to know who I am in the world, and to know who I am I must remember *whose* I am.

- Worship is a safe place to be told the truth about myself. God's presence is the centre of my security, the arena in which I am loved and know it. Only as I know myself as loved can I face myself as broken and give myself to the love of others.

- True worship is a doorway into justice. I align my life with the character of my maker. I place my small compassion against the plumb line of his undivided mercy. I let him break my heart for what breaks his, and ask, here, for the courage to act justly.

Do you know what the most frequent command in the Bible turns out to be? What instruction, what order, is given, again and again, by God, by angels, by Jesus, by prophets and apostles? What do you think – "Be good"? "Be holy, for I am holy"? Or, negatively, "Don't sin"? "Don't be immoral"? No. The most frequent command in the Bible is: "Don't be afraid. Don't be afraid. Fear not. Don't be afraid."

N. T. WRIGHT[260]

CHAPTER 5

Limitation:
Find Strength in the Faithbuilder

You have a **LIMITATION** story.
It is the story of God's presence in the places in your life,
and the places your life takes you,
that are hard for you.
The mission of God is an adventure
of discovering his purposes
even in the pain of exile.

For Such a Time

As Christians enter the twenty-first century, they do so as exiles, strangers and pilgrims, aliens in a strange land. They will need to learn the strategies of survival, and to sing the songs of Zion in the midst of Babylon.

KENNETH LEECH[261]

When you think of living in exile, which Bible character comes to mind first? The answer is most likely to be Daniel, whose story has inspired multiple generations to hold firmly to their faith in times of pressure and struggle. There is another figure, though, who personifies in just as powerful a story the reality of living in exile. She is Esther, whose experience in Susa in many ways mirrors that of Daniel in Babylon.

The most important moment in Esther's story is the challenge laid before her by her guardian, Mordecai: "If you keep quiet at a time like this, deliverance and relief for the Jews will arise from some other place, but you and your relatives will die. Who knows if perhaps you were made queen for just such a time as this?"[262]

This is without doubt the most familiar verse in this entire book. It is also the most misunderstood. Mention Esther to a group of Christian young people and this verse will in all likelihood be part of the conversation: "for such a time as this". We refer to it when people become rock stars; win competitions; prove themselves massively talented; pass their exams. Is it for such a time as this that God has given you these blessings?

What we miss entirely is the context.

What did Esther hear when Mordecai issued this challenge? Was it for such a time as this that she had been taken from her home; deprived of her liberty; forced to have sex with a man much older than herself who chose a different virgin each night, and called them back only if they truly pleased him? Was it for this that she was pampered for months to arouse him; that she walked in fear for her very life lest she displease him for one moment and be killed; that her exile had become a still-deeper slavery; that she had said goodbye to any dream she'd ever had of marrying a man for love, of raising a family; of building a home? Was it for this that God had done all this? Esther's story is not an account of God turning gifts and opportunities to gold. It is a story of misfortune transformed. Of slavery redeemed. Esther is forced to give away the one thing most precious to her – her virginity, her very body – and yet discovers that good can come from it. Consider these words from modern-day victims of trafficking. Can you hear an echo of Esther's voice?

Sophie, UK:

"Two years ago everything changed. I was trafficked. I was fooled. I was deceived by a man who said that he loved me. The tragedy is that I believed him. Now I know that love is not shown by forcing me to work on the streets, beating me up, force-feeding me, and turning me into someone with no mind of my own. I had become like a frightened rabbit. I was terrified that he would kill me. Death too often felt like my only way to escape."[263]

Memey, Indonesia:

"We were watched closely; there was no opportunity to escape. Our passports were taken away, and we did not have access to a phone either."[264]

Sopeah, Cambodia:

"I had no hope and was full of fear. It was hard to breathe. I had no self-worth, and I didn't want to live… Every day I had nightmares and could not sleep. I always seemed to have a fever too. I had panic attacks and intense fears."[265]

It is a great shame that in our love for Daniel as the hero of the exile we lose sight of Esther, the heroine. Her exile is more extreme than Daniel's ever was, her loss more real, and yet she finds, along with the great Jewish hero Joseph, that "God meant it for good".[266] Like Daniel, Esther personifies the experience of exile. Her call to work out her place in the mysterious purposes of God is not pursued in a time of plenty, with access to all the resources of Jerusalem at her disposal. It is worked out in a time of need. She is an alien, far from home. Her people are persecuted. Worse still, her own life has been cruelly disrupted. Even the small dreams she has nurtured have been shattered. She has been robbed of what little she had. Is it even possible that God can work "in such a time as this"? Everything Esther has to offer, even her self-worth, is taken from her. But she has one thing left – one thing neither exile, nor slavery, nor forced sex work can take from her: her availability for the purposes of God. As a powerless slave, in fear for her life, she changes the destiny and future of her nation. The only thing she has to give is her surrender, but it is all that God needs from her.

The message of this book is that God is sovereign over all our circumstances. Esther is often noted as the one book of the Bible in which God is not named – and yet it has his fingerprints all over it. The sovereignty of God is written on a larger canvas than the rituals and routines of our faith. Even in a pagan land his purposes remain. Esther teaches us what it means to surrender to God's mission even when our circumstances tell us only of his absence. This is a vital lesson in our understanding of the mission of God. It was the hardest lesson served up to the Jewish people – the season in their history they most viewed as negative – and yet without it their picture of God would be smaller, more limited. God used the limitation of their circumstances to show them that his love and power had no limits. It took the loss of Jerusalem for them to find out, once and for all, that Yahweh is the king of all the earth.

Exile is experienced as loss. In biblical terms it means:

- The loss of the visible furniture of God's victory. Our sense of God's triumph might be represented by the

Temple or the palace, or by the strong walls of the city. It might be the rhythms of worship that remind us of his presence, or the sight of the priests in all their robes. Maybe it's just having friends and family around us, sharing together the stories of our God. Perhaps it's not until these things are taken from us that we realize how much we have relied on them. Perhaps we have to lose our small securities to discover the hugeness of God's mercy.

- The reversal of God's workings in our lives. It's all too easy for us now, from the vantage point beyond the exile, to assume that we would have handled it quite smoothly, that it wouldn't have thrown our faith. Not so the people of Israel. Jerusalem was their proof that God was powerful. It was his gift to them, the fulfilment of his promises. Everything about the exodus moves towards this reality – the land, the city, the people safe at home in it. This is what God has given. Why would he take it away? In this sense exile is the polar opposite of exodus. God frees his people from their slavery, only to let them slide back into it again. Why would he do that?

- The disgrace of losing, in the full glare of publicity. The bitter words of the psalmist ring in our ears:

Our captors demanded a song from us.
Our tormentors insisted on a joyful hymn:
"Sing us one of those songs of Jerusalem!"
But how can we sing the songs of the Lord
while in a pagan land?[267]

What are the songs of Jerusalem? Here's one example: "Jerusalem is a well-built city; its seamless walls cannot be breached."[268] Could you sing that, when you'd just been invaded, your city sacked, and your friends and family carted off with you into exile? Here's another: "For the Lord declares, 'I have placed my chosen king on the throne in Jerusalem, on my holy mountain.'"[269] If God put him there, who took him away? Maybe his God wasn't quite so powerful after all. How about this, perhaps the best song of all:

> How great is the Lord,
> how deserving of praise,
> in the city of our God,
> which sits on his holy mountain!
> It is high and magnificent;
> the whole earth rejoices to see it!
> Mount Zion, the holy mountain,
> is the city of the great King!
> God himself is in Jerusalem's towers,
> revealing himself as its defender.[270]

Really? Is that how Babylon destroyed us? Is that how we came to be living in Susa? Because God was our *defender*? There's only one reason why those who have defeated us would ask to hear such songs – because they want to utterly humiliate us.

Exile is the experience of seeing undone all you thought that God was doing. It is hard not to interpret it as God letting you down. He was the one, after all, who promised not to.

And yet there is another side to exile. This period of loss and regret turned out to be, for Israel, a time of immense creativity. There is a discovery, in the loss of our small world, that God rules over a bigger world altogether. Exile, as it turns out, has a place in the plans of God. He uses the limitations of our circumstances to break us out of our limited world. We lose a city to inherit the earth. Like Esther, we discover that God can work, can triumph even, in such a time as this.

Perhaps you haven't been sold into sex slavery. Perhaps you are not the plaything of a king. But are there other ways in which your liberty has been curtailed? Are there circumstances in your life that mean you may not get what you want? Might it be that the purposes of God will be fulfilled not in your escape from these circumstances, but in your being available to God despite them? If you make a mental list of the things God has allowed for such a time as this, do you include the things you have struggled with; the exilic experiences you had hoped to escape from? Esther joins Daniel and Joseph, Jeremiah and Isaiah, and, yes, Jesus and Mary, in asserting that God's purposes can be discovered in the very place of exile.

Limitation: The Story So Far

> Scripture, like a symphony, does not have one theme or melody but many. It offers not so much a single song as a symphonic tone poem pregnant with music and meaning. All of life is here with texts composed from every situation. Scripture's ability to sound out the textures and colours of the human condition, is the reason we come to trust the Bible.
>
> RUSSELL ROOK[271]

In early 2016 the Musée des Beaux-Arts in Caen – my nearest gallery – mounted an exhibition essentially based on one painting. Such is the reputation of the painting in question that the exhibition drew significant crowds. I couldn't wait to go. There are only a handful of paintings in the world that have had such an influence on my life as this. The exhibition didn't disappoint.

Michelangelo Merisi da Caravaggio painted *The Supper at Emmaus*[272] sometime around 1606, just four years before his death. It is a stunning work, full of depth and insight. Caravaggio was known for his realism, for making figures from the Bible appear as ordinary people, often based on models from the streets of Rome. Here, though, his realism reaches new depths. It is as though he is reaching out for the meaning of the story, asking how the risen Christ might really have appeared. What might it feel like to be confronted with such a resurrection? The reason for the painting's global fame is that it was the second version the artist created of the same scene. The two paintings couldn't be more different.

In 1601 Caravaggio was commissioned by a prominent Roman businessman to create the first painting. True to his reputation, he recruited a collection of disreputable characters to sit as models and produced a work lavish in colour and opulent in its setting. Jesus, ruddy-cheeked and beardless, a long curl to his hair, sits at a table with a bowl of plump fruit in front of him. There is also a roast chicken, and wine in a fine jug. The furniture is expensive, the clothing of Jesus and his hosts richly coloured.

The 1606 painting could be by a different artist, so distinctive is its tone. Jesus is bearded, serious. He looks almost tired. This is Christ as "a mature man whose weary expression suggests the weight of both his recent ordeal and the endless mission to save humanity from its own folly".[273]

The colours are muted, the shadows deeper. There is a meal on the table, but it is peasant fare. The gathered group – the two disciples and the innkeeper and his wife, added to the scene by Renaissance tradition – are themselves rugged peasants: simple people, evidently poor. And yet the miracle is there. This is resurrection happening not among the fashionable elite of Rome, but in the shadows of an ordinary world.

For the Caen exhibition the 1606 painting was on loan from its home museum in Milan. It was set alongside Caravaggio's own sketches and several contemporary paintings of the same scene. A reproduction of the 1601 work, housed in London's National Gallery, was included. The setting of the exhibition served to highlight the sheer depth of the 1606 painting. Both works are technically brilliant – both deserve their place in art history – but there is a quality to the 1606 work that sets it apart. It is reflective, thoughtful, and respectful of its subject. It does not simply represent the resurrection. It tries in some way to understand it. It is "a tender portrayal of confidence in a redemptive Christ, who gently renews hope in the despairing disciples, and brings comfort to the poor".[274]

So what happened? What changed? How did the frivolous young painter of 1601, recruiting street people to sit for a bubbling, superficial *Emmaus*, become in just five years the thoughtful artist engaging with this powerful story and probing the truth of the resurrection? The answer is that *exile* happened.

Caravaggio had always been a party animal. He was often getting into fights and ran up fairly frequently against the Rome police. He had the patronage of the Pope, and was hugely successful as a painter, known for a while as "the greatest artist in Rome". He lived a rock-star lifestyle, until in May 1606 he got into an argument about the score in a tennis match, and killed his opponent. The death of Ranuccio Tomassoni changed everything. Neither his celebrity status nor his powerful patrons could save him, and Caravaggio was forced to flee Rome. He never returned, living the rest of his life in exile and dying in unknown circumstances before he could benefit from the pardon granted to him.

Exile brought disruption in the life of the young Caravaggio, but it also brought depth. His work was deeply changed by the experience. It is debatable whether he became a better painter, but there is no doubt that he became a better artist. The searing loss of exile brought out in him a deeper faith.

This is the how *limitations* work in the purposes of God. The greatest single example is the period between 605 and 536 BC, when a series of three invasions led to the destruction of Jerusalem and the transportation of God's people to Babylon. Exile represented, for the Jewish people, the loss of everything that Yahweh had given them. Jerusalem itself was progressively ransacked. The Temple was defiled, and then destroyed. The king and all his princes became prisoners. It was a time of devastating loss – and yet this was possibly the most creative time in Israel's theological history. New thinking was done. A wider vision emerged. For the first time there was talk of a "kingdom of God" that would trump all other kingdoms, and of a "Son of Man" who would deliver it. It is hard to see how the promise of Messiah could ever have become what it was without the exile. It was the Babylon years, more than any, that set the stage for Jesus.

Walter Brueggemann refers to the "prophetic imagination" that exile evokes in us. "This work of poetic alternative", he writes, "in the long run is more crucial than one-to-one pastoral care or the careful implementation of institutional goals. That is because the work of poetic imagination holds the potential of unleashing a community of power and action that finally will not be contained by any imperial restrictions and definitions of reality."[275]

For twenty-first-century followers of Jesus, the stories of exile are among the most powerful in the armoury of God. Those who know who God is can overcome even the great losses of exile – but they won't do it by hankering after all they have lost. They will do it by allowing God to awaken his dream in them: the dream that is bigger than Jerusalem and Babylon; that is sovereign over both. They will do it by taking up their lyre, by setting aside grief and regret, and saying to their captors, "I have a new song for you..." Because we *can* sing the Lord's song in a strange land. That's what mission is, in a time of exile.

Reading Between the Lions

> Exile is a dream of a glorious return. Exile is a vision of revolution: Elba, not St Helena. It is an endless paradox: looking forward by always looking back. The exile is a ball hurled high into the air.
>
> SALMAN RUSHDIE[276]

The Russian composer Sergei Rachmaninov saw his first symphony performed in 1896, to a disastrous reception. The performance was poor, the critics hated it, and he all but lost the will to write. For three years he faced an acute form of "composer's block". He couldn't write a note, and lost all self-confidence as a musician. Through a strange mixture of mainstream and alternative therapy he began to re-emerge as a composer, and the result was his Second Piano Concerto in C Minor, written in 1900. This was more positively received, and has gone on to become one of the world's best-loved compositions. It has often been used in films and theatre, and its intense, brooding opening chords are recognizable to millions. The minor key carries a certain sadness, but it also carries hope. In the lament there is a hint of elation – not of the empty triumphalism that ignores adversity, but of the deeper character that faces loss and yet lives. The concerto marked the resurrection of its composer's creativity – and it carries a resurrection tone. It is deeply Russian in character, recognizing that joy, as well as sadness, can have weight. God's joys are not found in the superficial, dancing like cartoon characters across the surface of things, but in the deep places, where pain as well as pleasure is acknowledged.

"Abandonment and displacement are the stuff of my favourite psalms," Bono writes in his introduction to the Psalms; "The Psalter may be a font of gospel music, but for me it's despair that the psalmist really reveals and the nature of his special relationship with God. Honesty, even to the point of anger. 'How long, Lord? Wilt thou hide thyself forever?'[277] or 'Answer me when I call'[278]."[279]

Some of the strongest of our sacred texts are written in a minor key. Why? Because exile as well as exodus brings fruit in our lives. God uses the limitations we experience to move us forward in his limitless purposes. A view of mission that always looks for exodus will not help us to live in the real world. Had Esther believed only in a God of exodus, she would have despaired. Her great discovery was that God was also real in exile; that his sovereignty was larger than her loss. Exile has the function, in the biblical account, of teaching us that loss as well as gain can bring God's blessings. Even more than this, it serves to teach us that it is only when we have nothing that we realize that God is everything.

When Tony Benn, formerly the Honourable Anthony Wedgwood Benn, published the first volume of his memoirs in 2004, he chose as a title *Dare to be a Daniel*. The volume recalls Benn's early years and his mother's nightly Bible readings. She always made a distinction, he says, between "the Kings of Israel who exercised power and the prophets of Israel who preached righteousness". Benn is in no doubt as to where her sympathies lay. "I was brought up to believe in the prophets rather than the kings,"[280] he writes.

This choice of title says a lot about the roots of Benn's radicalism, which he had always attributed more to "the man from Nazareth" than to Marx, but it also says something about Daniel – the Hebrew hero, who stood as a minority of one at the court of pagan kings and yet turned the fortunes of the empire around; the political operator who was also a man of prayer; the wise and tactful prophet who dreamed of a different future for God's people. Daniel remains one of the most influential figures in the biblical record. Generations of Jews and Christians have been empowered and inspired by his story.

Daniel serves in the Old Testament narrative as an embodiment of the nation of Israel in their journey through exile. In this sense arguments about the historicity of Daniel himself, and about exactly when the book was written or edited, are irrelevant to the text's power. The central character of the drama is Daniel but the story is about Israel. The hope of all Israel, the future of all Israel, is somehow carried in the life of this one man as he lives through – and survives – the fate all Israel has feared. Will exile destroy Israel? Will the promises of God be forgotten and the nation devoured? Will the very memory of God's victory be lost as the saga that began with the faith of Abraham, the adventuring of Joseph, and the liberating passion of Moses descends into tragedy and loss? Will the exile be the undoing of the exodus, leaving the Hebrews in as bitter a slavery as they began with? These questions hang in the air as we watch the story unfold. How will this new experience – exile; loss; the defiling of God's Temple; the "defeat" of God himself – affect their faith? Is there a plan and purpose to God's rule that can survive such a blow? Can faith stay strong in the furnace of affliction? Is there a divine courage for those who face the lions of a hostile culture?

Daniel becomes the focus of all these questions. In his faith, we see the faith of Israel projected. His sufferings are the sufferings of Israel. If he can find hope, there is hope to be found for all of us. If he can stay true to Yahweh in the face of Yahweh's defeat, perhaps we all can. The book of Daniel is more than a collection of stories aimed at encouraging struggling souls. It is more than a morality tale to uplift our hearts. It is an epic adventure, a myth on the scale of the Norse Sagas. Other tales can serve to encourage those facing difficult times and the loss of prosperity – Daniel serves those facing the loss of God. In this book God himself – represented in the victory over Egypt; the settling of the land; the building of the Temple; the sanctity of the holy city of Jerusalem; the royal Davidic line – seems lost to us. It is not we who have lost a battle, but God. Or so it seems.

Exile is a kind of death, in which not only Israel but Yahweh himself seems implicated. The God who has promised to stand against evil; who proclaims himself greater than the pagan gods; who will not allow the slavery in Egypt to continue; who rages against the pagans even as he clears them from the land: this God of victory, might, and power gives in, it seems, to a pagan army. He lets a pagan king defile the promised land, the holy city, and the sacred Temple. He allows pagan worshippers, quite literally, to walk all over him. Where is he? Is it all over for Yahweh? Is he powerless after all? Was Moses wrong about him?

The great secret of this story; the priceless jewel at its heart; the explosive discovery Daniel makes and delivers to all Israel; is this: that God himself is not fazed by the loss of God. Daniel's God, it turns out, is not too small for Babylon, but too big. He is victorious, he is in control, he is committed to fulfilling his plans; he is there for Israel. All these things are true, but not on the small scale in which the Hebrews had formerly viewed them. Rather, it is on a global scale that God is sovereign. It is as the universal king that he will reign. He is bigger, in Daniel, than the biggest human ruler: more powerful than the most powerful dictator. The loss of the Temple doesn't throw him because he is so much bigger than the Temple. The invasion of the land does not stop him, because he has plans for the whole earth. The exile does not distance him from his people, because there is nowhere they can go where he will not be found.

Exile does not faze Daniel, because it has not fazed his God. Temple worship was great and encouraging, and doubtless Daniel missed it as much as those who later hung their harps mournfully on Babylon's riverside trees, refusing to sing the Lord's song. But Daniel was not *dependent* on the Temple. He could worship God wherever he was: surrounded by countless crowds of strange and even hostile pagans; knowing that the monuments of Nebuchadnezzar's great city pointed not to Yahweh but to other, lesser gods; under pressure and under fire; trapped in a strange land a long way from home. Nor was Daniel dependent on being located in Jerusalem, or on being called to serve God's anointed king over Israel. Royalty, temple worship, civic life – all these Daniel missed, but on none of them was he *dependent*. He did not need the visible victory of God to trust in God's promises. His *internalized* faith turned out, in the event, to be stronger and more lasting than any *externalized* faith relying on the props and trappings of Jerusalem worship.

The central metaphor of Daniel's whole story, the thread that weaves through his life over a seventy-year-long public career, is that of "faith in a foreign land". Daniel thrives in a context in which the language and customs are alien to him; in which gods other than his own are worshipped; in which the expectations and aspirations of everyday life are not those of his birth or childhood. He learns early in life that there will be no props or scaffolding to bolster his faith: if it is not internally sustained, it will not last. He discovers that if he is to communicate, he must do so across a vast cultural and religious divide: the language of Zion will not serve him if he is to make himself understood in Babylon. He realizes that he must keep alive the dream of God's greater purposes. If he forgets, there is no one to remind him. He is an agent behind enemy lines, navigating an unfamiliar landscape to find his way in an uncharted culture.

Several aspects of Daniel's response to these challenges are significant to our own efforts to live out "faith in a foreign land":

1. He wastes no time on nostalgia. Daniel misses Jerusalem; there is no doubt about it. Like all exiles, he longs for home, and when he prays at his window it is to Jerusalem that he looks. But he has no time for "if-only" scenarios. His focus is on engaging with the culture in which God has placed him, no matter how difficult. Yesterday has little currency in the life of Daniel – today and tomorrow are paramount.

2. He is not afraid to learn. He throws himself into a passionate study of his new language, land, and culture: so much so that he stands head and shoulders above the non-Hebrew students. Daniel may be uncomfortable in this new context, but he does not fear it. He follows a hunch that Yahweh might be just as accessible and active from Babylon as from Jerusalem, and when he sees the emperor himself kneeling in repentance, he knows for sure that his hunch was right.

3. He embraces a life of discipline, simplicity, and service. From his early adoption of the Atkins Diet through his astute avoidance of involvement in palace political wranglings and petty jealousies, to his apparently lifelong habit of daily prayer, Daniel pursues a disciplined life. There is a dynamic of cultural relevance in Daniel, as he seeks to find his place and his voice in Babylon, but there is also an energized irrelevance. He is not afraid to be at odds with the culture in his spirituality and lifestyle. His centre of gravity is not culturally defined: it lies elsewhere.

4. He looks to God for a different future. To read the book of Daniel only in the past or present tense is to miss the

point: Daniel pursued God for revelation of the future. He had to know that exile was not the last word: that though Babylon seemed for a time to be dominant, God had other plans. He had to root his life in God's vision for the world, knowing that there was a coming kingdom so strong, so robust that all other kingdoms would be smashed by its arrival. His patient endurance in the present was informed and inspired by his faith for the future.

The ultimate triumph of Daniel is that he does better in Babylon than many of his fellow Jews had done in Jerusalem. The absence of the signs, symbols, and support mechanisms of religion does not rob him of his faith; it makes him stronger. Exile serves to purify, deepen, and strengthen his faith. It causes him to think harder, to pray longer, and to look deeper. The result is a series of prophecies that in many ways lay the foundations for the ministry of Jesus. God has a much bigger plan than to bless Jerusalem alone. Through the losses of deportation and dislocation, Daniel gains a deep, abiding, and exhilarating faith. Exile is good for him.

Exile meant for Daniel a loss of power and prestige. It involved relocation to a foreign culture and the learning of a new language. It meant facing hostility, and explaining faith in Yahweh to people entirely outside that experience. And yet it became, for him, not a curse but a blessing. It brought him into a life that he would never have enjoyed if the city of God had not fallen.

What faith adventures await us, beyond the walls of Christendom, out there in the "foreign soil" of a changed and changing culture? What depths of faith and wisdom might God have for us to discover? What dreams might he yet have to give us? The book of Daniel suggests that these blessings cannot be ours without the letting go – that renewal lies somewhere beyond relinquishment. There is an adventure of faith waiting for us in the twenty-first century. There are new languages to learn; new cultures to explore; whole new Babylons to be invaded by eccentric prophets.

Fruitful Exile

> The text invites people like us, at the door of capitulation, to think about an alternative. The proffered alternative is this: Remember who you are by remembering whose you are. Be your own person even in the face of the empire, of the dominant ideology, of the great power of death. Be your own person by being in the company of the great God who works in, with, and through the training programme of the empire for the sake of God's own people. Be your own person, because God has not succumbed to the weight of the empire.
>
> WALTER BRUEGGEMANN[281]

What can we do, then, to make of exile a fruitful experience?

Find connection with the purposes of God, despite the difficulties

Like the books of the "prophets of exile" – Jeremiah, Isaiah 40 – 55, and Ezekiel – the book of Daniel shows that a deeper, more robust faith emerges from the crucible of dislocation and loss. Exile, as devastating as it was for those caught up in it, bore rich fruit for the Hebrew people, for the ongoing revelation of God's plans, and for the theology of hope on which the coming of the Messiah was built. "What we see is that the great trauma of the exile, potentially disastrous for the faith, identity and even existence of Israel, actually becomes one of the most creative periods in its theology with lots of new works being written and older traditions collected. It is because of this that we have an Old Testament at all."[282]

It is important to recognize that exile is a fruitful setting for God's mission, because the New Testament suggests it is the normative condition for the Christian community. Filled with the power of the risen Christ, the church is sent *into exile* in the world, to bring the presence of God to every people, tribe, place, and culture.

When the disciples ask Jesus in Acts 1 "Will you now restore the kingdom to Israel?" they are assuming that Jerusalem will be restored as the epicentre of God's global plan, with people of every tribe and nation being drawn to God's visible, public, structured, and established new order. Jesus insists that this remains a future promise, and, in the meantime, his people are called to be his witnesses "in Jerusalem, and in all Judea and Samaria, and to the ends of the earth".[283] They are to carry the gospel into every culture – known and unknown, familiar and foreign. Like Eve and Adam sent out from the garden to tame the wilderness, they are to go out *into exile* with the gospel. The call of God will be an outward arc, a movement away from settledness and safety. Exile is the seedbed of the missional church.

This leads to the important New Testament concept of Christians as "resident aliens[284] living freely in the world and yet somehow strangers to it. The Greek terms *paroikeo* and *paroiko* present the local church as a "colony" of resident aliens in a given place and time. We are called to be both *resident* and *alien*, at home but not at home, in every place to which the Spirit of God scatters us. "1 Peter begins by identifying the readers with those in exile. ... As Daniel and his colleagues in Babylon had to learn how to sing the Lord's song in a foreign land, so too the Christians in Pontus, Galatia, Cappadocia, Asia and Bithynia are being encouraged to sing a new song, a song about Jesus and his saving grace, in the place where they too are scattered aliens."[285]

Ernest Lucas suggests three aspects of Daniel's life in exile that point to ways in which Christian colonies of "resident aliens" should view their culture:

1. Daniel's refusal to adopt a "ghetto mentality" in exile. He was ready to engage with this alien culture, even taking the opportunity to spend three years studying it in order to understand it in some depth. He accepted a responsible job in its power structure.

2. Within this context Daniel was concerned to retain his personal integrity. Engaging fully with the alien culture did not mean being absorbed in it with a loss of his distinctiveness, especially his commitment to God. At this point his stand is made privately; only a couple of Babylonian officials know of it.

3. Daniel adopted a non-confrontational, conciliatory attitude in his relations with the Babylonian officials. He did not make life unnecessarily hard for them or demand they behave in a way that would risk their jobs or lives. He found a creative way to achieve his end.[286]

Graham Tomlin paints a picture of just what it might mean to live as resident aliens:

> In every capital city, you can usually find communities of exiles. Chinese restaurants in San Francisco's Chinatown, Irish bars in Kilburn in London, Arab neighbourhoods in Paris. In all of them, communities try to recreate the atmosphere of home, so that when you step inside you can begin to feel what it is like to be in the real country itself. There will be reminders that you aren't actually there yet... The idea is that church is meant to be, as far as it can, a reminder of life under the rule of God.[287]

Realize that God is working in your second-choice world

"In our ideal world," Viv Thomas writes. "we choose our job, spouse, city, entertainment, company, community and religion at leisure with freedom. Most of us like to have our first choice..."[288]

Daniel, by contrast, is a primary biblical example of "second choice":

> The Babylonians carted him off to Babylon. This was precisely the place where he did not want to be; he wanted to live in Jerusalem. The people he did not want to relate to were all the people who lived in Babylon. The culture of Babylon, its gods, food, and language – all alien to him... His life was one long adjustment to other people's thoughts, fears, passions and addictions.[289]

This is the "second-choice world", an environment in which

you don't get what you want and must live in the shadow of other people's choices. Yet even here, God is with you. Even here, where you have not received what you hoped for, God is sovereign. The message of the prophets of exile was that the world is God's. You may be outside your first-choice world, but you are not outside the scope of God's power and provision. He can be with you, and he can work through you in any place you're sent.

Jeremiah tells the exiles to go even further. Not only to tolerate their second-choice world, but to give themselves to it. Let this be the place, he says, where you find God. It is to the exiles he addresses his most famous words of hope: "'For I know the plans I have for you,' says the Lord. 'They are plans for good and not for disaster, to give you a future and a hope.'"[290] Even in your exile, you are not forgotten. Even here, God's good intentions for you are active. Even here, he reassures them, God is present. "'If you look for me wholeheartedly, you will find me. I will be found by you,' says the Lord."[291] The message is clear – your exile doesn't change the plans God has for you, nor does it mean God isn't with you. You can find him in the very midst of your loss. How should you live this exile? "Build homes, and plan to stay," says Jeremiah. "Plant gardens, and eat the food they produce. Marry and have children. Then find spouses for them so that you may have many grandchildren. Multiply! Do not dwindle away! And work for the peace and prosperity of the city where I sent you into exile. Pray to the Lord for it, for its welfare will determine your welfare."[292]

Do these words seem familiar? Do you hear an echo of God's Eden mandate? "Be fruitful and multiply. Fill the earth and govern it."[293] Even in exile, God's original intentions stand.

It is still his desire that we bear fruit. More importantly, it is still possible. The ground that Eve and Adam had to tame was wilderness, yet fruit was promised. Is there any place on earth God's word won't stand? Don't let your second-choice world be a second-rate life. Let God meet you where you are. Let him give you meaning in your exile.

Set aside bitterness to embrace hope

Lastly, there is a call to set aside regret and bitterness and look for hope. Rob Lacey's free translation of Psalm 137 captures the despair of its composer:

> The Babylon rivers flowed along,
> But our tears nearly broke their banks;
> Our hearts were wading in the rivers back home,
> Our instruments dumb in this depression zone;
> And what? They expected us to sing our songs?[294]

The grief is understandable, but at some stage it has to end. If it were true that the loss of Jerusalem amounted to the end of God's plans, grief would be justified. We can all stop singing on the day God's plans are halted. But this isn't what the exile means. The destruction of Jerusalem is not the death of God. Rather, it is something he has allowed to happen, to grow our faith. He has robbed us of our dream because he has a bigger dream to show us. Regret and mourning only point us to the past; they set our face to what has been. Hope, on the other hand, points forward. It sets us looking for the new world God is bringing. Like the exiles of old, we who see the church declining so sharply in the West face, says David Smith, "a point at which God appears to be terminating our known world and inviting us to a new world in which the true nature of the church and its mission can be recovered".[295]

We have to let go "of the old world of king and temple that God had now taken", Walter Brueggemann says, "to receive from God's hand a new world".[296] Might it be that the new cannot be delivered until God prises from our cold, hard hands the old? Those who hear God's call to mission might learn not just to tolerate exile when it happens but to seek it: to hear God's call to mission precisely as a call to live and thrive in exile.

Finding Jesus on the Wild Side

Some of what I've learned about mission in exile, I learned from the late Lou Reed. I bought "Walk on the Wild Side" in 1973. It was the British 45" with "Perfect Day" as the B-side. I managed to get hold of the *Transformer* album not long after and was hooked. I'm not sure I entirely understood all the cross-dressing references, but that really made no difference. What I heard was an invitation to walk on life's wilder side. At the time I was hanging around with a group of young Christians variously referred to as Jesus Freaks or the Jesus Movement. They were inseparable from the hippy subculture of Bath. Everyone I knew was doing either drugs, Jesus, Hare Krishna, or Guru Maharaji. In some cases they were rotating all four. What these movements had in common was a disdain for the mainstream; a belief that Western culture had failed us, that the nine to five had nothing to offer. In this we were prescient of the post-modern theories that at the time were still being thrashed out in the universities and cafés of Paris. People moved fluidly between different cults and experiments because they were searchers, looking for a meaningful path into their future.

My part in all this was trying to decide whether to commit to this Jesus Movement I had encountered. I was certain it was a better life choice than drugs and was fairly sure it trumped the Divine Light Movement. Hare Krishna was a contender but still remained a little weird to me, and my application to train in Transcendental Meditation had been turned down because, at thirteen, I would need my mother's permission to sign up. So Jesus it would be, if anything. But I couldn't quite decide. I'd met some good people; had heard their arguments. I didn't want to let them down. But this was a big decision. Was I *sure*?

And then someone helped me. His name was Lou Reed and he had teamed up with David Bowie to make one of the defining albums of the twentieth century. We loved him because we sensed that his "wild side" was exactly where we wanted to live – not as addicts, but as people who did not accept either the comforts or the easy answers offered by our mainstream culture. We were "wild-side" people and Lou had given us our song. And here's the unexpected thing that happened. I thought about Jesus, and I thought about Lou and his wild-side people, and I knew, with a conviction I can hardly explain to this day, that this is where Jesus could be found. Jesus was on the wild side, with my generation, hearing our questions, believing in our search, sharing our disdain for easy comforts. Among addicts and, yes, cross-dressers, Jesus was walking on the wild side.

So my decision was made. I would join him there. With Lou's help, I would cross the tracks and find a Jesus who walked on the underside of life. Not an outcome, I suspect, that Lou was aiming for, or that he'd have approved of. But you never know – he was so contrary and counterintuitive in most of his decisions. He might just have liked a wild-side Jesus.

Walking on the wild side became for me a picture of mission. In a sense it is an image of exile – of the people of God leaving safety behind and moving out from the place we feel at home to the places we are strangers to. This doesn't mean that we are called to reject every comfort in the name of mission, or indeed to put ourselves at risk. What it does mean is that mission seems to call us from the centre to the margins. It is a very biblical image. God's command to Eve and Adam, backed by fire, was to live quite literally on the wild side of the garden wall. Abraham moved out from security to promise, from settled home to wilderness wanderings. Moses, we are told, heard the call of God to leave behind the "treasures of Egypt",[297] even though he was entitled. This wasn't because Egypt didn't matter to God – it was the very action by which he would in time "reveal his glory" to them.[298] If exile in the Bible is the journey from Jerusalem to Babylon, it is significant that both are implicated in the call of Jesus to his followers. They *will* bear witness in Jerusalem, but they will also touch Samaria, and in time make it all the way to Lands' End…[299]

The call, then, is not to ignore our "home country" as if only far-off lands matter to God. This was the thinking that all but killed the mission of the churches of Europe for centuries. Rather, we are called to leave *comfort* behind and seek God's purposes in the places that are hard for us, near and far. Wilbert Shenk suggests that this is very much the task of the missional church. "It is in the nature of mission", he writes, "always to seek the frontier where the struggle between faith and unfaith is most clearly and urgently drawn. The first essential of leadership, the one above all others with regard to mission, is to see the vision of the reign of God being established in these frontier situations and then to hold that before the church. All else is secondary."[300] The frontier may be a long-haul flight away, or it may be in the bedroom at the top of the stairs, sulking because you wouldn't let it stay up late on Facebook. It may be squatting in the warehouse at the bottom of your street because all the refugee camps are full and the traffickers have taken the money and run. It may be your neighbour; your enemy; your friend. Wherever the frontier is, it will be on the wild side of your particular garden wall. Mission is not faith-based tourism. It is self-emptying.

Our model, in the end, is the journey of Jesus. Like Eve, like Abraham, like Moses, he did not consider home – even a home with the Father and Spirit – as something to hold on to. He gave all; risked all; abandoned all to journey into the deepest, darkest prisons of humanity and free us all. His is the ultimate missionary journey, the very definition of the "sentness" of God. He blesses Jerusalem *and* Babylon; Egypt *and* the wilderness; you *and* your greatest enemy, by his embracing of self-giving love. Before Lou ever thought of it, Jesus walked on the wild side. And he does call us to follow. Paul puts it in the most graphic of terms: "Let this mind be in you..."[301] he says. If you want to walk as Jesus walked, then think as Jesus thought. Mission is no more or less than the imitation of Christ.

Complex Heroes

In Love's service, only wounded soldiers can serve.

BRENNAN MANNING[302]

"The exile" as an event is a single period in the history of Israel. Though lasting only seventy years, it is a time of great significance. The theme of exile, though, does not belong to this time period alone. In a sense it is woven through Scripture, as God shows time and again that he can be strong when we are weak and present when it seems all we can see is absence. Exile is a strategy God uses to overcome our weaknesses, and sometimes to overcome our strengths. We assume it would be a good idea always to be strong, but this is not the case. For one particular biblical character, the key to everything was learning to be weak.

J. R. R. Tolkien is known throughout the world as one of the most epic and heroic writers of all time. There is something about the way he creates characters that makes them compelling and believable. Who doesn't love Frodo? American author Roger Colby recently combed through the letters of the great writer to draw out "Tolkien's five rules for creating complex heroes".[303] The five rules are:

- Complex heroes must suffer
- Complex heroes are rewarded for suffering
- Complex heroes fail
- Complex heroes have fatal flaws
- Complex heroes are ordinary people

The beauty of Colby's insightful article is that it could have been written about the Bible. The heroes of Scripture are not perfect. They are real. They are complex characters seeking, in a complex world, to follow God. Nowhere is this more true than in the life of Samson,[304] who is remembered for two outstanding leadership traits: his mind-boggling strength and the mind-boggling foolishness that led to his losing it. For Samson the journey into exile was not so much about moving from one city to another as about understanding that being strong was not always what God wanted. The Jerusalem and Babylon of his journey are represented by the strength he thought would always prove God's faithfulness and the weakness through which, in the end, more was accomplished. Embracing God's desire to meet our weaknesses is a big part of pursuing mission in exile.

The book of Judges sums up Samson's glittering career by telling us "he killed more people when he died than he had during his entire lifetime".[305] Setting aside for a moment the difficulty we have, in our culture, with measuring success by counting bodies (the ancient world used death in much the way that Wall Street uses zeros), this is a stunning account of a life. It means that one of the strongest men in history achieved more in his moment of greatest weakness than in all the legends of his life. In the exile of his suffering, captive and blind, Samson finds out why he was alive.

What can we learn from this roller-coaster life about the relationship between strength and weakness? Here are three lessons you can apply to your own life and growth as you seek your place of greatest usefulness to God.

- Firstly, **though we long for simplicity, God is more**

fully revealed in complexity. Human beings love tidy answers. We like to know what's (always) right from what's (always) wrong and who's (definitely) in from who's (definitely) out. All too often, we associate the name of God with such certainties. But these stories show us that God is present in complexity. Samson's life is a mixed bag of clarity and confusion; of obedience and error; of triumph and tragedy. And somehow, miraculously, God is with him in it all. Professor Ian Stewart writes that, "if our brains were simple enough for us to understand them, we'd be so simple that we wouldn't". The same is true here. If the God we worship is simple enough for us to contain within our certainties, then by definition he has ceased to be God. Are there areas of your life where the simple answers aren't working any more? What might it take for you to find God in the complexity: to trust that he is at work even if you can't quite see it and don't quite understand it? A simple faith can be positive: a simplistic faith rarely is. Are you leading young people into an oversimplified view of their world, or can you lead them towards faith in a God unafraid of complexity?

- Secondly, **being strong in one area doesn't mean you are not weak in another**. No matter how many oranges you have, you can't make apple pie with them! Samson is not only physically strong; he is also very clever, outfoxing his enemies with his tricks and riddles. But he has a weakness for women – especially foreign women. It may not be immediately evident from a modern, multicultural perspective why going after foreign women was such an issue, but in Samson's day it was. One of the clearest instructions God had given to his people was *not* to marry the women of the land. In the terms in which this text is being presented, we are being told that our hero isn't just dumb: he is really, really dumb. His weaknesses are every bit as extreme as his strengths. The temptation – and we all face it as leaders – is to keep focusing on the strengths so as not to have to deal with the weaknesses. This is manageable up to a point – you don't have to be good at everything – but where your weaknesses are indicative of real character flaws, you do need to face up to them. Samson tried to build his leadership entirely on the basis of his strength. Perhaps he thought that he was so strong that nothing else mattered. But in the end it was his glaring weaknesses that floored him. Are you in danger of using your strength as a shield behind which to hide your weakness? Ask God regularly to "examine your heart", to highlight areas you should be dealing with. And when he speaks, don't change the subject! Are you a great musician? Perhaps you might like to learn to worship without music. Are you good with words? Learn the power of silence and servanthood. Do you excel at sport? Spend some time with people who don't – and learn from them. Celebrate your strengths: but let God do business with your weaknesses.

- Lastly, perhaps surprisingly, the story of Samson demonstrates that **your weakness may not be the enemy of God's purposes after all!** God may be working on key areas of weakness in your life, but here's the good news: he's big enough to use you even when you're weak. The end of Samson's life is intriguing and extraordinary. His foolishness has cost him his strength, his freedom, and his eyesight. He is reduced to a place of humiliation and servitude: a place he would never have come to if it weren't for the weakness he has shown. But, as he stands in that place, gathering such strength as he can and shaping one last, desperate prayer, he is able to achieve a victory greater than any he had imagined when free. God has not been a passive presence in the complexity of Samson's life; he has been active: weaving the threads together to achieve his purposes through a potent combination of his servant's strengths and weaknesses. Sometimes the very thing you are afraid of – poverty; imprisonment; redundancy; loneliness; change; persecution – is the thing God can most use to bring about his greater plan. All the time you are running from death, your maker is plotting resurrection.

It's hard to miss, of course, the sense of Samson as a prefiguring of Jesus: the one who by his death will not *kill* more than in his life but will *save* more than could be saved by any other means. It was "for the joy that was set before him" that Jesus endured the cross. There was a bigger picture, and he surrendered himself to it. Borrowing from a metaphor made famous by Albert Schweitzer, Tom Wright suggests that it was the calling of Jesus "...to throw himself on the wheel of world history so that, even though it crushed him, it might start to turn in the opposite direction".[306]

This is the picture with which the life of Samson ends. He

finally understands that he will best serve God not by being clever *or* by being strong, but by giving himself – wholly, unreservedly, and sacrificially. He surrenders himself, in the complexities of his strengths and his weaknesses, and asks God to do the rest. What more could any of us offer to the God we so want to serve? I am not the hero of God's mission. I am a complex character in the story he is writing. There are strengths that I bring, and weaknesses too. But whatever I bring, God will ultimately win: my highest priority is to surrender to him.

Response: Find Strength in the Faithbuilder

> Shadrach, Meshach and Abednego:
> "If we're chucked into this blazing oven,
> the God we work for could pull us out alive.
> He'll rescue us from your cruelty, King.
> Even if he doesn't and we fry, you should still know,
> there'd be no regrets – no way are we bowing down to your gods
> or your overgrown gold Action Man."
>
> DANIEL 3:17–18, *THE STREET BIBLE*[307]

Exile is the love of God proved even in my limitations. My world is broken open but God is still God. Limitation is a significant category in understanding the mission of God because:

- God uses exile as well as Exodus to teach us. It is in our places of loss and weakness, very often, that we are most able to discover who God is.

LIMITATION: FIND STRENGTH IN THE FAITHBUILDER

- The great figures of the Bible's story are *complex heroes*, who learn as much from suffering as from success. We, like them, are called to find God's presence in the full breadth of our human experience – good, bad, and ugly.

- Our problem, all too often, is that our God is too small, hemmed in by our religious practises and expectations. Only be separating us from these props can God begin to show us how big he really is.

- It is often in the place of exile that the dream of God's rule comes most sharply into focus. Losing our small comforts, we begin to yearn for the fulfilment of God's much greater purposes.

- Crucial to our full understanding of God is the discovery that he is with us in our moments of greatest pain as well as in those of joy. How will we make such a significant discovery if we are artificially kept from experiencing discomfort? How will we bring consolation and hope to others if we ourselves have never proved God's love in fire and flood?

To meet the penitent thief, Jesus had to hang on the other cross beside him, but, when the man turned to him there, he did not say only "Today I am with you on Calvary", but also "Today you will be with me in paradise." The sight of Jesus with us in our pain is the promise of our healing; the sight of Jesus sharing our death is the promise of our life.

DEREK TIDBALL[308]

CHAPTER 6

Incarnation:
Follow the Footwasher

You have an **INCARNATION** story.
It is the story of the journey God himself has taken
to come to you and end your alienation.
Mission is not what you can do for God.
It is everything that God has done for you.

Proud Mary Keep on Turning

Mission is Christian when, in its gaze towards the end, it looks beyond the horizon to God's new beginning: the beginning of eternal life, the beginning of the eternal kingdom, the beginning of the new earth, the beginning of the glory in which God's "all in all" will be present. Mission is expectation of the life of the world.

JURGEN MOLTMANN[309]

Luke's Gospel records an odd moment in the ministry of Jesus when the demands of fame clash glaringly with those of family.310 The emerging messiah is busy handling an increasingly demanding public schedule. His family presumably haven't seen him for a while, and they assume that maybe they should just try making an appointment.

They present themselves to his entourage and a message is transmitted: "Your mother and your brothers are standing outside, and they want to see you." Doubtless they are hoping he can find at least a narrow window in his day to fit them in, but the response they receive is dispiriting. "My mother and my brothers are all those who hear God's word and obey it," Jesus says. Meeting denied.

How must this have felt for Mary? She has carried him to term, borne him, and watched him grow, and from the very first has known that something huge, and strange, and possibly quite painful was to come. The first time she lost track of him, when he was still a child but unafraid to strike out on his own, she asked him, "Why have you done this to us?"[311] In truth, she already knew his answer. She had always known that she would one day have to give him up.

When God first sent his messenger, we're told, Mary was "confused and disturbed, trying to think what the angel could mean".[312] When old prophets see the child she hears the warning: *This one will hurt you. Your heart will break.*[313] Even as he grew, she thought back often to his birth, holding in her heart the many questions it had left her with.[314]

Mary didn't know exactly what it was that God was doing, but she knew that he was doing something, and she knew that it would centre on the child she bore. Her life is marked by two of the greatest prayers in history. To God, she says, "Let it be to me according to your word."[315] And to the servants at a family wedding, convinced that she's the one who understands what Jesus might be thinking, "Do whatever he tells you."[316] At the heart of these two declarations lies Mary's willingness to engage with the mission of God. She is available to God; she accepts his plan. What she has she gives, and she makes possible, through her surrender, the life of Jesus. Though she knows that doing it will pierce her soul, she releases to the world the son she loves.

As Eve is a hinge between the garden and the wilderness, as Shiphrah and Puah deliver the deliverer, as Miriam marks the transition from political freedom to worship, so Mary is the hinge between the promises of God and their fulfilment. Her soul rejoices in her God[317] because she knows that he has ended his long silence. Hope is stirring; the whisper of new beginnings. Mary senses in her spirit that Good News is coming. Her prayer is a profile of the coming kingdom,[318] as surely as that of Jesus in the synagogue.[319]

How does Mary model our participation in the purposes of God?

- She sees the end from the beginning. Mary doesn't know the detail of her son's intended role. She doesn't need to. It is enough, for her, that God is moving. In anticipation of Jesus' later command, she is willing to trust the Father and ready to receive the Spirit. Because of her we can all tell the story of the Son. Mary is a figure, above all else, of hope. For 400 years God has not spoken. His people have held their breath, while their situation goes from bad to worse. Has he forgotten them? Are his promises now void? No, Mary says. He *has* taken notice,[320] for he made this promise to our ancestors.[321]

- She plays her part and leaves the rest to God. I can't begin to think how many questions Mary must have had. Theological questions. Personal questions. Questions about her own future and that of her son. Questions on the future of her nation. She must have felt at times at the centre of a perfect storm, and she held them, stored them in her heart, because this was not the time for questions. This was the time for trust. Being inspired by the widescreen picture of God's plan is essential to participation in his mission. Needing to know every detail is not. Do you doubt that Mary's questions were all answered? On the resurrection morning? In the upper room at Pentecost? In Ephesus, where she retired with John and *saw* the church her son had come to build? There is a time for asking, and a time for waiting, and the only way to operate in both is to trust.

- She makes room for incarnation. This is her most moving miracle. Mary is asked, quite literally, to make space for God. Incarnation makes its home in her; expands her. Her body makes it welcome. She is asked to do, on our behalf what all of us will later have to do: to make room in our hearts, in our thinking, in our faith for God to become man. Mary is the first of us; the first to believe; to receive. The first disciple. She shows the way for us. The world will change when we receive, within ourselves, the true story of God's incarnation.

Protestant history has had major issues with the incarnation story. We steer clear of Mary, so sure are we that *Queen of Heaven* doesn't work. We relegate the first chapters of Luke to Christmas readings, and patronize the very truths they try to tell us. We say that Jesus was "born to die" and fail to see that like the rest of us he was born to live. I love Max Lucado's words about the plan of God, "as the echo of the crunching of the fruit was still sounding in the garden, Jesus was leaving for

Calvary",[322] but I wish that he'd said Bethlehem. It's Bethlehem he came to, and it's at Bethlehem that his work of reconciliation starts. It's true to say that Jesus died for me, but better still to say that he was born for me; lived for me; died and rose; ascended for me. That he sits now with the Father, praying for me. This is the story of his incarnation, all of it, and all of it matters.

Not only is this epic tale the true adventure of the incarnation, it is also the oldest creed of the church. Quoted by Paul in his letter to the church at Philippi,[323] the outline of Jesus' U-bend journey is the oldest worship song we know. It was on this that the first church built their faith: not on doctrines and dogmas about God's theoretical attributes but on the actual history of Jesus. Jesus, God and Man, has left his throne to journey into servanthood, becoming flesh, living and dying in our place, and God has raised him to the highest place where, as human as we are, he stands for us still. Jesus is our brother now, and God is all our own.[324]

What gave Mary the courage to trust God – not only when saying yes to receiving Jesus, but saying yes to letting him go? It was her vision of God's far horizon. She knew her people needed rescue. She knew that God had promised it. She believed that he would one day move. She accepted that if angels said the move was on, the move was on. She saw herself, and her baby, in the light of the promises of God. The first time he kicked, what did she feel? The beginning of new life.

Incarnation: The Story so Far

> The gospel is not a *what*. It is not a *how*. The gospel is a *Who*. The gospel is literally the good news of Jesus. *Jesus* is the gospel.
>
> CARL MEDEARIS[325]

INCARNATION: FOLLOW THE FOOTWASHER

In 2013 I was involved for the last time in creating the study material for the Spring Harvest conference in the UK. We had chosen as our theme "The Source". We wanted to explore the sense in which Jesus, in and of himself, is the very foundation of the Christian journey. This may seem a superfluous quest. Surely it is self-evident that Christianity derives from Christ. If Christians aren't following Jesus, what are they doing? Our hunch, though, in tackling this theme, was that there is a journey to be made, back to the person of Jesus as the source of our faith. It was our sense that:

- Too much in our world today that bears the name of Jesus does not bear his fingerprints. So much has been added to the faith since its first moments. So much, too, subtracted. The evident distance in common speech between the adjectives "Christian" and "Christlike" demonstrates this starkly. We wondered if our Christianity might just need to reconnect with Christ.

- The divisions visible and growing in the body of Christ seemed too often to be rooted not in the essentials of faith but in our added extras. It is the peripherals we seem so keen to fight about. Might we find each other once again as family if we journeyed back towards our common source?

- When it comes to mission, we saw a church in which ordinary people struggled to engage. It was as if the pure, simple story of Jesus had become so overlaid with clutter that most of his followers could no longer tell it. Too many people wearing WWJD bracelets; not enough knowing *why* or *how* he would do it.

The study involved in putting this programme together was a huge undertaking. It pushed me further than any previous such task. Somewhere in the middle of the process, engaging with the biblical texts and with what scholars from around the globe were saying, something unexpected happened. I can't pinpoint the moment, but I can tell you honestly that part way through my efforts to help the Spring Harvest teams and guests make a journey back to Jesus, I found that I was making the same journey. The quest to reconnect with the source became my quest. The reading, as it turned out, didn't stop once the material was written. I carried on, and to this day I am finding rich and remarkable new pathways through the jungle of contemporary theology. Three convictions shaped the writing of "The Source" and have continued since to reshape and renew my faith.

The first is that the story of Jesus, specifically the story of the incarnation, is the ultimate expression of God's purposes on earth. In one sense it is *a* story within the story of God. In another sense it is *the* story. It is from the incarnation that we come to see the Trinity. It is the incarnation that the fathers of the church spent centuries considering. It is the incarnation that makes us Christian. More, that saves the world. Yet the story that is told in many of our churches – proclaimed from our pulpits, coded in our worship, implied in our lifestyle decisions – is not the incarnation story. The magnificent journey that the early faith community embarked on in reconciling their conviction of Jesus as God with their belief in the one creator has been all but forgotten in our churches. We are heirs of the greatest story ever told, and we've forgotten how to tell it.

The second is that this story, firmly founded on the belief that in the particular life of Jesus of Nazareth the human

INCARNATION: FOLLOW THE FOOTWASHER

and divine have met, cannot be arrived at by a process of deduction and reason. There is so much about our belief system that does make sense, in the sense that even without faith you can perceive it. Sunsets and stars and swans in flight all point to something, and it isn't too great a leap to say that the something might be God. To say that Jesus is both God and man goes further. It does require a leap of faith. Not a leap in the dark, but a leap all the same. The identity of Jesus as both human and divine is a revelation of who God is and can only be received by faith. It is, therefore, the fundamental non-negotiable of Christian conviction. All around the edges are things it's easy to agree on, but at the centre of our faith there is a choice that it takes *everything* to make.

The third is that this choice, once made, changes everything. It challenges, not least, my false perceptions of who God is. Once I've moved from thinking Jesus is like God to knowing that God is like Jesus, I have an attic full of old religious junk to clear. Recognizing Jesus as the source, ruthlessly discarding all that does not derive from him, is like being born again, again. I have reread Genesis with new eyes; revisited Romans; found treasures in the Gospels that I never knew were there. I have seen in John and Paul, in Peter and the fathers of the church, a revolution I had previously missed. My worship life has changed, as has my world view; my complete commitment to the fullness of God's mission in the world. All this because I have determined to read everything through the lens of the incarnation of Christ.

I'm aware this sounds as if I've only just become a Christian, and to a certain extent I think that might be true. If Nicodemus could be as learned and respected as he clearly was, and still know nothing,[326] there's hope for all of us.

Throughout this process of discovering the incarnation, I have been conscious of my long-term quest to understand God's mission. My day job involves helping people to connect with God's purposes, and that's what this book sets out to do, but here is where the magic really happens. A fresh appreciation of the journey of Jesus is, for me, the single most important step in understanding God. How will we know what God is doing in the world, unless we see it here? This is the story that unlocks everything. Will you come with me on a quest to re-embrace the story of the incarnation of Jesus?

The Source Code

>Right at the start, before anything had happened,
>When nothing that would be made had yet been made,
>There was a source code for everything.
>The source code was the maker's way of making things,
>Because it was what he himself was made of.
>Each thing and every thing made by the maker
>Has the source code at its centre.
>Every ingredient, every invention;
>Every part and particle;
>Marked; stamped; infused
>With that which makes life possible.
>
>Later, after the making of many things,
>A quite remarkable specific thing happened.
>It was a singularity, a one-off:
>The source code of everything became a something.
>He entered into life;
>Pushed out legs;
>Took on a body and a beard;
>He was as human

INCARNATION: FOLLOW THE FOOTWASHER

As every human born before him,
But unlike any human ever born.
He was a straight line in a world of twists and turns;
A resounding YES to the second chance,
Against a chorus of condemning cries.
The source code walked the world
Whose fabric he himself had woven.
The one who made us was one of us,
And we saw that the maker's mark was on him.
Something shone from him that shook us all.
He sounded out a note so clear and true
That it is sounding still,
And the very noise of hell can't drown it out.

A man called John was sent to us
With a message from the maker –
To tell the world that the answer so long waited for was coming.
"I myself am not the answer," he told us,
"but I am here to tell you that the answer has been sent."
He knew that after him the maker's one true answer would arrive.
"Beside him I am nothing," he said;
"Compared to the answer that is coming
I am not even a question worth asking."

The true answer was spoken
When the source code walked among us.
We should have known him;
We should have recognised the maker in our midst,
But we were blind.
Only a few saw him for who he was:
And those few, though dead, are celebrating still.
So the source code came to us –

Born as one of us; walking with us.
It is from this very code that life has come to us
Life upon life, blessing upon blessing, cascading down upon us.[327]

Adam 2.0

There is no doubt that the Church's Easter proclamation is invested with cosmic, mythic claims, not unlike the cosmic, mythic claims made at creation and in the Exodus.

WALTER BRUEGGEMANN[328]

The "Roman Road" is a well-established method of reading Paul's letter to the Romans that tends to focus on the moral failures of humanity, on God's wrath, and therefore on the punitive dimension of Christ's death. A wide range of questions have been raised about this approach in recent years, not least because it seems out of sync with so many aspects of the Bible's narrative, and because it doesn't seem to be the story that the church fathers told. In the Roman-Road approach it is essentially the death of Christ that works atonement for us – it's hard to imagine what exactly his *life* was for. This approach allows me to celebrate the fact that Jesus died for me, but gives me no sense of what it might mean that Jesus lived for me – or that he lives for me still.

Ironically, it is a chapter in the letter to the Romans that most addresses this lack. Often ignored in popular accounts of the atonement, Romans 5 may be, in fact, its beating heart. What Paul does here is to set the life of Jesus as a counterbalance to the life of Adam. He does so because he is determined that we should know:

- That we are made right with God *because of what Jesus has done*.[329]

- That we stand now in a place of undeserved privilege before God.[330]

- That Christ came to us precisely in the place of our complete helplessness – he did for us what we couldn't do for ourselves.[331]

- That God's rescue plan therefore took place while we were still in a state of alienation.[332]

- That it is not only the death of Christ, but also his life, that saves us.[333]

All of this points to an objective reality in what Christ has done. His rescue of us is independent of our actions or response. To use a philosophical term, it is an *ontological* event: a reality that exists independently of our knowledge of it. Philosophers speak of the twin categories of *ontology* and *epistemology*. The first refers to what is real: ontology is the study of "how things are". The second speaks of our knowledge of what is real: epistemology is the exploration of "how we know how things are". The distinction is important because so much about our faith is subjective – it properly belongs to our epistemology. Not so, for Paul, the atonement. That which Jesus has achieved has been achieved independently of us. It needs nothing from us, we add nothing to it, and our response to it, whether positive or negative, does nothing. Atonement *is*, whether you know it is or not. It is in this sense that redemption takes its place alongside creation – and the promised day of restoration – as acts of "fiat": actions of God that he has completed by his own choice and power, ex-nihilo: from nothing.

Enter Adam.[334] Both of them. Paul uses the reality of sin in Adam to demonstrate the reality of forgiveness in Christ. His method is to place Adam and Jesus as mirror opposites[335] and demonstrate:

- That humanity is represented in each. Just as many can be said to be "in" the one Adam, so are we "in" Christ. Adam, as the first human, "contained" all humanity. Jesus, as God incarnate, did the same. The flesh that Jesus took on includes your flesh. In this sense God didn't only become *human*: he became *humanity*.[336]

- That the impact of both lives is ontological. There is bad news but there is good news in the mirror. First the bad: when Adam sinned, all sinned.[337] Sin came into the created order, and has made its home there since. We are born into it. We carry it. It is the crack that runs through everything. With sin comes death, and we all die. The good news, though, is that just as we are in Adam in his sin, so we are in Jesus in his death and resurrection.

- Better still, it turns out that the mirror isn't equal after all. There is an imbalance, a bias to the image. The victory of Jesus far exceeds the failure of his ancestor.[338] This is not a small distinction between the two – it is "a great difference". The grace of Christ is larger, by an unimaginable margin, than the pain of sin. Want to know how big a victory Christ has won? Take all the sins that have ever been sinned, and all the pain and death they've caused. Multiply it by infinity. That's how big the life of Jesus is.

The picture is breathtaking. All the evil of the world is traced back to its source in Adam, and all of it is outweighed by the life that finds its source in Jesus. The first time I saw this mirror effect my thought was "that makes sense". How *could* God's answer to our sin be smaller than the problem? How could God's act of incarnation be a less important event than the act of creation? How could it be an act on a smaller scale? The answer is that it couldn't be. This was the explosive reality the early church did business with. If *Jesus is God*, they said, *and we believe he is*, his incarnation is nothing short of a new creation.

As David Taylor says:

> The God we preach can end up not looking like the Word made radiant flesh, but like the Word who belongs to a Mensa club. He has the answers, all of which are true, but no real presence. He is the Right Idea who looks nothing like the resplendent, technicolor Son of Man — "hair a blizzard of white, voice a cataract, face a perigee sun" — whose beauty captivated the heart of St. John.[339]

If you have a view of God in which sin or its result, in any way, is bigger than the work of Jesus, you have parted company with the faith passed down to you. Jesus outweighs Adam by the mass of all the stars combined. And doubled.

Paul also tells us how it was that Jesus, in your place, reversed the fall. It was through his obedience. "Because one person disobeyed God," he writes, "many became sinners. But because one other person obeyed God, many will be made righteous."[340] Taking the place of humanity, Jesus offered to the Father the one thing Adam hadn't, and you can't – a life of obedience. He *obeyed* in your place. The life of perfect obedience God was looking for he's found, and he's found it in his Son. It is in this sense that Jesus becomes Adam 2.0. He takes the test that Adam failed, and he takes it in your name. In essence, "Adam" means "humanity". His story is the story of humanity. Now here's the implication of Paul's mirror imaging. In Adam, humanity failed God. In Christ, humanity obeyed. Jesus has already made the perfect offering of an obedient life. He has "fulfilled the law", obeyed its every comma. He has done everything the creator asks of us.

And just before he got up from the table, leaving his perfect-score exam paper for marking, he coughed to divert the examiner's attention, bent over to pick up a dropped pen – and quickly wrote *your* name on his paper. God has received the offering of an obedient life *from you*. You've already done it, because Christ has done it for you. I think we can agree this is good news.

Are we saying that the death of Jesus doesn't count? Far from it. We are saying, rather, that the whole journey of the eternal Son, from the moment he left his Father's side to the moment he returned in victory, was a journey of obedience including, miracle of miracles, the obedience of death. The one who by right and nature couldn't die accepted death on your behalf – as you. To tread again our well-trodden path to Philippians,[341] this is the story that saves you. The whole journey of Jesus is a journey of obedience and submission: to being human; to servanthood; to humiliation; and even to death. Jesus accepts all that is implied in becoming Adam 2.0, and emerges in victory. This is what we mean when we speak of the sacrifice of Christ. From the throne he left to the throne he regained, and every moment in between, is what he's done for us.

Incredibly, it doesn't end there. Like a meal where you didn't expect a cheese course or the petits fours after the coffee, and *then* you're told there is a digestif… the blessings of the ministry of Christ just keep on going. Jesus has made us "friends of God" Paul says,[342] and the impact of this moves in two directions. It means we *have been* made right with God and that we *will be* saved from condemnation.[343] It means we have been made friends and we will be given life.[344] That which Jesus has done for us he continues to do. Why? Because his incarnation isn't over. He stands at God's right hand on our behalf, still representing us. As priest, he now represents the people before God and God before the people.[345] Jesus is headmaster and head boy at the same time. It is one of the most neglected doctrines of the Christian faith that Jesus, in this continuing priestly role, is permanently reconciling us to God. He *is* reconciliation, in his very being, and the more we know him the more fully into reconciliation we are drawn.

Consider the words spoken by Jesus to his followers after his resurrection. To Mary in the garden he gives a message to be carried to Peter and the others: "Tell them, 'I am ascending to my Father[346] and your Father, to my God and your God.'" A little later, when they do at last see him, he tells them, among other things, "I am with you always, even to the end of the age."[347] So, I'm going to be with my Father, and I'm going to be with you, and I'm going to do them both forever.

Jesus is forever the bridge between humanity and God, forever the uniting of the two. He will forever tell the Father what it feels like to be human and forever open up to us the thoughts of God. This is why we can say that "there is (present tense) one God and one Mediator who can (forever) reconcile God and humanity – the man (still human, even now) Christ Jesus".[348] This is perhaps the most thrilling aspect of the incarnation story: that it isn't over yet.

Writer Adam Johnson unpacks how this idea can work in a new book called *Atonement: A Guide for the Perplexed*.[349] Bringing together diverse strands of thinking about the incarnation and atonement, he suggests that two key verses, both from the letters of Paul, succinctly capture Christ's achievement. The first, shared with the Christians of Corinth, suggests that "God was in Christ, reconciling the world to himself".[350] The second, written to the church in Colosse, tells us that "God in all his fullness was pleased to live in Christ, and through him God reconciled everything to himself".[351] From these two Johnson suggests the meaning of atonement is that *God was in Christ, reconciling all things to himself.* To honour the place of atonement in the plans of God, Johnson offers this, expanded, definition:

> The triune God, Father, Son and Holy Spirit, in the fullness of the divine perfections, was in Jesus Christ, the Messiah of Israel, bringing all created things in heaven and earth to the fulfilment of their God-given purposes through reconciliation with God.

The power of this statement is that it not only sums up the atonement, but at the same time describes the scope of the mission of God. It tells us:

- That atonement is God's work, not ours. God has taken action to bring God's creation back to God.

- That the action is completed by God as man, as Jesus. The humanity of Christ is as fully implicated in his action as his divinity. As "one of God" he comes to us and as "one of us" he saves us. The atonement is achieved from the inside of human life and experience.

- That this is a reconciling work. Atonement is at-one-ment, the making one of what has formerly been separated. All that has been fractured since Adam's trust of God broke down will now be healed. Creation is regained.

- Lastly, that this really does mean all things. There is no suggestion here that "souls" are saved. Whole people, and their whole world with them, are swept up in reunion with their maker.

These four principles put Christ's atoning work at the very centre of the story of creation. Jesus in his life and death completes the telling of God's story. He answers the questions raised on the edge of Eden. He turns in that ancient lock the key that only he can hold. All that was lost then – God's wisdom poured through people; the promise of a fruitful earth – is possible again. The lost vocation of Adam became the vocation of Abraham, the vocation of Abraham became the vocation of Israel, and at last, in Christ, the vocation of Israel is fulfilled.

The cross, Tom Wright says, is: "… the moment when the kingdom of God overcomes the kingdoms of the world. It is the moment when a great old door, locked and barred since our first disobedience, swings open suddenly to reveal not just the garden, opened once more to our delight, but the coming city, the garden city that God has always planned and is now inviting us to go through the door and build with him."[352]

Opening the Circle

> The single biggest, and really one-and-only, idea dominating the Gospels is this: the Gospels are about Jesus, they tell the story of Jesus, and everything in them is about Jesus.
>
> SCOT MCKNIGHT[353]

What does it mean to move, with Mary, to the incarnation as the next phase in the purposes of God? How does incarnation change our view of mission?

1. It tells us that this is in essence God's own story. God makes himself the central actor in his own unfolding plan. This event is all about us in the sense that it is *for* us, but as choice and action it is all about God. God himself is acting on behalf of his creation. The pattern established at the exodus is repeated and fulfilled. We are perhaps reminded of the words of Moses to his terrified companions: "Don't be afraid. Just stand still and watch the Lord rescue you today. The Egyptians you see today will never be seen again. The Lord himself will fight for you. Just stay calm."[354] This is why we talk so often about grace. The incarnation tells me once and for all that the Christian faith does not tell me what I can do to please my maker. It tells me, rather, everything that God has done for me. Tim Keller writes that "[r]eligion, as the default mode of our thinking and practices, is based upon performance: 'I obey; therefore I

am accepted by God.' The basic operating principle of the gospel, however, is, not surprisingly, an about-face, one of unmerited acceptance: 'I am accepted by God through Christ; therefore I obey.'"[355]

2. It tells us that this story is the heart and soul of God's wider story. It is the same but different; small enough to fit neatly into the wider narrative, but big enough to swallow it whole. To label your understanding of mission as Christian means to take seriously the centrality of Jesus. You cannot do serious business with the breadth of the mission of God unless you do business with this story. More than this, if our interpretation of Acts 1:8 is right, then this story is the entryway, the only on-ramp, for all those you would love to see engaging with God's purposes. All those who seek to climb the mountain of God must, sooner or or later, pass this way. Evangelism is not the explanation of a systematic set of propositions, as if $x+y-z=$eternal life. It is, rather, exposure to the personhood and life of Jesus. He is more than the key to mission; he *is* mission. Tim Keller sums up the promise of gospel-centred mission as "that you will find the figure of Jesus worthy of your attention: unpredictable yet reliable, gentle yet powerful, authoritative yet humble, human yet divine. (We) urge you to seriously consider the significance of his life in your own".[356]

3. It doesn't tell us, though, that this is all there is. The story of Jesus does not exhaust the narrative of God. Rather, it makes sense of the rest. Incarnation is the hermeneutic key to the New Testament and, as it turns out, to the Old.

Our faith becomes Trinitarian when incarnation collides with creation. Jesus changes how we see God's history. We have arrived at his story by reading forward from creation towards it, but you can equally read outwards from it – following the dual sight lines of Jesus back to Eden and forward into promise. What you can't do is do justice to God's purposes without this hub. Tom Wright explains that:

In Jesus himself, I suggest we see the biblical portrait of YHWH come to life: the loving God, rolling up his sleeves[357] to do in person the job that no one else could do, the creator God giving new life, the God who works through his created world and supremely through his human creatures, the faithful God dwelling in the midst of his people, the stern and tender God relentlessly opposed to all that destroys or distorts the good creation, and especially human beings, but recklessly loving all those in need and distress. "He shall feed his flock like a shepherd; he shall carry the lambs in his arms; and gently lead those that are with young."[358] It is the Old Testament portrait of YHWH, but it fits Jesus like a glove.[359]

This act of "reading out from" incarnation is in fact what happened in the first years of the church. The doctrines we now identify as Christian didn't come to us pre-packaged, like tidy volumes checked out from God's library. Rather, God himself came to us, his fullness squeezed into a single human life. It was meeting Jesus and adding to that meeting the strange claim that *this is God* that set in motion the adventure of the church. For the writers of the New Testament, Tom Wright says, "the story of Jesus was the unique turning point of all history".[360]

Why does this matter? Because it is just possible that this same pattern is important in our day. Perhaps we should be trying less to convince people of our arguments; trying less to demonstrate our "proofs", and leaning in a little more to showing Jesus. Perhaps the journey taken by Mary – and later by Peter and Paul, later still by Lydia and Timothy, and Polycarp and Clement and Irenaeus – can be our journey. Can we too move from the place of meeting Jesus to understanding who he is, and from that place to knowing God?

Cardinal Joseph Ratzinger, later Pope Benedict XVI, describes this journey:

> As early as twenty or so years after Jesus' death, the great Christ-hymn of the Letter to the Philippians[361] offers us a fully developed Christology stating that Jesus was equal to God, but emptied himself, became man, and humbled himself to die on the cross, and that to him now belongs the worship of all creation, the adoration that God, through the Prophet Isaiah, said was due to him alone.[362] Critical scholarship rightly asks the question: What happened during those twenty years after Jesus' Crucifixion? Where did this Christology come from? To say that it is the fruit of anonymous collective formulations, whose authorship we seek to discover, does not actually explain anything. How could these unknown groups be so creative? How were they so persuasive and how did they manage to prevail? Isn't it more logical, even historically speaking, to assume that the greatness came at the beginning, and that the figure of Jesus really did explode all existing categories and could only be understood in the light of the mystery of God?[363]

The pattern is that Jesus shows us the Father. The God who is Father, Son, and Spirit invites us into full participation in his life. There is a place at his table for each one of us. But he doesn't leave us to find our way there; to make the running; to overcome whatever barriers prevent us. Rather, he extends himself to us in Jesus, opening the circle of his love until we find it grown so large we are already in it. He brings us to the table. He comes for us. Sometimes the best way we can grasp these things is also the simplest, and in all the words of Jesus there are three that say it all. It is finished.[364] The job is done. Adam's curse has been reversed. A perfect life of obedience has been offered by a man to his God after all. All that needs doing for humanity to enter into full participation in the life of God has been done. How could there be a better entryway to understanding and embracing God's plans for me?

Love vs Judgment

> In Christ, there is nothing I can do
> that would make you love me more
> and nothing I have done
> that makes you love me less.
> Your presence and approval
> are all I need for everlasting joy.
> As you have been to me,
> so I will be to others.
>
> J. D. GREEAR[365]

Sherlock Holmes. Gregory House. Endeavour Morse. Such heroes move us when by brilliant deductive reasoning they see a situation as no one else has seen it and bring an outcome

INCARNATION: FOLLOW THE FOOTWASHER

no one has expected. Like a first-century Arthur Conan Doyle, the apostle John loves to place Jesus in a seemingly impossible situation and watch as he finds the secret door. Nowhere is this better illustrated than in the encounter with the woman caught in adultery.[366] The story turns on Jesus' words to the woman, a stranger to him: "Neither do I condemn you. Go and sin no more."[367] This phrase and the story it is found in show us as starkly as anywhere in Scripture the differences between Jesus and the religious leaders of his day.

It goes without saying that John, whose record of the encounter is the only reason we know about it, is aware of the deep irony of the situation. For a woman to be caught in adultery alone is evident nonsense. By definition, there is a man somewhere. This doesn't matter to the accusers because the confrontation isn't actually about adultery at all. It's about power and gender and the keeping of a code that overlooks the sins of an in-crowd while loudly denouncing the supposed sins of outsiders.

From the outset John confirms our hunch that this is a set-up.[368] It is Jesus these violent men are hoping to trap. To flush out the would-be messiah they resort to a cruel set piece in which they threaten the very life of a chosen victim: a sinner and therefore expendable. She is mere bait to them. The bigger fish they're out to catch is Jesus. Surrounded by armed men ready for an execution, the electricity of their pent-up rage held on a hair trigger, it is Jesus who must decide the woman's fate. The trap-setting challenge is stark – join us or defy us – but in a plot twist worthy of *Dr Who* Jesus does neither. Instead, he drops out of sight to write in the dust on the ground. In one balletic movement Jesus disassociates himself from their plan for violence, and by implication from the whole male heritage of his tribe. At the same time he breaks the intensity of their sight line, locked as it was on the woman. He gives her a moment to breathe, delaying for a few seconds the throwing of that first, vital, stone.

Having drawn their attention to himself, Jesus proposes a way forward for the stoning operation. They all want to stone the woman – there is a mob mentality at work – but they also know that someone has to go first. The decision to move from accusation to execution will be taken by the man who is first to let loose his rock. Who should that be? The oldest? The youngest? The most pious? The most angry? Who will have the courage to shift the baying pack from bark to bite, from the threat of harm to its delivery? "Since your scenario is supposed to be about sin and judgment," Jesus suggests, "How about this – let the one among us who has never sinned be the one to start the party."[369]

Something in Jesus' question, in his non-violence, in his refusal to be ruled by the mob, gets through, and one by one the men leave, subtly dropping their stones as they go. Jesus stoops down to the ground again to let them leave quietly, affording even them the dignity of a peaceful withdrawal. Which leaves him alone with the woman. She is, by John's implication, fully guilty of the crime she is charged with. She has not so much been accused of adultery as caught in the very act. Her guilt is not in question. So what is Jesus to do? Already she has seen that he is not like other men, who take their pleasure in private but publicly denounce those they take it with. This is a different kind of man; a whole new definition of manhood. What will Jesus say to her now?

"Go and sin no more."

This phrase is the heart of the dramatic encounter and is

hugely important to John's understanding of the ministry of Jesus. Preachers looking to retrofit a judgmental outlook onto the radical grace of Jesus often cite this phrase in evidence. Here, surely, is the confrontation with sin to balance the earlier refusal to condemn? What a relief to find that our saviour isn't soft on immorality after all. He didn't stone this woman for her adultery, but nor did he turn a blind eye to it. Like a silencer fitted on the barrel of an assassin's gun, this last-minute return to judgment mitigates the earlier display of mercy, leaving our insider–outsider religious world view intact.

Except that it doesn't. This reading sadly misses the entire meaning of the narrative, and the lesson John is asking us to learn. Far from representing a last-ditch return to judgment, the phrase "Go and sin no more" has the very opposite function: it tells us just how radical and counter-cultural the grace of Jesus truly is. In urging this woman to deal fully with the sin in her life, Jesus is affording her the dignity of deciding for herself, before God, what that sin is. Unlike the disbanded lynch mob, he will not tell her what, in his opinion, her sin consists of. He doesn't say, "Go and repent of your adultery." Rather, he says, "Whatever in your life is sin, do no more." He empowers her to be the activist in her own transformation and redemption; to come to her own understanding of what her sin is, and to deal with it accordingly.

This is a hinge moment in John's account of the incarnation. The coming of Jesus represents a movement that is both consistent with and radically different from the Hebrew approach to faith. Religion, in Jesus, will no longer consist of telling others the ways in which they have failed to reach God's mark. It will consist of empowering them to discover for themselves what God asks of them, and to draw close because they want to. Love, not guilt, will fuel the new engine of faith Jesus has designed.

"Our fundamental sin", Gregory Boyd suggests, "is that we place ourselves in the position of God and divide the world between what we judge to be good and what we judge to be evil. And this judgment is the primary thing that keeps us from doing the central thing God created and saved us to do, namely, love like he loves."[370] Far from being the work that we are called to, Boyd suggests, separating good from evil outside our trust and dependence on God is the very outcome of the fall. Judgmentalism is the hunger for *the knowledge of good and evil*[371] in action. The gospel of the Pharisees requires that they point out, quite publicly, the failings of this woman. To name her sin, and see that the penalty it calls for is delivered. This is not the role Jesus chooses. His goal, rather, is to let this woman find out for herself what her sin is, and to act accordingly.

This makes sense in terms of the wider biblical narrative because of what was lost in Eden. It was trust that ended when Adam and Eve disobeyed God. The scene is poetic and mysterious, but it seems clear that the choice to eat the fruit was an attempt to know good from evil apart from and outside of their relationship with God. It was an act of independence, a breaking of trust. What was God's proposal? The very pattern we have seen throughout his story: that men and women, through participation in the love and life of God, will have wisdom to live well in the world, and make it fruitful. It was participation in the life of God that Eve discarded, as did the Pharisees in Jesus' day. They wanted rules, not relationship. Their code could be expressed as "Behave as one who is righteous and God will accept you". The Jesus code reverses this. Behave as one who is accepted, he says, and God will teach you righteousness. He has only a few seconds with this woman, but everything he does embodies this.

- By stooping down, he eschews violence, and lets her know he has done so.
- By refusing to condemn, he shows her that this is not his starting point.
- By encouraging her to leave behind her unnamed sin, he empowers her to seek God for herself.

It is difficult to say that in these moments Jesus "loved" this woman, or that "loved" is how she would have felt, but there can be no doubt she would have sensed mercy, and grace, and that she might have walked away empowered to face her sin. Whatever it was. Perhaps adultery was not her problem. Perhaps it was a symptom, not the cause. Perhaps as she walked away she would have named her unforgivingness; her bitterness; her uncontrolled temper. What she would have known, for certain, was that Jesus had called her to a secret act of self-examination.

The pattern is that judgment – the knowledge of good and evil held independently of God's love and presence – always leads to slavery. Only love sets us free.

Speaking later in John's Gospel of the promised Holy Spirit, Jesus says that "he will convict the world of its sin, and of God's righteousness and of the coming judgment".[372] It won't be the job of the church or its leaders to point out to people their sin, but of the Holy Spirit. Why? Because repentance that is a response to the condemnation of others rarely takes hold. When my sins are helpfully listed for me by others I may feign penitence but it will rarely go deep. The sins I come to see for myself, on the other hand, I am highly motivated to be rid of. Like the Lost Son, it is when I "come to my senses"[373] that my conviction is deep enough to drive me home. It is to relationship that we are called. To repent is to return to God. "When I bow before his love he is not slow to come," Carlo Carretto writes. "Rather he has already come, for he loves me so much more than I, poor creature, can ever love him. And love shows itself in action, as for the Prodigal Son. Rising up is a fact, leaving the pigs is a fact. The soul must say with sincerity, 'Now I will arise and go to my Father.'"[374]

Don't let the voices of religion tell you what your sins are. Look into your own heart, where the laws of God are written. Let the Holy Spirit show you where you are broken. Then and only then will you find healing.

What impact does the story have on the way we engage with God's mission?

- It tells us that the Jesus way of handling sin is different from all that has gone before. Religion tries to change us so that God will like us. Jesus wants to change us from the inside, drawing us into God's love, and only from that place of deep security discussing our behaviour. Restored relationship is the goal, and rules don't get you there.

- It tells us that it's not our job to tell others their sin. If ever there was a lesson our churches need to learn, it is this. So convinced are we that only those who see their sin will come to God for healing, we play the helpful role of sin-describers. Nothing could be further from the work of God incarnate. The only sins you can ever help people shed are the sins they see for themselves. Your job, first of all, is to see yours.

- It tells us that it is our job to love, and from a place of love to pray for healing. If I love you – if I have become your friend – is it possible that you might trust me with the issues that are damaging your life? "Those who avoid the contamination of sinners are like the Pharisees. Those who earn the label 'friend of sinners' are like their Saviour."[375]

The Jesus approach actually places our sin in a different place in the order of things as we become his followers. In the world of the Pharisees, sin must be removed before I come to God's embrace – *I face my sin and therefore God embraces me*. In the Jesus view, sin will never be removed *until* I come to God's embrace. *Embraced by God, I face my sin*. This one small change in how you see things changes everything about the practice of God's mission. I love Brennan Manning's rant-like exposition of just what this might mean:

> Because salvation is by grace through faith, I believe that among the countless number of people standing in front of the throne and in front of the Lamb, dressed in white robes and holding palms in their hands (see Revelation 7:9), I shall see the prostitute from the Kit-Kat Ranch in Carson City, Nevada, who tearfully told me that she could find no other employment to support her two-year-old son. I shall see the woman who had an abortion and is haunted by guilt and remorse but did the best she could faced with gruelling alternatives; the businessman besieged with debt who sold his integrity in a series of desperate transactions; the insecure clergyman addicted to being liked, who never challenged his people from the pulpit and longed for unconditional love; the sexually

abused teen molested by his father and now selling his body on the street, who, as he falls asleep each night after his last "trick", whispers the name of the unknown God he learned about in Sunday school. "But how?" we ask. Then the voice says, "They have washed their robes and have made them white in the blood of the Lamb." There they are. There *we* are – the multitude who so wanted to be faithful, who at times got defeated, soiled by life, and bested by trials, wearing the bloodied garments of life's tribulations, but through it all clung to faith. My friends, if this is not good news to you, you have never understood the gospel of grace.[376]

Only by a commitment to such radical grace, and by a wholesale rejection of our inherited desire to stone people, will we be empowered to walk fully in the way of Jesus.

Cross Roads

Jesus Christ did not come into the world in order to conquer evildoers through an act of violence, but to die for them in self-giving love and thereby reconcile them to God. The outstretched arms of the suffering body on the cross define the whole of Christ's mission... Though suffering on the cross is not all Christ did, the cross represents the decisive criterion for how all his work is to be understood.

MIROSLAV VOLF[377]

The first Christians were not always as certain as many of us are today of the distinction between the life and the death of Christ. They knew that both mattered, but how to say which part "saved" them, or when in his biography Jesus moved from walking among us to actually redeeming us, they weren't too clear. This is why their songs told the whole story.[378]

What they did know was:

- That the incarnation of Jesus is decisive. Our whole salvation is dependent on it. Christ has come, and from Bethlehem to Calvary and beyond, he has saved us.

- That this action of saving love reaches its climax in his death. Atonement doesn't only *include* Christ's death: in a very real sense it is completed by it.

- In part this is because death is the ultimate act of Christ's obedience, the deepest depth of incarnation. Death is our biggest problem; our final enemy; the symbol of our brokenness. Unless death is beaten, we are not free. The Jesus who shares our life does not flinch from also entering our death.

- Because the whole journey of incarnation is a sacrificial path, it is most fully expressed in the ultimate sacrifice of death.

For all these reasons the cross has come quite rightly to be the symbol of our faith. We recognize that in Jesus we are reconciled to God, that by his incarnation he has saved us, and we mark this by remembering the place where his self-emptying underwent its most gruelling test. He has faced our every enemy – temptation, sin, Satan, and death itself – and all are beaten. It is helpful to see the cross as the very centre of the mission of God because all that God has done for us is present somehow in this one event.

Atonement itself is as wide as the sky – it is a huge concept, as epic in scale as creation itself – but the ways we interact with it are more simple, accessible, scaled to fit our human condition. Among these, the most significant is forgiveness. We embrace the cross when we learn to live in the giving and receiving of forgiveness. The cross represents the fulcrum of forgiveness at the heart of history. It is the one place the abused and the abuser both can come: the one to forgive; the other to be forgiven. Because of this it is the place that I can come, for the abuser and the abused in me to find their healing.

Having been wounded in a number of ways as a child, I gladly came to the cross as a place of consolation. God embraced me there; loved me in a way others had struggled to deliver. I could envisage the harm done to me transferred, instead, onto the broken figure of the messiah. A burden was lifted. Love healed me, and I was able to forgive. Imagine my surprise, then, as I grew in Christ and discovered that I was the abuser. Not in the same ways I had been abused, but in my selfishness, my inability to love, my insensitivity to the needs of those around me. The victims-only parking area at Calvary is a short-term zone. You're allowed to be in it for a while, but in due course you have to move on to the culprits' area. The beauty of the Calvary story is that the place God brought me to show me his love, to embrace and heal me, was the same place he brought me to knock the selfishness out of me. The God who called me beautiful was unafraid to name me broken, and the answer offered to me was to drink twice from the same fountain.

This works because the dynamics of the cross are stark and simple. The perfect Son of God, the one being in the universe who can claim to be beautiful but not broken, who deserves no reprimand, accepts in his own body the full impact of our brokenness. From cruelty to pollution, from acts of rape to acts of simple self-indulgence, all of it falls on him. And because it falls on him, it no longer weighs on us, neither the criminals who stand before him nor the victims of their crimes.

One of my sons, as a toddler, had an unbreakable attachment to baby bottles. We tried every strategy we could think of to get him to drink from a cup, but nothing worked. He just kept crying for the old ways: even when we explained what growing up was all about and he agreed it was a generally good idea, he still couldn't bear life without his bottle. Until my wife had a brainwave. We took our boy to a bridge over the River Avon in the very centre of Bath, and let him watch as we threw his bottles in the river. I know, it was an irresponsible act of littering – but there was a higher purpose at work. He watched the bottles float away. He saw them go. He cried a little, but he never asked for them again. Telling him the bottles were no more didn't do it. Showing him where they went did.

Is this too naïve a picture of the cross? That it exists to show us where the pain goes – the pain we inflict and the pain we endure?

Don't be surprised, as you come before the cross to ask forgiveness for your failings, to find yourself in company with those you have let down. And don't be shocked, when you come here for healing, to see the one who hurt you in the crowd. They're both here, because there's nowhere else for either one to go. Has there ever been a movement in the history of the world where the medicine for criminals and for the victims of their crime comes in one bottle? Where the same prescription heals the sinner and the sinned against? This is what the cross represents: it pours forgiveness over me, and it gives me power to forgive. And for the same reason. The harm that has been done to me breaks Jesus, and so does the harm that I have done.

In his biography *Long Walk to Freedom*, Nelson Mandela explains that it took the pain of prison to convince him of this truth. Locked away for years on Robben Island, deprived of liberty and dignity, he came to see that only through forgiveness could redemption come. "It was during those long and lonely years", he writes, "that my hunger for the freedom of my own people became a hunger for the freedom of all people, white and black. I knew as well as I know anything that the oppressor must be liberated just as surely as the oppressed."[379]

This is the why the cross matters, because it is the only place where both the tyrant and his slave can come for freedom. This is not all the cross means, of course. It is the very centre of forgiveness, but it is so much more. For Robert Webber, the discovery, late in life, of the sheer breadth of Christ's victory on Calvary changed everything:

> When I discovered the universal and cosmic nature of Christ, I was given the key to a Christian way of viewing the whole world.[380]

The cross changes everything, and it is right to see all that is achieved in incarnation focused, somehow, here. All that has gone before, from Abraham and Sarah to John and Mary, leads to this moment. If ever there was any doubt of how Jesus saw his own death, it is swallowed by those three words "It is finished".[381]

> The crucifixion was the shocking answer to the prayer that God's kingdom would come on earth as in heaven.[382]

Is it right, in the light of all that we have said about God's story; in our wider view of redemption; of creation; of God's mission in the world, still to speak of "coming to the cross"? It is, because God's story, wide as it may be, has a centre. No other single event holds within itself, so fully and perfectly, the depths of the story of God. Not everything you can know of God is told at Calvary, but everything you need to know can be seen from its vantage point. It is the undoing of the wisdom of humanity and the outpouring of the wisdom of God. It is a contradiction of all we thought religion would mean; an offence to our sensibilities. It turns the world on its head. And so it should. How could the death of God himself do any less?

Response: Follow the Footwasher

> Name another religion where an omnipotent, omniscient, and good God becomes human and dwells among us and dies for us. Name another religion that operates according to resurrection, and to grace.
>
> CAROLYN WEBER[383]

The Incarnation is a vital category in understanding the mission of God because:

- It represents the journey God himself has taken. The whole purpose of God – the original intention of our maker – comes into focus in the person of Christ. This is the "story within the story" that tells us who God is and how he loves us.

- It enables us to say not only that Jesus is like God, but that God is like Jesus. Here at last is a revealing of the mystery of our maker's identity. In Christ we see what previously we have not guessed at. Jesus is in this sense the source of our faith – the key by whom all else is read and understood.

- Incarnation tells us what God has done to deal with the problem of sin – not only in the death of Christ, but in his life of obedience and service. This is the event that changes everything – the announcement of new hope from humanity. All that was lost in the fall of the first Adam is regained in the life and death of the second.

- Because all Christian mission is, in the end, a response to the person and work of Christ. It is this that allows us to place the word "Christian" in our lives. In the macro we respond to Father, Son, and Spirit, but in the micro we begin with the simpler question *who is Jesus?*

Only reckless confidence in a Source greater than ourselves can empower us to forgive the wounds inflicted by others.

BRENNAN MANNING[384]

CHAPTER 7

Restoration:
Be Filled by the Firestarter

You have a **RESTORATION** story.
It is the story of the gifts God has given you,
the greater gifts he has for you,
and his plan that you should share them
with your neighbour.
Mission is joining God
in making the whole world new.

Purple Rain

The gospel has been a force for change throughout history and all over the world, wherever and whenever it has been effectively preached and wholeheartedly embraced, both in the lives of individuals and through them of the societies of which they form part.

ALISON MORGAN[385]

Buried in the Jewish story, often ignored but never absent, is the idea that from the start God had the whole world in his sights. Psalm 67 is a good example of this thinking. Not content to say "We are the chosen people" and leave it at that, this psalm goes deeper, to try to understand what being chosen might mean.

There is no doubt that it is a celebration of God's choosing of Israel: its opening line reiterates the words given to Moses by God as a blessing for the tribes of Israel.[386] These are words that for centuries have been recognized as a sign and symbol of the special status of Israel in the purposes of God. The psalm celebrates Israel's election. But it goes further. It celebrates the fact that Israel is chosen *so that the world might be blessed*. The blessing of Israel is not for Israel alone but for the nations.[387] All peoples[388] are to find joy in the overflow of the blessings of Yahweh. To be chosen is to be blessed for the sake of others. Israel is elected not only *from* among the peoples of the world but *for* all the world.

The result, this hymn of praise reminds us, is fruitfulness.[389] As the earth receives the blessing of God it releases back to him its fruits in grateful worship. The blessing of God breathes life into the world, and the world in praise presents its harvest. This is the image that was there in Eden; that hovers over the exodus; that has shaped and guided the people of Israel over centuries. Where God is honoured, fruit will come. Somehow, the psalmist believes, God will accomplish this through Israel. The beginning and the end of the adventure are captured in the poem's final line: it all starts when God blesses Israel, but it isn't over until the very ends of the earth know his name.[390] As for Israel, so for the church, Paul will later teach. We are blessed to be a blessing. No wonder Paul and the early church asserted that Jesus fulfilled the hope of Israel. Psalm 67:7 is a fourteen-word summary of the Acts of the Apostles.

The lofty ideals of Psalm 67 are a theory: they are the picture Israel longs for, not the life that Israel lives. For the church of the New Testament they are reality. The journey, from the special blessing of Jerusalem to a movement for the world, is what the stories of the Acts of the Apostles are about. What Jesus predicts in Acts 1:8 we see beginning as the book unfolds, and though the ends of the earth are not reached by chapter 28, there is no doubt by that time that they will be. Once the walls that divided Jews and Gentiles fall, there are no borders that grace will not find a way across.

Lydia, a successful businesswoman living in the Macedonian city of Philippi, is a perfect symbol of this process: the first fruits of a truly global church. Lydia represents the movement of the Spirit beyond the boundaries of Jewish expectations.

How did the death and claimed resurrection of Jesus – a Jewish travelling rabbi whose first followers were all Jewish and whose every point of reference was a Jewish world view – become a world-shaping faith? The obvious answer is that it was *because* of the resurrection. The event itself was too extraordinary, too category-defying, to be contained within the bounds of one small group. Much as this is a good theological answer, though, it doesn't quite explain what happened on the ground. For that, there are three key reasons why the faith that began in an all-Jewish prayer group in Jerusalem became the planet's most diverse religious movement. Christianity broke out of its Jewish setting:

> 1. Because Jesus himself wanted it to. In all his final discourses with his followers, Jesus points towards an "end of the earth" dynamic. By the time he has ascended into heaven, his disciples are in no doubt. He's made reservations at the restaurant at the end of the universe, and he expects them to join him there.

2. Because the Holy Spirit moved that way. At several key junctures in the story of the Acts, it is the Holy Spirit who pushes for a wider view. The baptism of Cornelius is a clear example, but so is the conversion of Lydia. Without the Holy Spirit stopping Paul in his tracks, there would never have been a crossing into Macedonia.

3. Because Paul came to understand it that way. Just a few chapters into the Acts of the Apostles it becomes clear that something big is going on under the surface. Jewish as he is, Paul has become convinced that Jesus is for everyone. He sees this earlier than Peter does, even though it is to Peter that God gives the vision. It is a source of conflict for them until at last the issue is resolved when Gentile churches begin to be established. It is Paul, though, who champions the call to Gentile faith, and fights to see that faith established widely.

History tells us that a cataclysmic event too late to be referred to in the book of Acts gave the biggest boost to Gentile faith expressions. In AD 70 Jerusalem was invaded and destroyed by Rome. The Jewish Christians fled in every direction, becoming missionaries by default. The authority of the "mother church" was lost for ever. Even this event would not have grown the church, though, if foundations for its spread had not been laid already. Had there been no hint of Gentile faith before AD 70, it seems likely that the church would have completely vanished.

Lydia, then, is part of this new age of the church. She represents the moment when the Christian movement finally breaks free from cultural captivity to Judaism and becomes its own force in the world. She is an early adopter in the new movement, the crucial "first follower" who will take Paul's mission to new heights. She is a huge step forward in God's restoration plan. Lydia lets us know:

- That the faith will be for Gentiles as for Jews. More importantly, those who are not Jews will not be made to convert first to Judaism before embracing Christianity. This had been the pattern, and was true even of Cornelius.[391] Pagans seeking God would first become Jewish proselytes and only afterward followers of Christ. As Paul came more and more to understand his faith, though, he saw that this was unnecessary. Seekers could jump straight from paganism to faith in Christ.

- That leadership will be for women as well as for men. There were women in the Jewish churches, and they did hold respected roles. Mary the mother of Jesus was among them.[392] But the truth is that the gospel, in its early months, was deeply male. Jewish culture was male-dominated, and it is no coincidence that Lydia, one of the early Gentile converts, is the first woman of any status mentioned in the Acts. The only three women mentioned earlier are Mary, Jesus' mother, whose attendance is simply noted, Sapphira,[393] wife of Ananias, who is hardly a role model of faith, and Rhoda,[394] a servant girl with a walk-on part in one of Peter's many adventures. Lydia is the first woman of substance to be mentioned, and the first as head of a household to host a church.

- That the church will be a stronghold of diversity. The first three members of the church in Philippi – Lydia,[395] the slave girl,[396] and the jailer – couldn't be more different.[397] Even as little more than a home group, the church includes already a great variety of people. Even in this one church the potential for a global faith is seen. Lydia represents the front end of the wave of growth that eventually will take the church across the world. She is proof, for Paul at least, that he was right to leave behind the more constricted Jewish view. God is on the move: those who dream his dream will follow where he leads.

- That this is just the beginning. It is to Lydia and her friends that Paul will write, years later, "I am certain that God, who began the good work within you, will continue his work until it is finally finished on the day when Christ Jesus returns."[398] Towards the end of his life's work Paul, now taken as a prisoner to Rome, repeats his admonition to the Jews, who have rejected his advances. "I want you to know", he says, "that this salvation from God has also been offered to the Gentiles, and they will accept it."[399] The sense is of a final passing of the baton, a prophecy that Jewish resistance to the gospel wouldn't end its spread, because non-Jews will gladly welcome it. Paul could not have known how resoundingly his words would be fulfilled.

In Lydia we see that the locus of God's purposes has become the church. The failed vocation of Adam, which became the vocation of Abraham and through him of Israel; which was taken up by Jesus and fulfilled on our behalf, becomes now, by his choice, the vocation of the church. It is in the church that men and women will participate in the life of God. It is through the church that the wisdom of God will be poured out to bring fruitfulness. God's original intention, which has never changed and holds its power still, is now the task and calling of the church. The mission of God becomes the mission of the church, not because it is no longer God's but because he draws us into partnership. We will be Christ's body on the earth, continuing the principle of incarnation. Because we now share in the full life of the Trinity, the Spirit will empower us to grow in our obedience. Jesus offers up on our behalf *his* life of obedience to the Father. By this action our communion with God is realized and Jesus shares his life with us so that we too can obey. The church is an earthbound movement of restoration through which God's original intention is recovered.

Paul must have thought his ship had come in when he stumbled upon Lydia. A successful businesswoman in her own right, she was devout and seeking after God. As soon as Paul explained to her his quest – to share the story of Jesus with the Gentile world – she wanted in. She was baptized, she brought her household to the church, and she offered her home as a base for Paul. After months of battling persecution; wrestling with his former colleagues in the Jewish leadership; stopped in his tracks by their stubbornness, Paul had at last found a more receptive audience. Is it any surprise he became convinced that God was calling him to work among the Gentiles?

One of the leading Pharisees of his generation, Paul was so well loved by the Jewish establishment that he was sent out from Jerusalem with the personal authority of the High Priest to persecute the Christians.[400] His journey ended in a different way, but nothing could change his roots and education: he was a Jew to the core.[401] It is extraordinary, then, that he not only converted to Christianity, but became the faith's chief ambassador to the Gentiles. Paul has two great motivations in his travels: he is determined to reach *the Gentiles* and he is committed to the spread of *the church*.

In the first instance, Paul has come to see that God's promises – the heritage of the chosen people that he has known from childhood – are now extended to the Gentile world.[402] Convinced of the sheer wonder and richness of these promises, Paul understands how astounding this revelation is, and that, having seen it, he must act on it. He senses the call of God not only to love the Gentiles but to *tell them*. The plan is breathtaking, and they have a right to know. This is not a burden he must shoulder; it is a gift and a grace he has been given.[403]

Secondly, Paul has come to see that in this new world-winning plan it is not the nation of Israel – racially, politically, and geographically defined – that will be the vehicle of God's purposes but the church: ethnically diverse and geographically dispersed. God's new family will draw people from every place and race, and it is through it, perhaps especially in its reconciled diversity, that the multifaceted wisdom of God will be made known.[404] This new human community will be the prism through which the pure light of God will fan out like a firework in a million magnificent colours. God promised to bless Abraham and through him to bless the world. Now in the same way the presence and blessing of God is to be experienced not only *in* the church but also *through* the church.

It's tempting to say that the church is the new Israel, but that's not actually how it works. In reality, Jesus is the new Israel, and the church is the body of Jesus on earth. Either way, the deal's the same: there is a new vehicle for the benefits of God's great wisdom to be poured out in his creation. This time it isn't limited – by ethnicity, geography, capacity, or law. Now God really *has* the whole world in his sights.

Lydia serves us as a powerful symbol of this change. This is a woman Paul, when he was Saul, might hardly have given the time of day, yet she becomes the focus of a whole new strategy for the expansion of the church. She is the first European convert, the beginning of a whole new adventure. She is a hinge between the limited, ethnically-centred and gender-restrictive world view of the Pharisees and the expansive, inclusive, world-changing vision of the apostles.

Restoration: The Story so Far

> Salvation includes the healing of broken relationships – with God, with others, with nature. It includes the healing of persons, justice for the oppressed and stewardship of the natural world. It operates on many levels – spiritual, psychological, physical, economic, social, and political. No aspect of the creation lies outside God's desire to bring restoration and wholeness.
>
> CLARK PINNOCK AND ROBERT C. BROW[405]

To understand how it is that the church shares in the vocation of Jesus and, through him, of Israel, it is vital to see that at the heart of the ecclesia lies the DNA of divine–human partnership. The model is the same as it has always been: participation in the life of God that leads to fruitfulness in the created world. Human beings are and always have been the lynchpin of God's plan. This is the relationship that God longed for with Eve and Adam; that he fostered with Abraham; that he invested in with Israel, and that he finally and fully realized in Christ. This is the role by which the church now takes its place in the history of the mission of God.

The pattern for the church, then, will be the pattern set out in Eden. God is inviting us from a relationship of trust to cultivate the earth, bringing his wisdom to the whole created order.[406] When Paul prays for his friends in the Ephesian church and, through them, for us all,[407] he uses words that are both Trinitarian and creational. His prayer begins with the Father,[408] honours the Son,[409] and rejoices in the work of the Spirit.[410] His vision for the church is deeply rooted in his understanding of creation. He sees the arc of the plans of God from their beginning before the creation itself,[411] through the achievements of Christ,[412] to the very future of the cosmos.[413] This magnificent backdrop, covering thousands of years of earth history in a few moments, traces the majestic strokes of God's plans for the world. We start our journey before the beginning of time, and move in ten verses to a place beyond its end. Could a "big picture" be any bigger?

And there is something else about this prayer that deserves attention, something characteristic of Paul's theology: his emphasis on *us*. Human beings, in Paul's panorama, are the primary agents and the central beneficiaries of the workings of God. "Church" is the word we use to describe just how this process works in the age of the Spirit. "Humans," Tom Wright says, "are the vital ingredient in God's kingdom project... Jesus rescued human beings in order that through them he may rule his world in the new way he always intended."[414]

Just as the people of Israel were blessed to be a blessing, so this kingdom of Jesus is established *in* us so that it can be mediated *through* us. No matter how huge the landscape is, the picture focuses on us. Human beings are, according to this prayer, blessed;[415] chosen;[416] predestined;[417] adopted;[418] redeemed;[419] forgiven;[420] included; marked and sealed.[421]

And these last two are the icing on the cake. This God, whose love for us is anchored in a commitment older than time and whose plans for us reach far into the future, meets us in the here and now by his Holy Spirit. His promises are behind us, his plans lie before us, but his presence is with us now. Paul wants the fledgling church to know that the present experience of the Holy Spirit is God's down payment on all that is to come. A deposit guarantees what is to come in both quality and quantity. The Holy Spirit both assures your destiny *and* shows you what it will be like. He is the flavour of your future – and not only yours, but that of the universe itself. Here is the explosive insight at the centre of Paul's vision of redemption: what God has done for you already in Christ and is doing for you now by his Spirit, he will realize fully in your future and somehow in the very fabric of the cosmos. Just as Eve and Adam were told that their obedience would lead, perhaps mysteriously, to a fruitful and fulfilled creation, so we are told that in surrendering to Christ we are the first fruits of a universal restoration. Like an astronomer exploring the vast night sky, Paul is astounded at the breadth of God's love. But like a microbiologist finding the patterns of life imprinted on the tiniest cell, he rejoices, too, in how intimate and personal that love can be. In the macro and in the micro; in the huge and in the human: God moves in transforming love.

This is the movement we come into when we join God's family, the church. The "in and through" dynamic is irreducible. There is no room in Paul's transforming vision for a faith that is purely personal, a gospel we receive but do not become participants in. The redeemer of the cosmos is drawing you into his life so that through his life you will be active in his world. As in the garden, these are not two movements but one – participation in the life of God and fruitfulness in his created world. There is inhaling and there is exhaling: both are breathing. Alan Hirsch and Lance Ford put it like this:

> Engagement with Jesus must move us beyond being spectators to being participants. If we wish to become like him, we must learn to participate in Jesus, actively applying him and his teachings to our lives. We cannot be disinterested spectators when it comes to following Jesus... It is those who allow Jesus to get into their hearts and heads who end up entering the kingdom.[422]

One sign of the fulfilment of the kingdom is the intrinsic diversity of the church. This is not the whole picture, but for Paul it is a very important part of it. It is not difficult to see the whole human family "represented" in Eve and Adam. You only have two figures to worry about, so their actions *are* the actions of humanity. If their vocation now falls, though, on God's new redeemed family, the church, what is that going to look like? How will we see that in Christ God is reconciled with all humanity? We will see it, Paul insists, in the visible community of the church. This is why, as Timothy Yates says, "Christianity cannot be a family religion, a tribal religion, or the religion of a particular people or nation. It cannot be a male religion. And it cannot be the political religion of a particular government or rule. If these religious forms develop, Christianity becomes so deformed as to be unrecognisable".[423] The founding of the church of Ephesus is described in Acts 18 and 19, beginning with Paul's encounters with the city's Jewish population.[424] Ephesus had a large cosmopolitan population, and the movement that began in the synagogue soon broke out, so that the name of Jesus came to be honoured by many of "the

Jews and Greeks living in Ephesus".[425] The church that grew up in the city was not made up of Jewish converts alone, but of Jews and Gentiles together. It is this miracle of reconciliation that Paul sees as the evidence of kingdom life. Writing to this new community, he stresses that the redeeming work of Christ is not only in them but *among* them, as those who were formerly enemies[426] become co-heirs of the same grace. All the promises that had seemed to be given to the Jews alone[427] are now made available, in Christ, to the Gentiles too. This reality, Paul insists, is a picture of the achievements of Christ. Human peace is possible because of the cross.[428] We can be reconciled to each other because we are both reconciled to God.[429] And because of Christ we have the same place of privilege in God's plan.[430] In the cultural diversity of the church, Paul sees the concrete, visible, and measurable impact of Christ's death. Without Christ, you would be enemies. With Christ, you are one. Reconciliation is the fruit of resurrection. And this is not just an Ephesus reality. It extends, through the interconnected relationships of the body of Christ, to the whole church. Paul is introducing us to a truly global faith. With the primary division of Jew and Gentile abolished, only one category remains: *all*. Across cultures and races, God is building one new family: we are joined together in Christ,[431] and in our multicoloured, many-tongued expressions, the Holy Spirit dwells.[432]

In the very different language of contemporary America, Shane Claiborne paints the equivalent picture:

> Some of us have worked on Wall Street, and some of us have slept on Wall Street. We are a community of struggle. Some of us are rich people trying to escape our loneliness. Some of us are poor folks trying to escape the

> cold. Some of us are addicted to drugs and others are addicted to money. We are a broken people who need each other and God, for we have come to recognize the mess that we have created of our world and how deeply we suffer from the mess.[433]

It is impossible to overstate the centrality of the community of the church in Paul's vision of the mission of God. We sense this when we eavesdrop on his prayers. When he prays for God's people, he longs that they will know strength and power;[434] will experience the indwelling presence of Christ;[435] will grasp the hugeness of God's love:[436] that we, the church, will be filled with the very fullness of God,[437] and the whole prayer raises a question. Why isn't Paul, the apostle to the Gentiles, the great evangelist, praying for the world *beyond the church*? If he was truly missional, isn't that what he would do? Why isn't he praying that those who don't know Christ will come to know him? The answer is that he is. He is praying for the world, because he believes, just as he has told us, that it is through the church that the world will be blessed. In the earthly ministry of Jesus the sovereign God was present, incarnate in the flesh of his Son: salvation and miracles followed wherever he went. Now this same God is present again, incarnate in the lives of his people.

This is the outcome of the gospel, the present work of the risen Christ. "It is surely a fact of inexhaustible significance," Lesslie Newbigin has said, "that what our Lord left behind him was not a book or a creed, nor a system of thought, nor a rule of life, but a visible community... He committed the entire work of salvation to that community."[438]

In our understanding of God's mission in the world, this means:

- That God's mission both produces, and is carried by, the church. Rather than saying that the church of God has a mission, it is more accurate to say that the mission of God has a church.

- That God's mission is fulfilled both *in* the church – not least in the visible dynamic of reconciled relationships – and *through* the church, in all the fruit that lives transformed by Christ produce.

- That the key to both dimensions is the full participation of the people of God in the life of God. Paul uses the term "equip" to suggest the functioning of the church as a living community resourcing our engagement in the life of God and thus our capacity to bear fruit for him.[439]

This church is a mustard-seed community that emerges wherever the mission of God is realized. Jesus predicted an organic, human movement when he said that he would present himself *wherever* two or more are gathered.[440] "When we are incorporated into God's family," Al Hirsch writes, "We all seem to become 'seeds' bearing the full potential of God's people within us."[441]

This is That

Those in whom the Spirit comes to live are God's new Temple. They are, individually and corporately, places where heaven and earth meet.

N. T. WRIGHT[442]

Though the possibility of this movement is secured in the life, death, and resurrection of Jesus, its delivery comes after his ascension. Pentecost is the birthday of the church, welcomed by its senior midwife, Peter, with the exclamation "*This is that!*"[443]

This is That, a popular show on CBC Radio Canada, recently caused an internet stir by reporting that dogs in Montreal would be required by law to understand commands in both French and English. They also revealed that during a visit by the Queen, Canadians would be temporarily required to drive on the right. Residents of Alberta were outraged to be told that the Calgary Aquarium was to close and, needing to empty the building, would be frying up all the fish and offering them to weekend visitors. None of the stories were true: Calgary doesn't even have an aquarium. The show is a satire, and has on its website the strapline "We make (up) the news". *This is That* is parody. It sounds like news, but is all comedy. A *parody* is an event or activity deliberately made to look like another when in fact it isn't – a comedy sketch delivered so perfectly in the style of a news show that listeners are fooled into taking it seriously. But what if you had the opposite situation? What if you had two events or activities appearing to be completely different when in fact they are the same? "*This is that*" would take on a whole new meaning.

This is Peter's job on the Day of Pentecost. The events that have shaken an early-morning Jerusalem are strange and unexpected, so bizarre that they appear to be evidence of drunken revelry. "This is weird," the people of the city say. "No," says Peter, "this is *that*."

By "that" he means the promise of the prophets, an event spoken of centuries earlier by leaders loved and respected by the Jewish people and deeply embedded in Jewish culture. He cites Joel and the Psalms. In a later sermon he will quote Moses and Abraham and suggests that "[s]tarting with Samuel, every prophet spoke about what is happening today".[444] What you see now, Peter says, is what God spoke about in ancient days. It is what he has always been speaking about. Samuel is thought of as the first of the Jewish prophets: if it started with him, and has continued ever since, then *everything* in Jewish history has been pointing to this day.

Peter could equally have mentioned Ezekiel: "And I will give you a new heart, and I will put a new spirit in you. I will take out your stony, stubborn heart and give you a tender, responsive heart. And I will put my Spirit in you so that you will follow my decrees and be careful to obey my regulations."[445]

He could have gone to Isaiah: "For I will pour out water to quench your thirst and to irrigate your parched fields. And I will pour out my Spirit on your descendants, and my blessing on your children. They will thrive like watered grass, like willows on a riverbank."[446]

Peter might equally have relied on the famous words of Jeremiah, surely not far from the minds of his audience as they gathered to celebrate the giving of God's rules. Pentecost, for the Jewish people, was Law-day, not Spirit-day. Yet Jeremiah had already spoken of "'the new covenant I will make with the people of Israel on that day,' says the Lord. 'I will put my instructions deep within them, and I will write them on their hearts. I will be their God, and they will be my people. And they will not need to teach their neighbours, nor will they need to teach their relatives, saying, "You should know the LORD." For everyone, from the least to the greatest, will know me already,' says the LORD. 'And I will forgive their wickedness, and I will never again remember their sins.'"[447] Was this how God would celebrate the birthday of the Law, by getting rid of it?

To these and many other places Peter could have gone, for everything that God was doing on the Day of Pentecost was consistent with his promises, a fulfilment of the plan he had held to from the very start. The Law was not to be abolished, but it had been fulfilled, and something new was rising in its place. The thread of Old Testament promises pointing to this day is long and strong. Archbishop William Temple wrote in the 1940s:

> It is no good giving me a play like *Hamlet* or *King Lear* and telling me to write a play like that. Shakespeare could do it – I can't. And it is no good showing me a life like the life of Jesus and telling me to live a life like that. Jesus could do it – I can't. But if the genius of Shakespeare could come and live in me, then I could write plays like this. And if the Spirit could come into me, then I could live a life like His.[448]

Why is it so important to Peter to identify the work of the Holy Spirit with this thread: not as parody, but as the fulfilment of what was promised?

Firstly, because *continuity* provides *context*. The current expression of the Holy Spirit's work may seem new, but it sits in the context of God's plans and purposes for Israel. The events of Pentecost are not a departure from the Jewish faith but the completion of it. This is the same God, Yahweh, coming to visit and inhabit his people. His original intentions haven't changed.

Secondly, because *comparison* aids *comprehension*. By citing the prophets, Peter is explaining what it is that God is doing. The heart cry of every Hebrew was to be able to obey God's Law. Living in tune with God was the goal the Jewish people longed for, the summit of the mountain they climbed. And this, Peter wants to say, is exactly what the Spirit makes possible. The Spirit is God coming to live in us; closer than breathing; enabling us to please God because the God we seek to please lives his life through us.

Thirdly, because *connection* makes for *credibility*. It's all very well being impressed by the sound of a great wind. Who wouldn't be intrigued by tongues of fire? And all those languages! Miracles and marvels will always draw attention. But who makes the miracles? Whose is the mind behind the marvels? Who does all this shaking *point* to? Peter wants us to know that these are not disconnected phenomena to be judged only by their own light. They are expressions of the presence of God. They connect us back to the God we know and want to know better.

The speed at which Peter recognizes what is happening and is able to highlight its context is remarkable in itself. He is no Old Testament scholar, but he sees immediately the significance of these events. His *"this is that!"* is not so much a speech of prepared exposition as a cry of spontaneous recognition. *This* is what they were talking about, for all those years in the synagogue. *This* is what my grandmother told me about. *This* is what I have longed for without even knowing it. It is as if the coming of the Holy Spirit answers questions he was hardly aware of asking, and fills a void he knew he had but couldn't name. *This*, he says, is *that*: the promise, the longing, the hunger of my heart.

The vital connection between God's present work and ancient promises is important because it allows us to know that the coming of the Holy Spirit *matters*. To speak of salvation in Christ without speaking of the present, vital work of the Holy Spirit is to tell half a story. The Passion without Pentecost is a football season without a Cup Final, a table laid for a meal that is never served. How many of our churches claim to worship Trinity but address their every prayer to a God who is binary? How many miss the fact that this is what Jesus lived and died to achieve? As Thomas Torrance often said, the whole gospel of the age of the Spirit can be summed up in Paul's prayer for his friends in Corinth: "May the grace of the Lord Jesus Christ, the love of God, and the fellowship of the Holy Spirit be with you all."[449] Grace because that is what Jesus has made possible. Love because that is what originates in the heart of the Father and animates all things. Fellowship, which is communion, because that is what the Holy Spirit draws us into. The incarnate Son has made possible our full participation in the life of God, but it is the Holy Spirit who makes it *actual*. This is the good news reserved for Jean-Paul Sartre. The Spirit brings the fullness of communion with the triune God into my existential reality.

Pentecost is the fulfilment of a long-held dream; the answer to a question asked so long ago that no one can remember the first time. This visitation of the Spirit is no random event. It has *purpose*. Since Eden God has longed for nothing as wildly as he longs for intimacy with you, to walk with *you* in a cool evening garden. The Holy Spirit hasn't come to tickle your toes; he has come to draw you into the life and love of the Trinity.

God's Gift Shower

> Imagine there was a power that lies hidden at the very heart of God's people. Suppose this power was built into the initiating "stem cell" of the Church by the Holy Spirit but was somehow buried and lost through centuries of neglect and disuse.... I now believe that the idea of latent inbuilt missional potencies is not a mere fantasy; in fact there are primal forces that lie latent in every Jesus community and in every true believer...
>
> ALAN HIRSCH[450]

What is the connection between the coming of the Spirit and the central place the church occupies in the mission of God? Is it simply that where we provide the ideas and activities the Holy Spirit is the power, like a generator hired to light our evangelistic tent crusade? Metaphors for the Holy Spirit revolving around energy and power seem to point in this direction. Jesus has told us what to do, the common argument goes, and it is up to us to do it: oh, and just in case we run out of steam, he's sent the Holy Spirit as our fuel. Is that how it works?

Not according to the Bible, or to the experience of the fathers of the church. The first disciple-making community grew into an understanding of mission that was thoroughly Trinitarian. It was the mission of the Father, Son, and Spirit. They associated the Holy Spirit with communion; it is he who makes it possible, in daily life, for us to share in the divine life. The prerequisite for fruitfulness is participation in God's life, and the Holy Spirit is the medium of our participation. He is God's power at work in us – the fuel analogy is not completely wrong – but his is not power that comes online only when we engage in directly "missionary" behaviour. He is power for the whole of our lives: a fusion of our life with God's. We experience the Spirit as empowerment for mission when we surrender to the Spirit as God's presence in our lives. Power flows from presence because:

- God's Spirit in us is the one who activates our fruitfulness. Participation in the life of God wakes us up, stands us up, and sets us up for purpose. Who wouldn't feel empowered as a result?

- The more our earthly life is drawn into participation in the life of God, the more "missionary" it becomes – not because we give up daily life to be on mission, but because our whole life offers God its fruitfulness.

- In this sense the Spirit is involved with us both when we are intentional about God's mission and when, by living life in his communion, we find that we are accidental missionaries.

- The key to both is the same: surrender to the Spirit of God. More of our ordinary life immersed in his extraordinary presence; more of our heart surrendered to his life; more of our days and moments "Spirit-filled".

One of the clearest ways to think about the Spirit, and the way most often chosen by New Testament writers, is to use the language of gifts. The understanding of the early church, in brief, was that:

- The Holy Spirit, drawing us into the life of God, will activate the gifts that God has given us. It is in him that we will find "the works he has prepared us for".

- Because we have lived for so long in the wilderness, and settling in the life of God is new to us, there will be new gifts that the Holy Spirit brings. So novel is the breaking in of God's life into ours that with it will come treasures thus far lost to us.

- Pentecost is the original gift shower, the pouring out of gifts to celebrate the new creation's birth. This is the language Paul adopts when he describes Jesus celebrating his ascension not by demanding gifts from us but by giving them to us.[451]

- It is the releasing of all the gifts God has for all his people that will usher in his kingdom on the earth.

The God Factor

Educationalist Ken Robinson reports a conversation with Paul McCartney, who says that he "went through his entire education without anyone noticing that he had any musical talent at all. He even applied to join the choir of Liverpool Cathedral and was turned down. They said he wasn't a good enough singer".[452] Perhaps they said he had no *talent*, or perhaps that he wasn't *gifted*. It is extraordinary how often in our culture we turn to biblical language when we want to talk about people who are in some way exceptional. The idea of *talent*, originally a Roman coin, comes from a story Jesus tells,[453] and describes *that which is given to us to invest and use*. In the same way, when we speak of being gifted, we imply that there is a giver. They say there are no atheists in foxholes but you'd think, sometimes, there were none on *The X-Factor* either, so often do the judges resort to biblical imagery. If you're an agnostic with a great singing voice, whom do you thank?

The fact that human giftedness requires the language of a giver is no accident. The spark within us, the potential we see in ourselves, is the world's strongest argument for creation. If the universe is random and unplanned, why Eva Cassidy? Not only is our giftedness a sign of our origin, it is also the best clue to *why* God made us. It is the release of this giftedness, the fulfilment of our potential, that God desires. The very health of the creation depends on it. Out of human giftedness, fruitfulness will come. It follows, then, that when the Holy Spirit comes to re-enact the original Eden intention, he will operate through giftedness.

The Holy Spirit is the means by which God's original intention will now reach fulfilment. It is the Spirit who enables us to participate in the life of God and who, by activating the gifts we have already and complementing them with new gifts we now need, enables each of us to play our part in bringing fruitfulness. The mechanics given to the church to help this happen are more gifts![454] Gifts given by the Spirit to the body of the church for its proper functioning, which is the releasing of its members' gifts. The whole operation is a kind of "gift exchange". Everything we are given is to be shared, so that others discover what it is they have been given, and they share, so that others find... And so on. Mission is, from beginning to end, the receiving and sharing of gifts. As Kester Brewin says:

> And so it is with almost every gift: God gives prophecy to one to share with all; he gives insight to this woman to help her counsel this man; he gives wisdom to a child to enrich an adult. All churches, wherever they

are and whatever tradition, need to become places in their communities where people can exchange gifts – not just spiritual gifts but any gifts... In the exchange of gifts, relationships are always catalysed, always strengthened.[455]

Participation, in this model, is a process of gift-discovery. You find your place in God's mission in the world when you:

- Discover your gifts. Ask God to reveal the gifts he has given you. What contribution were you designed to make to the flourishing and fruitfulness of creation?

- Receive new gifts. Invite the Holy Spirit to pour into you the new gifts the ascended Christ is giving you.

- Develop your gifts. In the community of the church, through participation in the life of God, ask the Holy Spirit to perfect his gifts in you.

- Deploy your gifts. In love of God and neighbour, all gifts are given to be shared. The paradigm of sharing is twofold: you offer your gift as worship and you use your gift to love and serve others.

As James Bryan Smith has said, "[God's] love can and must extend itself through our own hands and feet, expressed in our love for others. We were created for a purpose. Not simply to wait until we die and go to heaven, but created 'in Christ Jesus for good works'".[456]

In the New Testament vision of the church this is for *all* God's people. All in the sense of their number and all in the sense of their diversity. Even the prophet Joel, seeing just a glimpse of what could be, saw men *and* women in this gift exchange, old *and* young contributing.[457] For his era, this was a radical vision. For the apostles it became explosive. Every nation would be touched by this new movement; every language implicated. Slaves would give of their gifts and so would slave-owners. Children. Grandparents. Leaders. Followers. All would find that they are gifted; all would be offered more; all would have the opportunity to contribute. The gift-exchange economy of God will meet the needs of his plan because the complexity of his mission is matched by the diversity of gifts. To put the same assertion as a question: if all the people of God discovered, developed, and deployed their many gifts in loving service of their neighbour, would the world be changed? The plan says yes.

> As a new order, a new humanity, the church has always had within it the power to be an explosive force in society and in the history of the world. For it is called not to *contain* its message but to live and to proclaim its message, calling all people into a repentance from the old body, the old humanity, the old creation, Satan's kingdom, the former age, into the new body, the new humanity, the new creation, the new kingdom, the new age.[458]

Signs of Life?

> The Church exists for the world by being committed to the world... If it truly follows its Lord the Church is called to active service of its brethren, who are all created by the one Father. A church which only lived and worked for itself would not be the Church of Christ.
>
> HANS KÜNG[459]

Nine of the most prominent images used in the New Testament to describe the church are: branches on a vine;[460] a field of crops;[461] God's Temple;[462] the body of Christ with all of us as the parts;[463] the bride of Christ;[464] the body of Christ with Christ as the head;[465] a family;[466] God's house – with Jesus as the builder;[467] living stones being built into a spiritual house.[468] These are for the most part organic metaphors, pictures of living things; so much so that when Peter wants to paint the church as stones, he has to invent the novel and unlikely category of "living stones".[469] Biology suggests that a "living thing" is defined by certain fundamental properties, which can be expressed as:

- Living things are composed of cells
- Living things have different levels of organization
- Living things use energy
- Living things respond to their environment
- Living things reproduce
- Living things adapt to their environment[470]

It's not difficult to see, reading such a list, why some of us bemoan our church as "dead". Centuries of Christendom – where the movement of the Spirit is made subject to political advantage – have left us with an institution that all too often has the stones without the living: an organization that used to be an organism. How does the story of the mission of God speak to us? It tells us there is hope.

Like Abraham, we can look at the night sky and, instead of being intimidated by the stars, can be inspired. Do we dare to dream, barren as we are, that God has plans for us? Taking seriously our present circumstances, living fully in the now, we can yet fix our hearts on God's tomorrow. "From first to last, and not merely in the epilogue, Christianity is eschatology, is hope, forward looking and forward moving, and therefore also revolutionizing and transforming the present," Jürgen Moltmann writes. "The eschatological is not one element *of* Christianity, but it is the medium of Christian faith as such, the key in which everything else in it is set, the glow that suffuses everything here in the dawn of an expected new day…"[471]

Like Moses, we can see the people groaning in their slavery and yet know that they are not forgotten. God will come. He himself will rescue them. Walter Brueggemann beautifully describes the actions of the God of exodus: "In response to the slave cry, God moved the darkness and the sea, God mobilized creation on behalf of the needy slaves, God managed the chaos redemptively."[472] Is the God of exodus our God too?

Like Esther, we can know that, even in such a time as this, God is still moving. Like Daniel, we can seek him in our exile. Like Jeremiah, we can speak to one another words of hope, that God knows the plans he has for us; plans for good, not for disaster; to give us a future and a hope.[473] That even in our exile we will grow, and not diminish.

Like Mary, we can sense within ourselves the heartbeat of a new creation. We can tune our ears to hear the very ground we stand on groaning with the pains of birth.[474] We can invite the Holy Spirit to groan in us, gifting us with prayers too deep for words.[475] We can enter into God's advent and share with him the longing for the coming dawn, welcoming the signs of life where we see them.

Like Paul, we can listen for the whisper of the Spirit, the word that says *Stop here!*[476] *Go there!* We can pray that God will send to us, in dreams, the men and women who are crying out for him.[477] We can look on every riverside[478] and jailhouse[479] for the people of peace God has for us, and recognize his hand in even those who hound us.[480]

All these are present activities of the church, even in a time of social exile. They are the ways in which God's life in us is activated as the Holy Spirit meets our imagination. Whatever circumstances we find ourselves in, God will work through the church, through our lives, to squeeze into our world every drop of blessing, every fragment of grace he can get through. The ultimate arena of his action is not within the church; it is across the whole creation. Even our planet is not large enough to exhaust the love and plans of God. Nothing short of a cosmos renewed will satisfy him. Jesus became incarnate so that stars and galaxies might rejoice at the reach of his redemption, and he will have the party he has paid for. Looking for the glory of God to be fully expressed inside the church is like spending a day at Heathrow and thinking you've visited London. We are a launch pad and a landing place, an airstrip cleared in the jungle so that kingdom blessing can be poured into our world. We are the delivery mechanism, not the product – the scooter, not the pizza. The creation renewed is the meal.

> Just as the presence of the Holy One among the Israelites was to permeate every aspect of their lives, so now this is how it is to be throughout the creation, as groups of followers live the life of the kingdom in their particular places.[481]

Nor are we, in ourselves, the arbiters of salvation. The church doesn't save lost people; Jesus does. Seeing the church as the gateway to salvation, the turnstile of faith, is a distortion that bends the gospel out of shape. Christ is the gateway, and the door, and the arbiter of all salvation. Salvation is in Christ; it is in what Christ has already done. This is the radical, world-changing message of the New Testament. It is finished. The deal is done. Whatever is necessary for your redemption has already been delivered. We can declare it and we can describe it, but only Jesus can redeem. The church is the body of Christ and, in some very important ways, as a living, human, earthbound community, we extend and continue the ministry of Christ: but *not* when it comes to salvation. Saving humans is his work alone. It is largely because Europeans have for so long been attending church to get their tickets punched for heaven that we have so misunderstood the gospel. The church cannot do what Jesus has already done. We are the announcer, not the news.

It's so hard, isn't it? The gospel is all about healing: about bringing our lives into the drop zone of God's marvellous redemption and seeing the changes come. We surrender our self-righteousness to Christ; we give up trying to please God and let him fill our very beings with his Spirit and… we change. In key and often visible ways, we get better. In some of our middle-class ghettoes the changes are more subtle, but we all know the stories. Drug-dealers who don't deal any more. Wife-beaters who don't beat. Selfish people freed of their selfishness. Loving heroes finding out that you win by losing. The hearts of the fathers turned to their children. Redemption uplift. We see it and rejoice in it and it is, indeed, beautiful. But then, oh then, we begin to notice a pattern. Those displaying these great fruits of salvation are *in* the church; those not yet doing so are not. The *in*, it seems, at least in some of the ways that matter to us, are righteous, the *out* less so. We begin to believe that this is what the church is: a membership association for the righteous. A club for the clean-living. A holy huddle. We start to think that the church is the goal of God's mission instead of its means. The drift is there and, time after time, this is what we become. But it is not what we *are*. Whatever the church is meant to be, it is not this. A place to worship the one who is righteous, yes. A gathering to honour the one who has obeyed on our behalf. But never, never an in-club for the holy. This is the mystery of the salvation God has worked for us in Christ. It is always bigger, always deeper, always better than the small accommodations we have made for it. The Old Testament average for underestimating the scope of God's salvation is by a factor of 7,000 to one.[482]

We are not winners. We are losers who have reached the point of owning our lostness. Yes, we experience a measure of healing. Yes, we can find ourselves, by grace and the wisdom of God, growing towards a more stable place for our families, a safer haven for our children; but, no, we don't have access to next week's lottery numbers. We are a community of the redeemed and redemption begins not with our wealth but with our poverty.

The key word used in the New Testament of the church is an "ecclesia" or "assembly". Outside church circles, the word could describe a group of citizens coming together to discuss the future of their city. It is a meeting of minds, a community of concern. Those willing to take some share of the responsibility for the future of their society come together to exchange ideas and see if they can move forward together. The word is used in this exact sense in Ephesus, when a group of citizens gather to discuss the disruption Paul and his team are causing.[483] The description of this citizens' assembly – *the people were all shouting, some one thing and some another. Everything was in confusion. In fact, most of them didn't even know why they were there*[484] – might just be a clue to why Paul later borrowed the word to describe the church! The importance of this image, though, is its emphasis on a shared identity, a commitment to community, and a common future. At its most stripped-down level, this is the church: a group of Christ-followers coming together to play their part in seeing the kingdom of God established in the earth. It gets more complex than that, of course, but that's where we start.

There is a similar metaphor at the end of the Old Testament that gives a sense of what the church, at its most basic, is to be. In the book of Malachi, the prophet has delivered his oracle, calling the people of God to a level of faithfulness and obedience they have long since abandoned. His message is for the whole nation of Israel, but it is those who first respond who are referred to in the book. "Those who heard God spoke to one another," we are told, "and a book of remembrance was made."[485] These are the early adopters, those who hear and understand the message. Knowing full well that it is intended for a larger group still, they want to record their names as if to say, "We, at least, have heard. We're hoping others will hear, too, but for the moment we want to note that we are saying yes". The action has the same sense as that of Joshua when he says, having read aloud the law of God, "as for me and my house, we will serve". We the church are not the whole nine yards of God's intentions. We are not the full Monty. We have tasted his blessing, but he has so much more. The best *is* yet to come.

The sense is of first followers, people who know full well that the call they have responded to is bigger than their number but who desire all the same to make public the commitment they have made. Recent research has demonstrated how significant these first followers are to every social movement. As a group of first followers, the New Testament churches had a deep sense of the scale and scope of God's call. They knew that the message they had heard was intended for a much bigger crowd; that God was very much at work beyond the borders of their shared experience. What are we, then, if we are not the prize? We are the early responders; the first fruits of the harvest; the Beaujolais Nouveau. It is right and good that we should recognize each other. A book of remembrance *should* be made. As long as we remember that the harvest, when it comes, will be much bigger. The adventure has only just begun.

At the Table of Peace

> Relax. Enjoy your friends. Enjoy their company along with the company of Jesus. Point him out, freely, without fear or intimidation. You're not responsible to sell Him to them. You're simply saying what you've seen. You're not the judge. You're the witness.
>
> CARL MEDEARIS[486]

What about "personal evangelism"? Is there a place in this complex model of God's mission for faith transmission? There is, but it may not be what you expect. It certainly won't be as stressful as you've expected.

The first personal evangelism team of the church age was sent out even before it began.[487] Before Pentecost, before even Calvary, Jesus sent out teams to explore mission. Much has been made of the instructions he gave them, but in plain terms they are these:

1. Go somewhere.

2. Find people of peace.

3. Have a meal with them and talk.

4. Watch Satan fall like lightning from the sky.

Really? Eat a meal, talk, and Satan falls. Is that it?

It is, for two reasons: because you're talking to the right people, and because you're talking to them at the table. These two conditions, which you can read both literally and metaphorically, are the conditions within which the exchange of stories works.

Who are the right people? They are people of peace. This means very simply that when you approach them peacefully they receive you peacefully. It means they are open to human exchange. They are described in the Old Testament as those who have not "kissed an idol".[488] They are people with an openness in their hearts, who show it by being open to each other and to you. People of peace are everywhere. They may not be religious people. Sad as it is to report it, religious people can be the least peaceful because their universal truth claims often lead them into conflict. True people of peace are open to you as a fellow human being. The model here is hospitality, as it is so often with Jesus, as it was with Abraham when the whole adventure of mission began.[489] The trick, of course, is that to find a person of peace you have to be a person of peace. "'Whenever you enter someone's home,' Jesus says, 'first say, "May God's peace be on this house."'[490] If your first word isn't peace it is unlikely that the second will be either.

This "trick" goes deeper than might first appear. By being

people of peace we give permission to others to be peaceful too. We make the first move and lay down our arms, because only then is a space created in which those who might or might not previously have chosen peace have the opportunity to do so now. These principles are used in forging reconciliation at the highest level of global negotiations. Here Jesus asks us to use them in the everyday. We *are* people of peace because the mission we're engaged in is God's mission of peace; we *seek* people of peace because they are the ones who will recognize and welcome the Prince of Peace when he shows up: the whole operation is an operation of peace. "The church is a movement launched into the life of the world", Lesslie Newbigin says, "to bear in its own life God's gift of peace for the life of the world."[491]

Why is the table important? Because it is the place we meet as equals. The origin of the word "companion" is the sharing of bread – my companion is the one I break bread with. The table normalizes us as human beings. We are drawn to it by our common need for food. It defines our shared humanity. It makes us vulnerable to one another because the hand that passes bread cannot, at the same time, hold a sword. Before we ever find, in conversation, things we differ over, we have established as our base the things we don't. The table is both literally the best place to do mission and metaphorically the best way.

Tim Chester has explored this model of "relaxed sharing" by highlighting the vital role of common meals in the life and ministry of Jesus: the kingdom explored around the table of the everyday. He cites Robert Karris, who concludes that, throughout Luke's Gospel in particular, "Jesus is either going to a meal, at a meal, or coming from a meal".[492]

Chester writes:

> *How* did Jesus come? He came eating and drinking. ... Jesus spent his time eating and drinking – a lot of his time. He was a party animal. His mission strategy was a long meal, stretching into the evening. He did evangelism and discipleship round a table with some grilled fish, a loaf of bread and a pitcher of wine.[493]

Honest human exchange, the telling of stories, is what mealtimes are for. Not, as it turns out, because they are the right time to sell double glazing. This model of conversational, story-based faith-sharing in the context of relaxed relationship helps us to establish what evangelism *is not*. In this setting it isn't:

- **A series of clichés, platitudes, or motivational catchphrases.** Real communication, linked to real events and experiences, doesn't need to fall back on such shortcuts.

- **A detailed exposition of God's story.** Faith-sharing in a relationship is part of a process, not all of it. Who knows what other initiatives and resources God is going to call on? Be yourself. Be part of a chain. Don't try to be a mastermind.

- **A task whose success or failure is on your shoulders.** Your responsibility is to be authentic, truthful, sensitive, and compassionate. The rest, according to Jesus, is the work of the Holy Spirit. When two people of peace sit down for a meal together there is no external goal – their communion is the prize.

- **A theology exam.** Nobody is waiting to pass or fail you.

- **A combination lock** where only one specific sequence works.

Some of the things that, in this context, personal faith-sharing might just *be* are:

- **An invitation to journey.** If there comes a context in which you are encouraging someone to take the next step in their journey with Jesus, it is always just that – one step. Effective discipleship is not counted in scalps but in growth and fruitfulness. What is the next thing that God might be inviting this person to do?

- **A link in a chain.** You will never be the only voice an individual hears. Even if there's no one else about, the Trinity make three, so at the very least you're one of four. More likely one of many, many more.

- **A challenge to know and tell your own story.** It's surprising how difficult it can be to answer the simplest of questions. How has the encounter with Jesus affected your life?

- **An integration of words and actions.** You may well value words above actions, but in the end those who see or hear you will draw from both.

- **An expression of dialogue.** The best conversations are mutually edifying. Genuine exchange always, in some measure, goes both ways.

- **Grounded in listening.** "Listen early, speak late" is a good rule. Better still: listen early, listen again, then listen to make sure you've heard well; then consider the possibility of speaking unless continued listening would be more helpful.

- **A kingdom operation,** shaped by the widest possible view of God's purposes. What makes your words good news? To whom?

Can you reimagine the process of evangelism through this paradigm of sharing meals and telling stories? Such an approach will require easy, positive relationships of mutual respect with people who choose not to be called Christian.

A Personal Easter?

At the heart of this approach is the suggestion that you can best share the love and truth of Christ by telling your own story: authentically relating how Christ has changed *your* life. The principle applies to the wider story of God's work in your life, but perhaps especially to the gospel's core events: the death and resurrection of Jesus. Instead of describing what *in theory* you think has happened as a result of these events, can you explore, and explain, the impact these events have had on you? What has it meant for you to bring to the cross your burdens; your anxieties; your shame? What does it mean in your life that Christ is not dead but risen? It is surprising that we talk so often of the Easter events and yet struggle to connect them with our own life journey. Can you find your personal connections? Are you ready to share these with others?

My own journey took a radical turn when I understood this process. Having lived in a more or less evangelical milieu for four decades, I am used to conversations about Jesus.

Competing theories of the atonement and lurid descriptions of the cross seem to feature strongly in the circles I have moved in. I have heard people I call friends, and some I don't, extol with deep conviction their particular account of how the cross of Jesus works. It is only in recent years, however, that I have dared to ask the question, how has it worked *for me*?

When I began to explore this question honestly, two things emerged. The first was an admission that some of the things my friends were claiming for the cross had simply never happened to me. I didn't want to say that those things might not be real for others – not out loud, in any case – but I had to have the courage to say it for myself. The second honest conviction that emerged was that while some supposedly important things hadn't happened, something very definitely had. I could not give an account of my own life that didn't include the enormous benefits of encountering Christ. So I began to ask myself, what did happen? If I had to tell the story without doctrine or dogma – my story, not the story of the theologians – what would I say? I realized I had always been afraid to ask this question, in case the answer was nothing. What if you take away the platitudes and nothing stands?

The answer wasn't nothing. As I explored my own history, I found a quite substantial something. The simplest way of expressing it is to say that, for me, what the cross achieved was this: in Christ I found the possibility of being completely forgiven, and the courage to completely forgive. There is more to my story, of course,[494] but these are its headlines, and unlike efforts I have made in the past to "explain" the gospel, these are real.

So I stopped trying, to the extent that I had tried in the past, to tell God's story for him, and concentrated instead on telling mine. It was a relief, to be honest, because I'm better at it. It does seem to me that in the past we have sometimes been guilty of lying for the sake of the gospel. We add supposed spiritual experiences that in truth have never happened because we think they make God's story more attractive. It is perhaps for this reason that so many of us have retreated, over recent years, from any sense of sharing faith. I welcome the honesty, but I'm not so sure retreating is a good idea. If it is a lie to say that something happened when it didn't, it is equally a lie to act as if it didn't when it did. What Jesus asks of us, instead, is honesty, and there is freedom in the model of faith-sharing that results.

Response: Be Filled by the Firestarter

> Our calling is not to reinvent the Christian faith but, in keeping with the past, to carry forward what the church has affirmed from its beginning. We change, therefore, as one of my friends says, "not to be different, but to remain the same."
>
> ROBERT WEBBER[495]

Restoration is a vital category in understanding the mission of God because:

- It represents the aspect of mission in which the focus of God's purposes moves from the incarnation of Christ to the birth of the church. This is where we come in!

- By the indwelling of God's Spirit, we are enabled to participate in the life of the trinity and to begin to live the life we were always intended to live.

- The individual work of Christ becomes, in this way, a worldwide movement of transformation, aimed ultimately at the healing of all things.

- This is where the intentions of our maker come full circle, as we are empowered once more to image him in the earth; to reflect his character and nature and through the gifts he has given us to bring fruitfulness to the creation. *Original Intention* is fulfilled as we rejoice in our own gifts and reveal the gifts of others.

> We are to be the billboards of the gospel in the extraordinary ordinariness of our daily lives – extraordinary because of the renewing power of the Holy Spirit, ordinary because of the common creational stuff of our daily existence. It is in that profoundly this-worldly and mundane sense that creation, to use Calvin's arresting phrase, is the theatre of God's glory.
>
> AL WOLTERS[496]

Endword

"Two households, both alike in dignity, in fair Verona, where we lay our scene..." The opening words of Shakespeare's Romeo and Juliet have captured audience imaginations for centuries. Without counting foreign-language productions, the play has been reimagined for the screen at least forty-six times; from ballet to Bhangra; from Leonard Bernstein's epic *West Side Story* to Baz Luhrmann's 1996 Radiohead-tinged extravaganza. The adventure moves us every time. We think of it as the greatest love story ever told.

Except it isn't. Not by a long way. That accolade would have to be reserved for a story that began before the very dawn of time and will still be unfolding at its end: the story of God's love for the world he has made. So caught up are we in God's narrative, so familiar with its scenes and themes, we forget that at its core it is a simple love story. When we read the Old Testament, particularly, we lose sight of love and see only bloodshed and judgment, the shadowy past of our God "before he became a Christian". But we are wrong. Jesus shows us once and for all that God has always loved us, that love has been his nature from the start, and, once we know it, we realize that it's been there, like a hidden code, throughout the Old Testament's journey.

This is the same love that the prophet Malachi tells us will "rise with healing in its wings"[497] until his people "leap with joy like calves".[498] This love will rebuild the family of

Israel, turning "the hearts of fathers to their children and of children to their fathers".[499] In the closing moments of the Old Testament narrative, the God who called Abraham, who met with Jacob, who protected Joseph, and raised Moses to lead his people to freedom comes to them once more to remind them that he did all this *for love* and that his love will ultimately heal and restore them. What more beautiful note could the ancient Scriptures end on? What better words could be spoken before four centuries of silence are broken with the cry of John the Baptist: "Behold, the Lamb of God, who takes away the sins of the world" (John 1:29)?

God says, "I have loved you – wait until you see just how much. This story isn't over yet...."

Endnotes

1. Danny Wallace, http://www.join-me.co.uk/about/ (accessed 7th March 2016).
2. Danny Wallace, *Join Me: The Man Who Started a Cult by Accident*, London: Ebury Press, 2004.
3. David Bosch, *Transforming Mission: Paradigm Shifts in Theology of Mission*, Maryknoll, New York: Orbis, 1991, p. 1.
4. Bosch, 1991, p. 9.
5. Ephesians 4:13, NLT.
6. Ephesians 4:12.
7. Matthew 6:10, NLT.
8. Samuel Escobar, *A Time for Mission: The Challenge for Global Christianity*, Leicester: IVP, 2003, p. 175.
9. For more, see my *Church Actually: Recovering the Brilliance of God's Plan*, Oxford: Lion Hudson, 2012.
10. Lesslie Newbigin, *The Gospel in a Pluralist Society*, Grand Rapids, MI: Eerdmans, 1989, p. 116.
11. Eugene Peterson, *Eat This Book*, London: Hodder, 2008.
12. Gerard Kelly, *The Prodigal Evangelical: Why Despite Everything I Still Belong to the Tribe*, Oxford: Lion Hudson, 2015.
13. Michael Novelli, *Shaped by the Story*, Grand Rapids, MI: Zondervan, 2008.
14. Genesis 2:16.
15. Revelation 21:4.
16. Michael Novelli, *Shaped by the Story*, Grand Rapids, MI: Zondervan, 2008.
17. Richard Foster and Kathryn A. Helmers, *Life with God*, London: Hodder and Stoughton, 2008.
18. Hebrews 12:1.
19. https://en.wikipedia.org/wiki/Crowdsourcing (accessed 7th March 2016).
20. Corrie ten Boom, *The Hiding Place*, Ada, MI: Chosen Books, 35th Anniversary edition, 2006.
21. Eugene Peterson, *Eat This Book*, London: Hodder and Stoughton, 2008.
22. John Steinbeck, *East of Eden* (Penguin Modern Classics), London: Penguin, 2000.
23. https://www.goodreads.com/work/quotes/1031493-paradise-lost (accessed 10th March 2016).

ENDNOTES

24. Genesis 3:20.
25. Genesis 3:6.
26. Genesis 2:24; see Matthew 19:5 and Ephesians 5:31.
27. John 14:2–3.
28. Lesslie Newbigin, *The Open Secret: An Introduction to the Theology of Mission*, London: SPCK, 1995.
29. Kate Adie, *Nobody's Child: Who Are You When You Don't Know Your Past?* London: Hodder & Stoughton, 2006.
30. http://www.ntwrightpage.com/Wright_JIG.htm#_edn8 (accessed 17th March 2016).
31. Genesis 2:16, NIV.
32. Genesis 3:8, 9.
33. Genesis 3:10, NLT.
34. Genesis 3:11, NLT.
35. Genesis 1:28.
36. Habakkuk 2:14, NLT.
37. Matthew 6:10, NLT.
38. Ephesians 3:10, NLT.
39. Revelation 21:2-4, NLT.
40. A. J. Köstenberger and Peter T. O'Brien, *Salvation to the Ends of the Earth*, Leicester: Apollos / Inter-Varsity Press, 2001.
41. Genesis 3:22–24.
42. Miroslav Volf, *Exclusion and Embrace*, Nashville, TN: Abingdon Press, 1996, p. 129
43. Colossians 1:6, NLT.
44. Colossians 1:9–10, NLT.
45. Walter Brueggemann, *Deep Memory, Exuberant Hope: Contested Truth in a Post-Christian World*, Minneapolis, MN: Fortress Press, 2000, p. 69.
46. Psalm 37:11.
47. Matthew 5:5, NIV.
48. 2 Corinthians 1:22, Ephesians 1:14.
49. Romans 8:18–23, NLT.
50. Genesis 1:3, 9, 12, 18, 21, 25, 31.
51. Revelation 21:4, NLT.
52. John P. Baker, *Salvation and Wholeness*, London: Fountain Trust, 1973, p. 17.
53. Numbers 6:24–26, NLT.
54. Zechariah 14:20, 21, NLT.
55. Zechariah 8:13, NLT.
56. Zechariah 9:9.

57. 2 Corinthians 9:7–10.
58. Matthew 6:24.
59. 1 Timothy 6:10.
60. Hans Rookmaaker, *Modern Art and the Death of a Culture*, IVP, 1975.
61. Deuteronomy 4:9–10.
62. Deuteronomy 6:2, 7, 20.
63. Deuteronomy 11:19 and 32:46.
64. Psalm 78:1–8.
65. Psalm 103:17–18, Psalm 128:5–6.
66. Proverbs 13:22.
67. Dietrich Bonhoeffer, *Creation and Fall: Temptation*, New York: Touchstone, 1997.
68. Brennan Manning, *Ruthless Trust: The Ragamuffin's Path to God*, Colorado Springs, CO: NavPress, 2006.
69. Genesis 18:11.
70. Hebrews 11:11–12.
71. See Genesis 18:12–15.
72. Genesis 21:5–7.
73. Genesis 17:16.
74. Hebrews 11:11.
75. Genesis 17:16.
76. Os Guinness, *The Call: Finding and Fulfilling the Central Purpose of Your Life*, Nashville, TN: Thomas Nelson, 2003.
77. Genesis 17:5, 16.
78. Genesis 18:18.
79. Genesis 12:2.
80. Tom Sine and Christine Aroney-Sine, *Living on Purpose: Finding God's Best for Your Life*, Grand Rapids, MI: Baker Books, 2002, p. 11.
81. Judges 6, 7 and 8.
82. Judges 6:25–28.
83. Judges 6:12.
84. Judges 6:14.
85. Judges 16:30.
86. 1 Samuel 1, 3, 7–10, 12–13, 15–16.
87. 1 Samuel 3:1–21.
88. 1 Samuel 3:10.
89. 1 Kings 22:8ff.
90. Colossians 4:7, Ephesians 6:21.
91. 1 Chronicles 4:9.

ENDNOTES

92. Judges 4:1–16 and 5:1–23.
93. Judges 5:12.
94. Judges 17:6, 21:25.
95. Rowan Williams, *The Dwelling of the Light: Praying with Icons of Christ*, Grand Rapids, MI: Eerdmans, 2003.
96. See http://www.sacredheartpullman.org/Icon%20explanation.htm, http://www.holy-transfiguration.org/library_en/lord_trinity_rublev.html, and https://en.wikipedia.org/wiki/Trinity_(Andrei_Rublev) (all accessed March 8th 2016).
97. Genesis 18:3.
98. Genesis 19:1.
99. Hebrews 13:2.
100. Genesis 18:13.
101. Hebrews 11:10, Revelation 21:2.
102. Resources abound, but one excellent overview, available online, is David T. Williams, *The "two hands of God" imaging the Trinity*, iUniverse, Inc, 2003. Available at http://www.davidtwilliams.com/books/twohands.pdf (accessed 9th March 2016).
103. Miroslav Volf, *Exclusion and Embrace*, Abingdon Press, 1996, p. 129.
104. Miroslav Volf, *After Our Likeness: The Church as the Image of the Trinity*, Grand Rapids, MI: Eerdmans, 1998.
105. http://www.sacredheartpullman.org/Icon%20explanation.htm (accessed 8th March 2016).
106. 1 John 1:1–4, 1 John 2:20–23, 1 John 3:23, 1 John 4:1–3, 1 John 5:1, 5, 6, 9–13, 20, 2 John 1:7–10.
107. 2 Corinthians 13:14, NLT.
108. See Philippians 2:6–11, one of the earliest fragments of the church's liturgy we have.
109. Acts 1:6–8, NLT.
110. Ephesians 3:18, 19.
111. Ephesians 3:15.
112. Ephesians 3:20.
113. Ephesians 4:14, 15.
114. From the hymn "Glory be to God on High", *Hymns for the Nativity of Our Lord*, London: William Strahan, 1745.
115. Acts 10:1–4.
116. Acts 10:44.
117. Acts 10:47–48.
118. Acts 17:24–29.
119. Acts 17:30, 31.

120. Christopher Wright, *Christian Mission and the Old Testament: Matrix or Mismatch*, www.martynmission.cam.ac.uk
121. Hebrews 11:9–10, NLT.
122. Hebrews 11:8–10.
123. Galatians 3:6.
124. http://www.geagort.com/urban-mission-en/city-changers-alan-platt/?lang=en, accessed March 9th 2016
125. Os Guinness, *The Call: Finding and Fulfilling the Central Purpose of Your Life*, Nashville, TN: Thomas Nelson, 2003.
126. Brennan Manning, *The Furious Longing of God*, Colorado Springs, CO: David C. Cook, 2009.
127. https://www.whitehouse.gov/blog/2013/02/04/rosa-parks-stamp (accessed 9th March 2016).
128. http://www.washingtonpost.com/wp-dyn/content/article/2005/11/02/AR2005110202154.html (accessed 9th March 2016).
129. Exodus 1:17(a).
130. Exodus 1:12.
131. Exodus 1:16.
132. Exodus 1:17.
133. Exodus 1:19.
134. Exodus 1:20.
135. Exodus 2:2.
136. Exodus 1:21.
137. Matthew 6:1.
138. Tremper Longman III, David E. Garland, *Expositor's Bible Commentary*, Grand Rapids, MI: Zondervan, 2008.
139. See for example Matt Barr, "I'm Not White I'm Jewish", http://genius.com/Bibleraps-im-not-white-im-jewish-lyrics (accessed 9th March 2016).
140. Deuteronomy 6:21.
141. http://www.sefaria.org/Pesach_Haggadah,_Magid,_We_Were_Slaves_in_Egypt.2 (accessed 9th March 2016).
142. Harvey Perkins, "Let My People Go", in Anderson and Stransky (eds), *Mission Trends No 3: Third World Theologies*, Grand Rapids, MI: Eerdmans, 1976, p. 193.
143. Philip Greenslade, *God's Story: Through the Bible Promise by Promise (Cover to Cover)*, Farnham: CWR, 2001, pp. 126, 128.
144. Gailyn Van Rheenen, *Missions: Biblical Foundations and Contemporary Strategies*, Grand Rapids, MI: Zondervan, 1996, p. 17.
145. Genesis 2:16.
146. James P. Byrd, *Sacred Scripture, Sacred War: The Bible and the American*

Revolution, Oxford: Oxford University Press, 2013, p. 195.
147. http://www.americanrhetoric.com/speeches/mlkivebeentothemountaintop.htm (accessed 9th March 2016).
148. Dietrich Bonhoeffer, *Meditations on the Cross*, Louisville, KY: Westminster John Knox Press, 1998.
149. Gregory Boyd, *God at War*, Downers Grove, IL: IVP USA, 1997, pp. 13, 19.
150. Vinoth Ramachandra, *Faiths in Conflict? Christian Integrity in a Multicultural World* Downers Grove, IL: IVP Academic, p. 97.
151. Derek Tidball, *The Message of the Cross (The Bible Speaks Today)*, Nottingham: Inter Varsity Press, 2001, p. 59.
152. Bryant L. Myers, *Walking With the Poor: Principles and Practices of Transformational Development* Maryknoll, NY: Orbis Books, 1999.
153. Bryant L. Myers, *Walking With the Poor*, Orbis Books, 1999.
154. John 8:44.
155. Genesis 3:1; 2 Corinthians 11:3.
156. Revelation 12:10, NLT.
157. Genesis 3:11.
158. 1 Peter 5:8.
159. Genesis 3:1.
160. John 12:31(a).
161. John 12:31(b).
162. Romans 8:21, NLT.
163. Walter Brueggemann, *Biblical Perspectives on Evangelism: Living in a Three-Storied Universe*, Nashville, TN: Abingdon Press, 1993, p. 31.
164. John 11:39, NLT.
165. http://historymatters.gmu.edu/d/5057/, (accessed 9th March 2016).
166. Yann Martel, *The Life of Pi*, Edinburgh: Canongate Books, 2002.
167. Exodus 2:14.
168. Exodus 3:6.
169. Exodus 14:13.
170. Exodus 20:20.
171. 1 John 4:18, NIV.
172. John 11:1–44.
173. John 11:39, NLT.
174. Max Brooks, *World War Z: An Oral History of the Zombie War*, New York, NY: Three Rivers Press, 2007.
175. J. K. Rowling, *Harry Potter and the Deathly Hallows*, London: Bloomsbury, 2007.
176. Stephen Dray, *Exodus, Free to Serve*, Wheaton, IL: Crossway Bible Guides, 1993, p. 23.

177. Exodus 3:5.
178. Exodus 3:1 – 4:17.
179. Ephesians 6:6; Colossians 3:24; 1 Peter 2:16.
180. Gary Haugen, *Good News about Injustice: A Witness of Courage in a Hurting World*, Nottingham: IVP, 1999, p. 72.
181. Exodus 1:11–14.
182. Exodus 1:15–17.
183. Terence Fretheim, *Interpretation: Exodus, A Bible Commentary for Preaching and Teaching*, Louisville, KY: Westminster John Knox Press, 2010, p. 18.
184. Isaiah 61:1–2; Luke 4:18–19.
185. Matthew 22:37.
186. Henri Nouwen, cited in Dallas Willard, *Renovation of the Heart: Putting on the Character of Christ*, Colorado Springs, CO: NavPress, 2004.
187. Walter Brueggemann, *Theology of the Old Testament: Testimony, Dispute, Advocacy*, Minneapolis, MN: Fortress Press, 2005.
188. Ronald J. Sider, *Good News and Good Works: A Theology for the Whole Gospel*, Grand Rapids, MI: Baker Books, 1999.
189. Duffy Robbins in *The Core Realities of Youth Ministry* by Mike Yaconelli, Grand Rapids, MI: Zondervan/Youth Specialties, 2003.
190. Numbers 12:2.
191. Numbers 12:4–10.
192. Numbers 20:1.
193. Micah 6:4.
194. Exodus 15:1–18.
195. Exodus 15:20–21.
196. Genesis 31:27.
197. Joseph Ratzinger, Pope Benedict XVI, *Jesus of Nazareth*, translated from the German by Adrian J. Walker, New York: Doubleday, 2007.
198. Dr Rowan Williams, *The Times*, London, 19th October, 2005.
199. Robert Webber, *Ancient-Future Faith*, Grand Rapids, MI: Baker Books, 2000.
200. Terence E. Fretheim, *Interpretation: Exodus*, Louisville: Westminster John Knox, 1991.
201. Exodus 25:1 to 31:18 and 35:1 to 40:38.
202. Terence E. Fretheim, *Interpretation: Exodus*, Louisville: Westminster John Knox, 1991.
203. Exodus 9:16.
204. Exodus 14:21–22; Matthew 8:27.
205. Terence E. Fretheim, *Interpretation: Exodus*, Louisville: Westminster John Knox, 1991.

ENDNOTES

206. Exodus 16:3.
207. Deuteronomy 6:12.
208. Exodus 17:3.
209. Numbers 13:31–33.
210. Exodus 32:1–8; Deuteronomy 4:15–16.
211. John 1:14.
212. 1 Corinthians 3:16.
213. 1 Peter 2:5.
214. Dallas Willard, interview at http://www.dwillard.org/articles/artview.asp?artID=112 (accessed 10th March 2016).
215. I Kings 18:21.
216. 1 Kings 18:36, 37, NIV, emphasis added.
217. Judges 2:17; 8:27; 8:33.
218. Deuteronomy 27:15.
219. Deuteronomy 29:16.
220. Isaiah 40:18–20; 41:6–7; 44:9–20; 46:1–2; Jeremiah 10:1–10; Psalm 115:1–8.
221. Ezekiel 8:10.
222. Daniel I. Block, *The Gods of the Nations: Studies in Ancient Near-Eastern National Theology*, Grand Rapids: Baker Academic, 2000, p. 70.
223. Matthew 12:34, NIV.
224. Attributed to Fr Pedro Arrupe SJ, 1907–1991, http://www.ignatianspirituality.com/ignatian-prayer/prayers-by-st-ignatius-and-others/fall-in-love (accessed 10th March 2016).
225. Matthew 15:17–19, NLT.
226. See Matthew 5:8, 5:28 and 6:21.
227. Romans 8:29.
228. Matt Redman and Friends, *Inside Out Worship*, Heart of Worship Trust, 2005.
229. Rowan Williams in the foreword to Ruth Burrows OCD, *Love Unknown: The Archbishop of Canterbury's Lent Book 2012*, London: Continuum, 2011.
230. Carlo Carretto, *Love is for Living*, London: Darton, Longman & Todd, 1976, p. 12.
231. Cited in Richard Attenborough, The Daily Mail Online, 2008, http://www.dailymail.co.uk/femail/article-1052245/Richard-Attenborough-The-film-bosses-wanted-Gandhi-sexy--played-Richard-Burton.html (accessed 10th March 2016).
232. http://www.songlyrics.com/foy-vance/joy-of-nothing-lyrics/ (accessed 10th March 2016).
233. Philippians 2:5–11.

234. 2 Samuel 12:13.
235. 2 Samuel 11:1 – 12:25.
236. Romans 3:4.
237. Psalm 139:13–16.
238. Psalm 51:5.
239. Psalm 51:10.
240. Psalm 51:18.
241. Mike Yaconelli, *The Core Realities of Youth Ministry*, Grand Rapids, MI: Zondervan/Youth Specialties, 2003.
242. Psalm 51:14.
243. Evelyn Underhill, *Abba: Meditations Based upon The Lord's Prayer*, London: Longmans, 1940.
244. Amos 6:1.
245. Amos 6:4.
246. Amos 6:4.
247. Amos 6:6.
248. Amos 6:6.
249. Amos 6:5.
250. Amos 5:23–24, NLT.
251. Amos 1:1 and 7:14.
252. Amos 7:10.
253. Amos 7:15.
254. Amos 5:21–23.
255. Amos 4:8–11.
256. Amos 5:5.
257. Amos 2:6; 4:1; 5:11; 5:12; 8:4; 8:6.
258. Amos 9:13–15.
259. Jean-Pierre de Caussade, *The Sacrament of the Present Moment*, translated by Kitty Muggeridge, San Francisco: Harper Collins, 1989.
260. N. T. Wright, *Following Jesus: Biblical Reflections on Discipleship*, London: SPCK, 1994, p. 56.
261. Kenneth Leech, *Through Our Long Exile: Contextual Theology and the Urban Experience*, London: Darton, Longman and Todd, 2001, p. 229.
262. Esther 4:14, NLT.
263. http://sophiehayesfoundation.org/about/ (accessed 10th March 2016).
264. http://www.unodc.org/unodc/fr/frontpage/2012/November/put-yourself-in-my-in-my-shoes-a-human-trafficking-victim-speaks-out.html (accessed 10th March 2016).
265. http://sassysouls.weebly.com/stories.html (accessed 10th March 2016).

266. Genesis 50:20.
267. Psalm 137:3–4.
268. Psalm 122:3.
269. Psalm 2:6.
270. Psalm 48:1–3.
271. Russell Rook and Gerard Kelly, *Route 66: The Spring Harvest Theme Guide*, Elevation, 2011.
272. See https://en.wikipedia.org/wiki/Supper_at_Emmaus_(Caravaggio),_Milan (accessed 10th March 2016).
273. Ingrid D. Rowland, *The Battle of Light and Darkness* New York Review of Books, 12th May 2005, cited at http://www.theway.org.uk/McElligott.pdf (accessed 10th March 2016).
274. Helen Langdon, *Caravaggio: A Life*, New York: Farrar, Straus and Giroux, 1998.
275. Walter Brueggemann, *Hopeful Imagination: Prophetic Voices in Exile*, Minneapolis, MN: Fortress Press, 1986, p. 96.
276. Salman Rushdie, *The Satanic Verses*, Viking, 1989.
277. Psalm 89:46.
278. Psalm 5:1–3.
279. Bono, "Introduction" to *The Book of Psalms*, Edinburgh: The Canongate Scriptures, Canongate, 1999.
280. Tony Benn, *Dare To Be A Daniel: Then and Now*, London: Hutchinson, 2004.
281. Walter Brueggemann, *Finally Comes the Poet: Daring Speech for Proclamation*, Minneapolis, MN: Fortress Press, 1989, p. 121.
282. John Holdsworth, *Dwelling in a Strange Land: Exile in the Bible and in the Church*, Norwich: Canterbury Press, 2003, p. 19.
283. Acts 1:8.
284. Hebrews 11:13; 1 Peter 1:1, 2:11.
285. Peter Phillips, *1 Peter as Rhetorical Liturgy*, Derby: Cliff College, 2004.
286. Ernest Lucas, editorial comment, October 2004.
287. Graham Tomlin, *The Provocative Church*, London: SPCK, 2002, p. 61.
288. Viv Thomas, *Second Choice: Embracing Life As It Is*, Carlisle: Paternoster, 2000, p. 3.
289. Viv Thomas, *Second Choice: Embracing Life As It Is*, Carlisle: Paternoster, 2000, pp. 5, 13.
290. Jeremiah 29:11.
291. Jeremiah 29:13–14.
292. Jeremiah 29:5–7.
293. Genesis 1:25.

294. Rob Lacey, *The Street Bible*, Grand Rapids, MI: Zondervan, 2002.
295. David Smith, *Mission After Christendom*, London: Darton, Longman and Todd, 2003, p. 35.
296. Walter Brueggemann, *Hopeful Imagination: Prophetic Voices from Exile*, Philadelphia: Fortress Press, 1986, p. 4.
297. Hebrews 11:26.
298. Romans 9:17; Exodus 9:16.
299. Acts 1:8.
300. Wilbert R. Shenk, *Changing Frontiers of Mission*, Maryknoll, NY: Orbis Books, 1999, p. 183.
301. Philippians 2:5, KJV.
302. Brennan Manning, *Abba's Child: The Cry of the Heart for Intimate Belonging*, Colorado Springs, CO: NavPress, 2015.
303. http://writingishardwork.com/2012/05/14/tolkiens-5-tips-for-writing-complex-heroes/ (accessed 10th March 2016).
304. Judges 13:1 – 16:31.
305. Judges 16:30.
306. Cited in Tom Wright, *The Lord and His Prayer*, Grand Rapids, MI: Eerdmans, 1996.
307. Rob Lacey, *The Street Bible*, Grand Rapids, MI: Zondervan, 2002.
308. Derek Tidball, *The Message of the Cross*, (The Bible Speaks Today), Downers Grove, IL: Inter Varsity Press, 2001, p. 162.
309. In Timothy Yates, (Ed.), *Mission – An Invitation to God's Future*, Sheffield: Cliff College Publishing, 2000.
310. Luke 8:19–21.
311. Luke 2:48.
312. Luke 1:29.
313. Luke 2:35.
314. Luke 2:19.
315. Luke 1:38, NKJV.
316. John 2:5, NLT.
317. Luke 1:46.
318. Luke 1:46–55.
319. Luke 4:18–19.
320. Luke 1:48.
321. Luke 1:55.
322. Max Lucado, http://aquotation.com/quote/max-lucado/journey-cross-began-long-before.html (accessed 10th March 2016).
323. Philippians 2:6–11.
324. Still from the hymn *All Glory be to God on High*.

ENDNOTES

325. Carl Medearis, *Speaking of Jesus: The Art of Not-Evangelism*, Colorado Springs, CO: David C. Cook, 2011.
326. John 3:10.
327. Gerard Kelly, *The Source: Be, Say, Do*, Theme Guide, Spring Harvest, 2013.
328. Walter Brueggemann, *Biblical Perspectives on Evangelism: Living in a Three-Storied Universe*, Nashville, TN: Abingdon Press, 1993, p. 24.
329. Romans 5:1.
330. Romans 5:2.
331. Romans 5:6.
332. Romans 5:8.
333. Romans 5:10.
334. Romans 5:12–20.
335. Romans 5:14(b).
336. Romans 5:18.
337. Romans 5:12.
338. Romans 5:15.
339. David Taylor, *A Holy Longing*, in *Christianity Today*, February 2010.
340. Romans 5:19.
341. Philippians 2:6–11.
342. Romans 5:11.
343. Romans 5:9.
344. Romans 5:10.
345. Hebrew 4:14–16.
346. John 20:17.
347. Matthew 28:20.
348. I Timothy 2:5, my additions.
349. Adam J. Johnson, *Atonement: A Guide for the Perplexed (Guides for the Perplexed)*, London: Bloomsbury T&T Clark, 2015.
350. 2 Corinthians 5:19, NLT.
351. Colossians 1:19–20, NLT.
352. Tom Wright, *How God Became King: Getting to the Heart of the Gospels*, London, SPCK, 2012.
353. Scot McKnight, *The King Jesus Gospel: The Original Good News Revisited*, Grand Rapids, MI: Zondervan, 2011.
354. Exodus 14:13–14.
355. Tim Keller in the foreword to J. D. Greear, *Gospel: Recovering the Power that Made Christianity Revolutionary*, Nashville, TN: B and H, 2011.
356. Tim Keller, *King's Cross – The Story of the World in the Life of Jesus*, New York, Dutton: 2011.

357. Isaiah 52:10.
358. Isaiah 40:11.
359. Tom Wright, *Jesus and the Identity of God*, originally published in *Ex Auditu* 1998, http://ntwrightpage.com/Wright_JIG.htm (accessed 10th March 2016).
360. Tom Wright, *How God Became King: Getting to the Heart of the Gospels*, London, SPCK: 2012.
361. Philippians 2:6–11.
362. Isaiah 45:23.
363. Joseph Ratzinger, Pope Benedict XVI, translated from the German by Adrian J. Walker, *Jesus of Nazareth*, New York: Doubleday, 2007.
364. John 19:30.
365. J. D. Greear, *Gospel: Recovering the Power that Made Christianity Revolutionary*, Nashville, TN: B and H, 2011. Used with permission.
366. John 8:1–11.
367. John 8:11.
368. John 8:6.
369. John 8:7.
370. Gregory A. Boyd, *Repenting of Religion: Turning from Judgement to the Love of God*, Grand Rapids, MI: Baker Books, 2004.
371. Genesis 2:17.
372. John 16:8.
373. Luke 15:17.
374. Carlo Carretto, *Letters from the Desert*, London: Darton, Longman & Todd, 1972.
375. Tim Chester, *A Meal With Jesus: Discovering Grace, Community and Mission Around the Table*, Wheaton, IL: Crossway, 2011.
376. Brennan Manning, *The Ragamuffin Gospel: Good News for the Bedraggled, Beat-Up, and Burnt Out*, Revised Edition, Multnomah Books, 2008.
377. Miroslav Volf, *Christianity and Violence*, Yale University Divinity School, http://repository.upenn.edu/cgi/viewcontent.cgi?article=1001&context=boardman (accessed 10th March 2016).
378. Philippians 2:6–11, again.
379. Nelson Mandela, *Long Walk to Freedom*, London: Abacus, 1995, p. 171.
380. Robert Webber, *Ancient-Future Faith*, Grand Rapids, MI: Baker Books, 2000.
381. John 19:30.
382. N. T. Wright, *Simply Jesus: A New Vision of Who He Was, What He Did, and Why He Matters*, London: Harper Collins, 2011.
383. Carolyn Weber, *Surprised by Oxford: A Memoir*, Nashville, TN: Thomas Nelson, 2011.

384. Brennan Manning, *Abba's Child: The Cry of the Heart for Intimate Belonging*, Colorado Springs, CO: NavPress, 2015.
385. Alison Morgan, *The Wild Gospel*, https://www.fulcrum-anglican.org.uk/articles/wild-gospel-bringing-truth-to-life/ (accessed 10th March 2016).
386. Numbers 6:22–26.
387. Psalm 67:4.
388. Psalm 67:5.
389. Psalm 67:6.
390. Psalm 67:7.
391. Acts 10:2.
392. Acts 1:14.
393. Acts 5:1–11.
394. Acts 12:13.
395. Acts 16:11–15.
396. Acts 16:16–18.
397. Acts 16:19–34.
398. Philippians 1:6.
399. Acts 28:28, NLT.
400. Acts 9:1–2.
401. Philippians 3:4–6.
402. Ephesians 3:2, 6.
403. Ephesians 3:7–8.
404. Ephesians 3:10.
405. Clark Pinnock and Robert C. Brow, *Unbounded Love*, Downers Grove, IL: InterVarsity Press, 1994, p. 112.
406. Ephesians 3:10.
407. Ephesians 1:2–14.
408. Ephesians 1:2–3.
409. Ephesians 1:4–12.
410. Ephesians 1:13–14.
411. Ephesians 1:4.
412. Ephesians 1:5–8.
413. Ephesians 1:9–14.
414. N. T. Wright, *Simply Jesus: A New Vision of Who He Was, What He Did, and Why He Matters*, London: Harper Collins, 2011.
415. Ephesians 1:3.
416. Ephesians 1:4.
417. Ephesians 1:5.
418. Ephesians 1:6.

419. Ephesians 1:7.
420. Ephesians 1:7.
421. Ephesians 1:13.
422. Alan Hirsch and Lance Ford, *Right Here Right Now: Everyday Mission for Everyday People*, Grand Rapids, MI: Baker Books, 2011.
423. Timothy Yates, in *Mission – An Invitation to God's Future*, Sheffield: Cliff College Publishing, 2000.
424. Acts 18:19.
425. Acts 19:17.
426. Ephesians 2:11.
427. Ephesians 2:12.
428. Ephesians 2:14.
429. Ephesians 2:16.
430. Ephesians 2:18.
431. Ephesians 2:20.
432. Ephesians 2:22.
433. Shane Claiborne, *The Irresistible Revolution: Living as an Ordinary Radical*, Grand Rapids, MI: Zondervan, 2006, p. 188.
434. Ephesians 3:16.
435. Ephesians 3:17.
436. Ephesians 3:18.
437. Ephesians 3:19.
438. Lesslie Newbigin, *The Household of God*, London: SCM, 1954.
439. Ephesians 4:12.
440. Matthew 18:20.
441. Alan Hirsch, *The Forgotten Ways: Reactivating the Missional Church*, Grand Rapids, MI: Brazos Press, 2006.
442. N. T. Wright, *Simply Christian: Why Christianity Makes Sense*, San Francisco, CA: Harper, 2006.
443. Acts 2:16, KJV. I'm grateful to my good friend Martin Young for highlighting the significance of these words.
444. Acts 3:24, NLT.
445. Ezekiel 36:26–27, NLT.
446. Isaiah 44:3–4, NLT.
447. Jeremiah 31:33–34, NLT.
448. William Temple, cited by John Stott, *The Mode: Becoming More Like Christ*, Keswick Convention, 2007.
449. 2 Corinthians 13:14, NLT.
450. Alan Hirsch, *The Forgotten Ways: Reactivating the Missional Church*, Grand Rapids, MI: Brazos Press 2006.

451. Ephesians 4:8, compare Psalm 68:18.
452. Ken Robinson with Lou Aronica, *The Element: How Finding Your Passion Changes Everything*, London: Viking, 2009.
453. Matthew 24:14–30.
454. Ephesians 4:11,12.
455. Kester Brewin, cited in Eddie Gibbs and Ryan K. Bolger, *Emerging Churches: Creating Christian Community in Postmodern Cultures*, Grand Rapids, MI: Baker Academic, 2005.
456. James Bryan Smith, *The Good and Beautiful Community*, London: Hodder and Stoughton, 2010.
457. Joel 2:17–18.
458. Robert E. Webber, *Common Roots: The Original Call to an Ancient-Future Faith*, Grand Rapids, MI: Zondervan, 1978, 2009.
459. Hans Küng, *The Church*, London: Continuum, 2001.
460. John 15.
461. 1 Corinthians 3.
462. 1 Corinthians 3.
463. 1 Corinthians 12.
464. Ephesians 5: 22–27.
465. Ephesians 4.
466. 1 Timothy 5.
467. Hebrews 3.
468. 1 Peter 2.
469. I Peter 2.
470. http://infohost.nmt.edu/~klathrop/7characterisitcs_of_life.htm (accessed 10th March 2016).
471. Jürgen Moltmann, cited in Tony Lane, *The Lion Concise Book of Christian Thought*, Oxford: Lion, 1984.
472. Walter Brueggemann, *Biblical Perspectives on Evangelism*, Nashville, TN: Abingdon Press, 1993, p. 55.
473. Jeremiah 29:11.
474. Romans 8:22.
475. Romans 8:26.
476. Acts 16:7.
477. Acts 16:9.
478. Acts 16:11.
479. Acts 16:36.
480. Acts 16:18.
481. Craig Bartholomew, *Where Mortals Dwell: A Christian View of Place for Today*, Grand Rapids, MI: Baker, 2011.

482. 1 Kings 19:18.
483. Acts 19:29.
484. Acts 19:32.
485. Malachi 3:16.
486. Carl Medearis, *Speaking of Jesus: The Art of Not-Evangelism*, Colorado Springs, CO: David C. Cook, 2011.
487. Luke 9:1–6, Luke 10:1–12 and 17–20.
488. 1 Kings 19:18.
489. In Genesis 18, remember?
490. Luke 10:5.
491. Lesslie Newbigin, *The Open Secret: An Introduction to the Theology of Mission*, London: SPCK, 1995, p. 48.
492. Tim Chester, *A Meal With Jesus: Discovering Grace, Community and Mission Around the Table*, Wheaton, IL: Crossway, 2011.
493. Tim Chester, *A Meal With Jesus: Discovering Grace, Community and Mission Around the Table*, Wheaton, IL: Crossway, 2011.
494. I wrote about this experience in *The Prodigal Evangelical: Why, Despite Everything, I Still Belong to the Tribe*, Oxford: Lion Hudson, 2015.
495. Robert E. Webber, *Ancient-Future Faith: Rethinking Evangelicalism for a Postmodern World*, Grand Rapids, MI: Baker Books, 1999, p. 17.
496. Al Wolters, *Creation* in *Comment* Magazine, March 2010, http://www.cardus.ca/comment/article/2022/ (accessed 10th March 2016).
497. Malachi 4:2(a).
498. Malachi 4:2(b).
499. Malachi 4:6.